T0191581

Lecture Notes in Computer Science　　10826

Commenced Publication in 1973
Founding and Former Series Editors:
Gerhard Goos, Juris Hartmanis, and Jan van Leeuwen

Editorial Board

More information about this series at http://www.springer.com/series/7408

Rafael Capilla · Barbara Gallina
Carlos Cetina (Eds.)

New Opportunities
for Software Reuse

17th International Conference, ICSR 2018
Madrid, Spain, May 21–23, 2018
Proceedings

 Springer

Editors
Rafael Capilla ⓘ
Universidad Rey Juan Carlos
Madrid
Spain

Carlos Cetina ⓘ
Universidad San Jorge
Zaragoza
Spain

Barbara Gallina ⓘ
Mälardalen University
Västerås
Sweden

ISSN 0302-9743   ISSN 1611-3349   (electronic)
Lecture Notes in Computer Science
ISBN 978-3-319-90420-7   ISBN 978-3-319-90421-4   (eBook)
https://doi.org/10.1007/978-3-319-90421-4

Library of Congress Control Number: 2018940155

LNCS Sublibrary: SL2 – Programming and Software Engineering

This Springer imprint is published by the registered company Springer International Publishing AG
part of Springer Nature
The registered company address is: Gewerbestrasse 11, 6330 Cham, Switzerland

Foreword

This volume contains the proceedings of the International Conference on Software Reuse (ICSR 18) held during May 21–23, 2018, in Madrid, Spain. The International Conference on Software Reuse is the premier international event in the software reuse community. The main goal of ICSR is to present the most recent advances and breakthroughs in the area of software reuse and to promote an intensive and continuous exchange among researchers and practitioners.

The conference featured two keynotes by John Favaro, Intecs SpA (Italy) and Alberto Abella from MELODA (Spain). We received 29 submissions (excluding withdrawn submissions). Each submission was reviewed by three Program Committee members. The Program Committee decided to accept 11 papers (nine full papers and two short ones), resulting in an acceptance rate of 37.9%. The program also included one full-day tutorial, one invited talk, and a panel about the future of software reuse.

This conference was a collaborative work that could only be realized through many dedicated efforts. We would like to thank all the colleagues who made possible the success of ICSR 2018: Barbara Gallina, Carlos Cetina, Mathieu Acher, Tewfik Ziadi, Roberto E. López Herrejón, Gregorio Robles, Jens Knodel, Carlos Carrillo, and Alejandro Valdezate. We also thank the ICSR Steering Committee for the approval to organize this edition in Madrid.

Last but not least, we would like to sincerely thank all authors who submitted papers to the conference for their contributions and interest in ICSR 2018. We also thank the members of the Program Committee and the additional reviewers for their accurate reviews as well as their participation in the discussions of the submissions. Finally, we thank Danilo Beuche for his tutorial and the members that participated as panelists including the support from people of The Reuse Company (Spain).

March 2018

Rafael Capilla
Barbara Gallina
Carlos Cetina

Organization

General Chair

Rafael Capilla   Universidad Rey Juan Carlos, Spain

Program Co-chairs

Barbara Gallina   Mälardalen University, Sweden
Carlos Cetina   Universidad San Jorge, Spain

Doctoral Symposium Chair

Gregorio Robles   Universidad Rey Juan Carlos, Spain

Workshops and Tutorials Chair

Roberto E. López Herrejón   ETS – Université du Québec, Canada

Tool Demonstrations Chair

Jens Knodel   Caruso-dataplace, Germany

Publicity Chair

Mathieu Acher   University of Rennes 1, France

Publication Chair

Tewfik Ziadi   University of Pierre and Marie Curie
                              (University of Paris 6), France

Local Chair

Carlos Carrillo   Universidad Politécnica de Madrid, Spain

Program Committee

Mathieu Acher   IRISA - University of Rennes, France
Paris Avgeriou   University of Groningen, The Netherlands
Ibrahim Bagheri   Ryerson University, Canada
Eduardo Almeida   RISE Labs - Federal University of Salvador de Bahia,
                              Brazil

Abstracts of the Keynote Talks

New Opportunities for Reuse in an Uncertain World

John Favaro

Intecs SpA, Pisa, Italy
john.favaro@intecs.it

Abstract. Twenty-five years ago, as the software reuse community was being established, the outlines of a research program in reuse were clear and its dimensions could be well-described with the application of the Three-C's model of Concept, Content, and Context. In the years that followed, researchers pursuing that program elaborated results in the precise specification of reusable artifacts, from feature modeling to component contracts (Concept); implementation, such as powerful generative methods (Content); and models and frameworks ensuring correct and effective integration (Context). Success was such that reuse has become a part of the everyday development process, and the death of general software reuse research has been hypothesized in some quarters. That hypothesis is premature. The world of applications is much more uncertain today, and that uncertainty is challenging reuse in all of its dimensions. Our previous understanding of Context is breaking down under the ambitious autonomous applications in robotics, IoT, and vehicles, whereby components are now being reused in scenarios that can no longer be completely characterized (the unknown-unknowns). Equally ambitious applications of advances in machine learning are challenging our previous understanding of Content, whereby the training and self-modifying implementation of such learning components becomes quickly inscrutable to humans, and dynamic variability in components and product lines is challenging our understanding of what implementation even means today. Even the idea of Concept is being challenged as attempts are made to reuse poorly specified knowledge artifacts in support of innovation management. Uncertainty brings new challenges with it, but it also brings new opportunities. The uncertain world of today's applications is laying the foundations for the next research program in software reuse.

The Challenging Future of Open Data Reuse

Alberto Abella

MELODA, Madrid, Spain
alberto.abella@meloda.org

Abstract. Since the first open data portal was launched in 2010 in Spain more than 20.000 datasets have been published. Nowadays, more than 100 active open data portals, mostly coming from the public sector, have been launched and E.U. open data website encompasses around 800.000 datasets coming from 31 countries as an active ecosystem. Although there is an increasing demand for open data reusable assets there is a need to estimate the social and economic impact of new investments and resources. Today, open data managers must deal with two main issues: (i) the available data reflects a poor management of the current open data portals' managers, including an astonishing percentage a complete absence of analysis of the use of published data, and (ii) a lack of sound models to assess this impact. Currently, two disciplines have emerged to cope with these challenges: data governance and open data coordination. Data governance creates a new business function in the company to care about the organization's data. Open data coordination refers to the need to make linkable the published data. The promising linked data paradigm struggles to link 'every' data published in the web due to the overwhelming amount of datasets published. In this keynote talk we will discuss a timeline describing the main achievements in the open data during the last decade and how to face the current challenges of open data reuse.

Reuse in (re)certification of Systems

Barbara Gallina[1] and Jabier Martinez[2]

[1] Mälardalen University, Västerås, Sweden
barbara.gallina@mdh.se
[2] Tecnalia, Derio, Spain
jabier.martinez@tecnalia.com

Abstract. The reduction of time and cost for the creation of a safety case is an urgent challenge that industries must face in the context of safety-critical product lines. A safety case is a contextualized structured argument constituted of process and product-based sub-arguments to show that a system is acceptably safe and thus "assure society at large that deployment of a given system does not pose an unacceptable risk of harm". Safety assurance and assessment processes required by standards and jurisdictions use to span several years and consume a large number of resources. To reduce time and cost, reuse capabilities are being investigated. At the core of this effort, there is the objective to provide a generic metamodel capturing concepts of safety compliance processes. This is opening many doors towards a common model-based certification framework that can simultaneously target diverse domains such as the automotive, railway, avionics, air traffic management, industrial automation, or space domains. Then, different recurrent scenarios of (re)certification are being studied with their own characteristics and challenges. For example, in the system upgrade scenario we aim to identify the parts of the safety assurance project that can be reused for the upgraded system. In the cross-standard reuse scenario, the same system certified against a standard needs to be certified with another standard or, in the case of jurisdictions, checking compliance with a country jurisdiction that differs from the current one. In the cross-concern reuse scenario, a system certified against a given standard (e.g., security related) requires to be certified with a standard targeting a different concern (e.g., safety). The AMASS project (Architecture-driven, Multi-concern and Seamless Assurance and Certification of Cyber-Physical Systems) continues previous efforts to define the Common Assurance and Certification Metamodel (CACM) and a tool-based platform is being developed. Among its functionalities, advanced techniques are provided enabling reuse by combining process lines, product lines and safety case lines.

Acknowledgments. This work is supported by the European ECSEL JU AMASS project 692474 (VINNOVA in Sweden, and MINETAD in Spain).

Managing Variability with Feature Models (Tutorial)

Danilo Beuche

pure-systems GmbH, Magdeburg, Germany
danilo.beuche@pure-systems.com

Abstract. Many organizations develop software or software –intensive products, which are can be seen as variants or members of a product line. Often the market demands variability and the software organization expects productivity benefits from reuse. In any case, complexity of the software development increases. Variability and variant management plays a central role in this, when it comes to mastering the complexity.

1 Topic

The tutorial aims at providing the essential knowledge for managing variability in product lines using feature models. It explains the concept of feature models and their role in product line engineering, such as how feature models can be used to control development and also product configuration. The tutorial is highly interactive and includes several practical exercises for the attendees. In this tutorial we cover the use of feature modelling for controlling the variability throughout the product line engineering process. Therefore, this tutorial covers the following topics:

- The importance of explicit variability modelling.
- Methods for managing variability in a product line.
- Concepts and Methods for creating correct and maintainable feature models.
- How to use feature models to control variability in product line assets.

With these topics we cover technological, organizational and business aspects of variability management for product lines, enabling practitioners to start with feature modelling on a solid basis. The intended audience are practitioners that want to learn how to carry out variability modelling (with feature models) for product line successfully.

2 Plan

The tutorial consists of three parts:

1. Introduction
    a. Product Line Basics
    b. Development Scenarios

Contents

Variability Management

Variability Management in Safety-Critical Software Product Line Engineering

André Luiz de Oliveira[1]($\boxtimes$), Rosana T. V. Braga[2], Paulo C. Masiero[2],
Yiannis Papadopoulos[3], Ibrahim Habli[4], and Tim Kelly[4]

[1] Federal University of Juiz de Fora, Juiz de Fora, Brazil
andre.oliveira@ice.ufjf.br
[2] University of São Paulo, São Carlos, Brazil
{rtvb,masiero}@icmc.usp.br
[3] University of Hull, Hull, UK
y.i.papadopoulos@hull.ac.uk
[4] University of York, York, UK
{ibrahim.habli,tim.kelly}@york.ac.uk

Abstract. Safety-critical systems developed upon SPLE approach have to address safety standards, which establish guidance for analyzing and demonstrating dependability properties of the system at different levels of abstraction. However, the adoption of an SPLE approach for developing safety-critical systems demands the integration of safety engineering into SPLE processes. Thus, variability management in both system design and dependability analysis should be considered through SPLE life-cycle. Variation in design and context may impact on dependability properties during Hazard Analysis and Risk Assessment (HARA), allocation of functional and non-functional safety requirements, and component fault analysis. This paper presents DEPendable-SPLE, a model-based approach that extends traditional SPLE methods, to support variability modeling/management in dependability analysis. The approach is illustrated in a case study from the aerospace domain. As a result, the approach enabled efficient management of the impact of design and context variations on HARA and component fault modeling.

Keywords: Variability management · Safety-critical systems · Dependability

1 Introduction

Safety-critical systems (SCS) are computer systems in which the occurrence of failures may lead to catastrophic consequences. Due to the benefits of large-scale reuse, Software Product Line Engineering (SPLE) and component-based approaches have been largely adopted by the industry in the development of SCS, especially in automotive [7, 32] and aerospace domains [8, 14]. However, safety-critical systems developed upon an SPLE approach have to address guidance defined in safety standards, e.g., ISO 26262 [18] for automotive, DO-178C [31] and SAE ARP 4754A [10] for aerospace. These standards establish that dependability properties of a SCS should be analyzed and demonstrated at different levels of abstraction before its release for

© Springer International Publishing AG, part of Springer Nature 2018
R. Capilla et al. (Eds.): ICSR 2018, LNCS 10826, pp. 3–22, 2018.
https://doi.org/10.1007/978-3-319-90421-4_1

operation. The adoption of an SPLE approach for developing safety-critical systems demands the integration of safety engineering into SPLE processes [14, 28]. Compositional dependability analysis techniques [6, 27, 30] provide the automated support for safety engineering, and seamless integration between system design and dependability analysis. Thus, system design and dependability analysis can be performed in a single model, contributing to reduce the complexity of the product line dependability analysis. Whereas safety-critical SPLE involves safety engineering, variability management in dependability analysis should be considered through software product line (SPL) life-cycle. Dependability analysis can be defined as the identification, early on the design, of potential threats to system reliability, availability, integrity, and safety, their potential causes, and measures to avoid or minimize their effects.

In safety-critical SPLE, dependability analysis should be performed aware of the impact of variation in the design and usage context on dependability properties to enable the systematic reuse of both architectural design and dependability information. Variation in the system design and usage context may raise different hazards, with different causes, and different risk that they may pose for the overall safety. As dependability properties may change according to the selection of product variants and their context, variability in dependability modeling should also be managed in safety-critical SPLE. Thus, mapping links between context and design variations and their realization in the dependability analysis, i.e., Hazard Analysis and Risk Assessment (HARA), and component fault modeling, should be defined in the SPL variability model. Existing variability management techniques [1, 15, 17, 32–34] provide support for managing variation at requirements, architecture, components, source code, and test cases. However, these techniques were not originally designed/or used to support variability management in dependability models developed with the support of compositional analysis techniques, e.g., OSATE AADL [6], HiP-HOPS [30], and CHESS [27].

Variability management in SPL dependability analysis/modeling enables the traceability of the variation in the design and context throughout dependability assets, and the systematic reuse of both architectural components and dependability information. Such reuse contributes to reduce the complexity, effort and costs in performing dependability analysis for specific product variants, since such analysis is not performed from scratch. Therefore, with the support of compositional safety analysis techniques, artefacts such as fault trees and Failure Modes and Effects Analysis (FMEA), required by safety standards for certification of safety-critical systems, can be automatically generated for a given product variant from the reused dependability information. Dependability analysis can only be treated as a product line asset if the variability model contains information about variation points and their realization in the dependability model. Therefore, the dependability model should be included in the SPL core assets, to enable the systematic reuse of dependability information together with other SPL assets, reducing the costs of generating safety assets for a larger number of product variants built around the SPL core assets. Although the reuse of dependability information provided by an SPLE approach is an attractive idea, existing approaches to support it are focused on the reuse of fault trees and FMEA [5, 12, 13, 26, 32], which can be automatically generated from reusable product line dependability analysis information. This paper presents DEPendable-SPLE (DEPendable Software Product Line Engineering), a model-based approach that extends traditional SPLE methods, to address dependability/safety analysis in SPLE, enhancing domain engineering with HARA, functional safety and integrity requirements allocation, component fault modeling activities, the support for variability modeling/management in dependability analysis, and application engineering with variant-specific dependability analysis, product derivation, fault trees and FMEA synthesis. This is required for certification of safety-critical systems in compliance with safety standards, e.g., ISO 26262 Parts 3 and 4 for automotive, and SAE ARP 4754A safety process for avionics. The application of the proposed approach is illustrated in a realistic unmanned aircraft system SPL. The proposed approach distinguishes from traditional SPLE methods by considering the impact of design/usage context variations on dependability analysis, thus, integrating variant management into compositional dependability analysis. Such integration allows the systematic reuse of both SPL architecture and dependability information. The remaining of this paper is organized as follows. Section 2 presents an analysis of existing variability types in safety-critical SPLE and their relationships. Section 3 presents the DEPendable-SPLE approach to support variability management in dependability analysis, and its application in a realistic aerospace SPL. Sections 4 and 5 detail related work, conclusion, and future work.

2   Product and Usage Context Variation and Their Impact

Variability in safety-critical SPLs can be: system (product) or contextual variability [17]. System variability can occur in: capability, operating environment, domain technology, implementation technique, or quality attribute features [19, 24]. Capability comprises features regarding end-user visible characteristics. Operating environment comprises features associated with the target environment where a given software product is operated. Domain technology relates to features representing specific domain techniques or tools that can be used to implement the SPL assets. Implementation techniques are features regarding specific implementation strategies, e.g., redundant or non-redundant control system architectures in the avionics domain. Quality attribute refers to features that the SPL products must address such as usability, maintainability, and data integrity checking. Usage context features relate to where and how the SPL is used. Such classification has been considered through this paper. Combinations among these features act as key driver during safety-critical SPL design, dependability analysis/modeling, and product derivation/instantiation. Such multi-perspective features and combinations among them have a direct influence in SPL architectural decisions and dependability analysis aimed at safety certification. The following sub-sections presents the Tiriba Flight Control SPL, used through this paper, and an analysis of the impact of variation in product and usage context features on the SPL design and dependability analysis. Such analysis, which is one of the contributions of this paper, was performed by analyzing the following system architectures and their respective dependability models: aircraft braking system [11], door controller [25], Tiriba UAV [33], and automotive braking system [29] product lines. Their architecture models were specified in AADL and Simulink, and their dependability models were specified in AADL/Error Annex, and HiP-HOPS analysis techniques.

2.1   Tiriba Flight Control Product Line

Tiriba Flight Control avionics product line (TFC-SPL) is part of the Tiriba UAV-SPL [2], which comprises a control subsystem with the following goals: to start the flight mode (direct, stabilized, or autonomous), processing and setup flight commands, keeping flight conditions, and executing commands sent by the navigation subsystem. Two different TFC product variants in different usage contexts were considered through this paper. Although Tiriba was originally designed in MATLAB/Simulink, to illustrate the integration of variability management and compositional dependability analysis techniques, TFC architectural and dependability models were specified in AADL and AADL Error Annex [6]. Base Variability Resolution (BVR) toolset [34] and the developed AADL/Error Annex adapter were used to support variability management in both architecture and dependability models. TFC-SPL was designed following an extractive strategy by analyzing the original Tiriba flight control subsystem Simulink model [33]. TFC-SPL comprises the *Pilot Mode* variation point, which contains four pilot mode options/variants: *Manual Pilot* is mandatory, *Assisted Pilot*, *Autonomous Pilot*, and *Autopilot* are optional. *Manual Pilot* mode is a human operator sending commands to the unmanned aircraft vehicle (UAV) from a ground control station. *Autopilot* executes a pre-defined route. *Assisted Mode* allows the operator sending commands to the UAV configured with *Autopilot*. *Autonomous Pilot* allows the UAV performing actions according to its current environmental conditions captured by pressure sensors. *Assisted Pilot*, *Autonomous Pilot*, and *Autopilot* can be combined into several different ways, allowing seven different flight control variants. TFC product variants can operate in a range of different contexts defined by combining *Airspace*, *Application*, and *UAV Size* variation points [2]. The composition of *pilot mode* and *usage context* variants leads to 84 different TFC variants. Since it would be prohibitive considering all these variants to perform dependability analysis, only TFC manual and autonomous (TFC-MAT) and all pilot modes (TFC-ALL) product variants, *Controlled and Uncontrolled airspace* context variants, illustrated in Fig. 1a, were considered through this paper.

TFC-SPL architecture comprises 4 subsystems and 14 components, which are composed by 252 model elements and subcomponents. An excerpt of the TFC SysML main block diagram is shown in Fig. 1b. *Mode Switch* encapsulates the *pilot mode* variation point, whilst *Command Switch* encapsulates the variation point inherent to the source from the pilot commands, e.g., manual pilot subsystem, sent to the UAV. *Basic Command Processor (BCP)* and its ports represent the realization of the *Autonomous* pilot mode. *PWM Decoder* output port connected to *Command Switch* block represents the realization of the *Manual Pilot* mode in the design. The realization of *Autopilot* is given by: *Autopilot* subsystem, *PWMDecoder.FlightControls* output connected to *FlightStabilizer* and *CommandSwitch* model elements, and *FlightStabilizer.AutopilotSettings* output port connected to *AssistedModeSwitch*. Finally, *ModeSwitcher.ControlMode* output port connected to *AssistedModeSwitch* and *CommandSwitch* elements represent the realization of the *Assisted Pilot* mode.

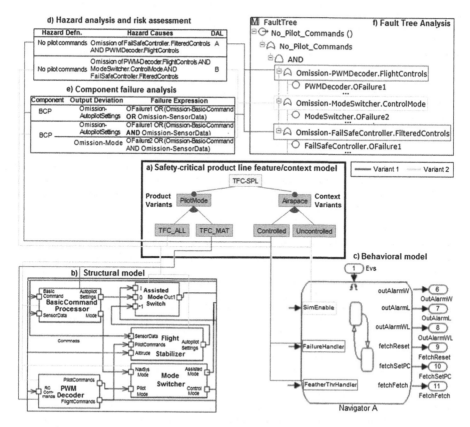

Fig. 1. Impact of product/context variations on design/dependability analysis.

2.2   The Impact of Variation on SPL Design

Interactions among usage context features define constraints that may impact on design decisions aiming safety certification, in which different design choices must be taken according to the targeted context. In both non-critical and safety-critical SPLs, variation points and their variants defined in a feature model have a directly impact on the derivation of variant-specific structural/architectural and behavioral models. In the development of safety-critical systems, the system architecture is often expressed in data-flow oriented models, and the system behavior is expressed in Finite State Machines (FSMs). In data-flow oriented architectural models, structural variability can be found in systems, subsystems, components, their ports and connections via flows from input to output ports, which may change according to the targeted usage context. For example, considering the TFC-SPL [33], developed upon Simulink model blocks, the selection of TFC-MAT variant from *Pilot Mode* variation point (Fig. 1a) implies in the selection of *PWM Decoder* and *Basic Command Processor* components, their ports and connections (Fig. 1b) during the product derivation process.

The realization of TFC-MAT and other product variants in the structural model are highlighted in Fig. 1 with lines linking features (Fig. 1a) to their realization in architectural components and their ports (Fig. 1b). It is important to highlight that variation in the usage context combined with variation in product features, and isolated variation in the usage context may also impact on the derivation of variant-specific structural and behavioral models. For example, considering the TFC-SPL, the selection of *Pilot Mode* product and *Airspace* usage context variants impacts on the derivation of redundant or non-redundant components in a variant-specific architecture model. Still in TFC-SPL, product features associated with *assisted, autopilot, autonomous*, and *manual* pilot modes, i.e., *all pilot modes* (TFC-ALL) product variant (Fig. 1a), are materialized in the architecture by all Tiriba flight control components, their ports and connections (Fig. 1b). Architectural variation inherent to TFC-MAT and TFC-ALL variants and usage context variation can be further propagated throughout Tiriba mission controller behavioral model expressed in a FSM (Fig. 1c).

In safety-critical SPLE, variation in product and usage context features may also impact on the system behavior, which can be expressed in a FSM. Thus, FSM *states, state transitions*, and *events* that trigger state transitions may vary according to the selection of the targeted product/usage context. Variation in FSM can directly impact on elements of the system architecture, changing data port values, configuration of components, and their connections. FSM variability can be firstly found in the number and in the structure of the *state flows* associated with different product variants and their usage context. Variation in a *state flow* can be found in its *input* and *output* data, *states*, and *state transitions*. A *State* can have different local *variables* with different values, and it can be involved in different *transitions* according to the targeted product and usage context variants. *State Transition* variation can be found in *source* and *target* states, in the *event* that triggers the transition, its *execution priority* order and *outgoing events*. A transition *Event* may be triggered by different *mode/states* with different *guard conditions*. A *guard condition* is a condition that should be satisfied for the transition from a *source state* to a *target state*. *Transition events* may also have timing constraints. For example, an event is dispatched on an interval of one second after a system failure. *Effects* of a *transition event* represent changes in *state variables*, which might vary according to the targeted product variant and context. Finally, *state transitions* may dispatch different *outgoing events* affecting both behavior and structure of a given product variant. Examples of *outgoing events* are changes on *states* and *variables* from other FSMs, and changes in structural elements such as *systems, subsystems, subcomponents*, their *connections*, and *port* values.

Variation in FSMs can be found in Tiriba UAV optional mission-related features [33]. Variability in the selection of these features was specified in a FSM that defines the Tiriba mission controller using a mechanism of transitions conditioned to variables that define variability, as illustrated in Fig. 1c. Thus, when *Entry Segment Simulation* is selected, a simulation is performed whenever the UAV starts a new mission segment (Fig. 1c), in order to find out the suitable approach to switch between two mission segments. When *Feather Threshold* feature is selected, the UAV route is adjusted whenever the aircraft deviates more than a certain limit from the planned mission route, i.e., correction start state transition in the FSM [33]. Finally, when *Failure Handler* is selected, the UAV is able to return to specific positions where a picture was not captured during the mission [33]. The activation/deactivation of mission controller features are defined by alternative flows with *Boolean* conditional variables (Fig. 1c), which allow enabling/disabling flows and FSM states according to the selected product/context variants. Thus, for each mission-related feature, there is a variable whose value defines which FSM states and transitions will take place in the final product. *SimEnable* is a *Boolean* variable that controls the activation/deactivation of the behavior related to the *Entry Segment Simulation*. When this feature selected, this variable is set with *true* value. The same is valid for selection/deselection of *Failure Handler* and *Feather Threshold* features.

Usage context features may have influence in the selection of product features that impact on the FSMs, changing the system behavior. Thus, when *uncontrolled* airspace context and TFC-ALL variants are chosen, *SimEnable* variable is set *true* activating the transition to the *Simulating* state in a variant-specific mission controller FSM. When *controlled* airspace context and TFC-MAT variants are selected, *Feather Threshold* and *Failure Handler* variables are set *true*, activating the *correction start* and *good simulation* state transitions.

2.3   The Impact of Variation on SPL Dependability Analysis

In addition to the impact of product and usage context variants on architectural and behavioral models in conventional SPLs, such variation may be propagated throughout dependability analysis in safety-critical SPLs. Thus, variation in SPL architectural and behavioral models, defined in product and usage context variants, can be further propagated throughout the SPL safety lifecycle, impacting on HARA, and allocation of safety requirements (i.e., Functional-Safety Concept in ISO 26262). Figure 1 illustrates the impact of variation in Tiriba SPL design, i.e., architectural (i.e., block diagram in Fig. 1b) and behavioral (i.e., FSM in Fig. 1c) models and usage context (Fig. 1a), on product line HARA and allocation of safety requirements (Fig. 1d), and their propagation throughout component failure modeling (Fig. 1e), Fault Tree Analysis (FTA) and FMEA (Fig. 1f) dependability-related activities required to achieve safety certification. The production of dependability-related artefacts contributes to increase the costs of the system development. Thus, understanding how SPL product and usage context variants impact on dependability analysis contributes to achieve the systematic reuse of both design and dependability artefacts, reducing the certification costs of individual SPL products. Combinations among product and usage context variants may be useful to derive scenarios, which can be used to guide dependability analysis in safety-critical SPL architectures. Thus, different failure conditions can lead to system-level failures (*hazards*) with different probability, severity, criticality levels, and different safety requirements can be allocated to avoid/minimizing hazard effects on the overall safety according to design choices and targeted contexts. Safety requirement is the required risk reduction measures associated with a given system failure or component failure. Variability types in dependability analysis are detailed in the following.

Variability in HARA. During hazard analysis, different *hazards* and *hazard causes* can emerge according to the targeted product and usage context variants. Figure 1d shows an example of variation in Tiriba SPL hazard analysis and risk assessment.

The causes for *no pilot commands* hazard are omission failures in *FailSafeController* and *PWMDecoder* component outputs when TFC-MAT product and *controlled* airspace usage context variants are chosen (Fig. 1a). On the other hand, omission failures in *FailSafeController, ModeSwitcher*, and *PWMDecoder* component outputs are the causes for the occurrence of the same hazard when TFC-ALL variant and *uncontrolled* airspace context are selected. In risk assessment, variation can be found in *probabilistic criteria*, e.g., *likelihood* and *severity* in SAE ARP 4754A avionics standard, used to classify the risk posed by each system hazard for the overall safety. In Tiriba SPL risk assessment, different risk probability and severity were assigned to *no pilot commands* hazard, according to the targeted product and usage context variants. Thus, the probability of occurrence of an omission of pilot commands is 10^{-9} per hour of operation, with a *catastrophic* severity when TFC-MAT product and *controlled airspace* usage context variants are chosen. On the other hand, the probability of occurrence of this hazard is 10^{-7} per hour of operation with a *hazardous* severity when TFC-ALL product and *uncontrolled airspace* context variants are chosen.

Variability in the Allocation of Safety Requirements and Integrity Levels. Still in HARA, after classifying the risk posed by each identified hazard and contributing component failure mode, variation can be found in the allocation of *functional safety requirements* and *Safety Integrity Levels* (SILs) to mitigate the effects of system or component failures on the overall safety. Variation in *functional safety requirements* can be found in architectural decisions that must be taken to eliminate or minimizing the effects of a system or component failure, which might change according to the targeted product and usage context variants. For example, in the Tiriba UAV product line, the control system architecture can be *Redundant* when *controlled airspace* usage context is chosen. A *non-redundant* architecture can be adopted when the UAV is intended to operate in an *uncontrolled airspace* [2].

Variation in the allocation of SILs relates to the variation on the mitigation mechanisms to handle the risk posed by a given system hazard, component failure mode, or component, which might change according to the targeted product and usage context variants. This may impact on the SPL development process, in which different system engineering activities, e.g., verification, validation, and testing should be carried out to address the targeted level [3]. Process-oriented safety standards, e.g., DO-178C and ISO 26262, define a set of safety objectives that should be addressed per SIL. Safety objectives define a set of activities to be performed and artefacts to be produced. DO-178C defines five levels of integrity named Development Assurance Levels (DALs). Level A is the highest stringent integrity, and level E is the less stringent. ISO 26262 automotive standard also defines five levels of safety integrity where QM is the less stringent and level D is the stringent. Addressing higher stringent SILs demand the most stringent safety objectives, system engineering activities, and software artefacts, increasing the development costs. Allocating less stringent SILs to less-critical SPL components and more stringent SILs only to highly critical components can contribute to reduce the SPL development costs. An example of variation in integrity levels is observed in the allocation of DALs to mitigate the effects of the occurrence of *no pilot commands* hazard, during the Tiriba SPL dependability analysis (see Fig. 1d). So, DAL A should be assigned to mitigate the effects of this hazard in TFC-MAT variant operating in a *controlled airspace*. On the other hand, DAL B should be assigned to mitigate the effects of this hazard in TFC-ALL variant operating in an *uncontrolled* airspace. Such variation may be further propagated throughout the decomposition of SILs allocated to hazards throughout contributing failures modes and components. Variation in SIL decomposition, which can be performed with automated tool support [30], is outside the scope of this paper. It is important to highlight that when developing reusable components, all variability aspects of a component should be considered from the initial stages of the SPL lifecycle, and the most stringent SIL assigned to that component in different contexts should be assigned to that component to ensure its safety usage across the SPL. Thus, product and contextual variability will not change the mitigation mechanisms for that component in specific product variants.

Variability in Component Failure Modeling. In the safety lifecycle, component failure modeling is intended to identify how components contribute to the occurrence of potential system-level failures identified during hazard analysis. Variation in component failure modeling can be found in *component output deviations* that contribute in some way for the occurrence of system failures, which might change from a targeted product/context variant to another. Different *input deviations, internal failures*, or combinations among them (named *failure expression*), which contribute to the occurrence of a given *output deviation*, may also be raised in different product/context variants. Variation in the design, i.e., in architecture and behavior models, may also impact on how component failures *propagate* throughout other components. Thus, *output deviations* of a given component may be propagated throughout different components according to the chosen product/context variants. Different product/context variants lead to different connections among components, via their ports, so it may change the way in which failures are propagated throughout the system architecture.

Variation in HARA can be propagated throughout how components contribute to the occurrence of system hazards. Tiriba *Basic Command Processor* (BCP) component failure modeling, shown in Fig. 1e, illustrates examples of variation in *output deviations* and combinations among *component failures* leading to *output deviations* in two different product/context variants. *Omission-autopilotSettings* output deviation may be raised when TFC-MAT product and *controlled* airspace context variants are chosen, whilst one additional output deviation, i.e., *omission-mode*, can also be raised when TFC-ALL product and *uncontrolled* airspace context variants are chosen. Such variation can also be propagated throughout the causes that lead to the occurrence of a given component output deviation. The causes of an output deviation can be stated in a failure expression using logical operators (AND, OR, NOT) that describe how combinations among internal and input failures of a component may lead to the occurrence of an output deviation. Such variation can be found in the causes of the *Omission-autopilotSettings* output in both product variants. An internal omission failure in BCP component or an omission in both BCP inputs can raise an *Omission-autopilotSettings* output in TFC-ALL variant. Conversely, an internal omission failure in BCP or an omission failure in one of its inputs may raise an *Omission-autopilotSettings* in TFC-MAT variant.

Probabilistic criteria values, e.g., *likelihood, severity, failure and repair rates*, which can be assigned to a given hardware component, may also vary according to the targeted product and usage context variants. An example of such variation was found in the assignment of failure rates to *Barometric Processor* hardware component from the Tiriba UAV-SPL. The component failure rate is 10^{-9} per hour of operation when TFC-MAT variant is chosen, and 10^{-7} per hour when TFC-ALL variant is selected. Variation in component failure modeling can be further propagated throughout **fault trees and FMEA** dependability artefacts, which can be automatically generated, with the support compositional dependability analysis techniques [6, 27, 30], from HARA and component failure modeling. Such variation can be seen in fault tree gates and nodes (Fig. 1f), and in the way how components contribute to hazards in a FMEA table from different product variants [5, 28, 29, 32]. Thus, variation in hazard causes can be evidenced in the structure of a fault tree as illustrated in Fig. 1f, in which *PWMDecoder* and *FailSafeController* component output deviations are top-level failures of *no pilot commands* fault tree when TFC-MAT variant is chosen. On the other hand, an output deviation in *ModeSwitcher* component together with other two aforementioned output deviations, are the top-level failures of *no pilot commands* fault tree when TFC-ALL product variant is chosen. Finally, variation in HARA, allocation of safety requirements, component failure modeling, fault trees and FMEA results are propagated throughout the structure of a variant-specific assurance case. An assurance case is a defensible, comprehensive, and justifiable argument supported by a body evidence which demonstrate that the system acceptably safe to operate in a particular context [22]. Assurance case is recommended by standards for certifying safety-critical systems in both automotive [18] and aerospace [10] domains. The analysis of the impact of product and context variants in assurance case is outside the scope of this paper.

3   DEPendable-SPLE

Interactions among product and usage context features can be used to establish safety certification criteria that might impact on SPL architectural decisions and dependability analysis. This section presents DEPendable-SPLE, a model-based approach that extends traditional SPLE methods, with support for HARA, allocation of safety requirements and component failure modeling dependability-related activities, variability modeling/management in both SPL domain and application engineering phases as illustrated in Fig. 2. In domain engineering, four steps related to dependability analysis and variability realization modeling were defined. The last step extends the variability modeling step, established in conventional SPLE methods, by considering

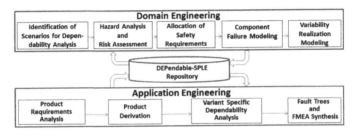

Fig. 2. An overview of DEPendable-SPLE approach.

feature realization in the dependability model. This is intended to support the systematic reuse of dependability information in SPL application engineering.

In SPL application engineering, the following steps were defined: product requirements analysis (i.e., product feature modeling), product derivation, which extends conventional SPLE product derivation process by linking features to their realization in the dependability model, and dependable-related activities: product dependability analysis, and fault trees and FMEA synthesis required to achieve the systematic reuse of dependability information, reducing product safety certification effort and costs. Compositional dependability analysis [6, 27, 30] and variability management techniques [1, 32–34] can be used to support DEPendable-SPLE dependability analysis and variability management steps, both in domain and application engineering. DEPendable-SPLE is applicable independently from the underlying variability management and compositional dependability analysis techniques. It should be used together with traditional SPLE methods [4, 19, 23] for developing dependable safety-critical SPL architectures. The steps shown in Fig. 2 are described and illustrated, by considering TFC-MAT and TFC-ALL product variants from TFC-SPL, in the following.

3.1   DEPendable-SPLE: Domain Engineering

In the first step, dependability analysis scenarios are defined from the analysis of interactions among product and context features. After scoping SPL dependability analysis to a set of targeted scenarios, HARA, allocation of safety requirements, and component failure modeling dependability steps are performed iteratively and incrementally for each scenario. Finally, features are linked to their realization in architecture and dependability models during safety-critical SPL variability realization modeling.

Identification of Candidate Scenarios for SPL Dependability Analysis. *Inputs:* the feature model containing the specification of product and usage context features and their interactions, SPL structural and behavioral models, and analyst's domain knowledge. *Purpose:* identifying, from the analysis of interactions among product and usage context features, variants (*scenarios*) relevant for the stakeholders, by combining features that may be considered to guide SPL dependability analysis. The identification of scenarios encompasses the following tasks: *(i)* to identify combinations among product features, which represent system functions and their interactions in structural and behavioral models, to derive product variants; *(ii)* for each identified product variant, combinations among features are analyzed to establish potential usage contexts in which the given product variant can operate; and finally, *(iii)* by combining the identified product/context variants, different scenarios can be derived. For example, from the analysis of TFC-SPL product/context variants, a range of candidate scenarios can be derived. Scenarios might support safety analysts in extracting the required domain knowledge to perform SPL dependability analysis. However, since it would be prohibitive performing such analysis covering all product/context variants, the analyst's domain knowledge, and relevant product variants for the stakeholders can be used as criteria to assess candidate scenarios to perform dependability analysis [3, 28, 29].

Outputs: combinations among product and usage context variants relevant for the stakeholders. In TFC-SPL, the TFC-MAT/*Controlled* and TFC-ALL/*Uncontrolled* scenarios were considered to perform dependability analysis.

Hazard Analysis and Risk Assessment. *Inputs:* targeted scenario relevant for the stakeholders, SPL structural/architectural and behavioral models. *Purpose:* After choosing a given scenario earlier identified at the previous step, HARA can be performed aiming at identifying combinations among component failures leading to system-level failures named hazards. Hazards can be specified by means of logical expressions involving potential failures in SPL architectural components that might lead to system failures. These failures are generally stated in terms of failure types that typically include: *omission, commission, value, early* or *late* failure modes. Firstly, interactions among core architectural components are analyzed to identify potential hazards that can emerge from such interactions. Later, optional, alternative, and mutual inclusive/exclusive architectural components, representing variation defined in the targeted scenario, are analyzed to identify potential hazards that can emerge in such scenario. This step results in a list of variant-specific hazards. Next, risk assessment is performed to estimate/classify, based on probabilistic risk tolerability criteria defined in the targeted safety standard, the risk posed by each identified hazard. *Outputs:* list of identified hazards and risk classification for each analyzed scenario. TFC-SPL HARA was performed with the support of domain experts, by considering TFC-MAT and TFC-ALL and their usage context, which were analyzed from the perspective of SAE ARP 4754A risk assessment process. During HARA, variation in *no pilot commands* and *value pilot commands* hazards and their risks were identified in both two aforementioned variants (Fig. 1d) as described in Sect. 2.3. *No pilot commands* can emerge in a TFC variant whenever both pilot modes, e.g., manual pilot and autopilot, are omitting their outputs. An incorrect value for pilot commands can emerge when all pilot modes provide wrong flight commands, e.g., wrong coordinates.

Allocation of Safety Requirements. *Inputs:* HARA results. *Purpose:* From the analysis of HARA results, functional safety requirements and SILs are allocated aimed at eliminating/minimizing hazard effects on the overall safety. SILs should be allocated to each identified hazard according to their risk classification. Moreover, SILs allocated to system hazards can be further decomposed throughout contributing components and their failure modes. Such decomposition can be performed with automated support of SIL decomposition genetic/meta-heuristic algorithms [30]. Finally, allocation of functional safety requirements aims at identifying system functions that can be added to the architecture for eliminating/minimizing the impact of a hazard or a component failure on the overall safety. Redundancy is an example of functional safety requirement. When a new functional safety requirement is added to the SPL architecture, dependability analysis should be performed again to evaluate the impact of the newer functionality on the overall safety in the context of the targeted scenarios. *Output:* system functions added to the system architecture, SILs assigned to mitigate hazards and component failures. In TFC-SPL, DALs from different stringencies were assigned to hazards in different TFC variants (Fig. 1d), as described in Sect. 2.3.

Component Failure Modeling. *Inputs:* SPL architecture model and HARA results. *Purpose:* From the analysis of the identified hazards that can emerge in a particular scenario, assumptions about how architectural components can fail and contribute to the occurrence of each identified hazard can be made. In this step, firstly, a particular component is chosen, followed by the identification of potential output deviations that can contribute to the occurrence of each identified hazard. Next, potential causes of each identified output deviation should be specified by analyzing potential combinations among component internal failures and input deviations that may lead to the occurrence of each output deviation. Such analysis continues whilst there are architectural components to be analyzed. *Output:* a set of component failure data showing how components can contribute to the occurrence of system hazards in each targeted scenario. In TFC-SPL, different component failures may contribute to the occurrence of the identified system hazards in different TFC variants and usage contexts. Thus, component failure modeling was carried out, and 106 failure logic expressions were added to 47 Tiriba flight control model elements. Figure 1e illustrates an example of variation in the specification of failure logic for the BCP component. Different output deviations may be raised from this component in different product variants. Omission of *AutopilotSettings* and *Mode* outputs may be raised, contributing to the occurrence of hazards when TFC-ALL variant is chosen. However, only an omission of *AutopilotSettings* output contributes to the occurrence of hazards when TFC-MAT product variant is chosen. Besides, different combinations among component input deviations and internal failures contribute to the occurrence of *Omission-autopilotSettings* output in both TFC-MAT and TFC-ALL variants (column *Failure Expr.* in Fig. 1e). Thus, when variability in the dependability model is solved for TFC-ALL variant, only component failure logic associated with this variant is included in a variant-specific dependability model. Variation in the DALs allocated to TFC hazards is further propagated throughout DALs allocated to mitigate the effects of contributing component failure modes. Variant-specific SIL decomposition can be performed automatically with the support of metaheuristics and genetic algorithms [30]. Additionally, product line SIL decomposition can be derived from the automated analysis of multiple variant-specific SIL decomposition results [28]. Early on the design, it can support the elaboration of a cost-effective safety-critical SPL development process. Finally, different component failure data lead to different fault propagations, i.e., combinations of component failures leading to hazards. Such variation is then propagated throughout fault trees and FMEA. In order to support the systematic reuse of the TFC-SPL dependability model, the impact of design and usage context variations on dependability information is managed during the variability modeling.

Variability Realization Modeling. *Inputs*: SPL feature, architectural, behavioral, and dependability models. *Purpose*: This step expands the *variability modeling* step defined in traditional SPLE methods [4, 23], aimed at establishing mappings between features to their realization in the architecture, to enable variability management in the dependability model. Thus, in this step, mappings linking product/context features to their realization in architectural, behavioral, and dependability models are defined. It can be performed with the support of extensions from existing variant management techniques. This step encompasses the following tasks: *(i)* specification of design and dependable-related variation points and their variants from the analysis of product/context features, and scenarios used to guide dependability analysis; *(ii)* mapping design variants to their realization in the SPL architecture by: defining model elements to be included/excluded when design variants are chosen/resolved during product derivation; and finally, *(iii)* mapping dependable-related variants to their realization in the dependability model by: linking each scenario considered during dependability analysis to the corresponding HARA, risk assessment, allocation of safety requirements, and failure data associated with each variant-specific component. *Output*: The end of this step yields a variability model, which links features to their realization in both architecture and dependability models. TFC-SPL feature and variability models were specified with the support of BVR toolset and BVR AADL Error Annex adapter. Details about how to configure a BVR variability model for a given SPL can be found elsewhere [34]. BVR fragment substitutions were defined to show how variability in the TFC-SPL AADL architecture and Error Annex models are solved when TFC-MAT/*Controlled* and TFC-ALL/*Uncontrolled* structural and dependable-related variants are chosen. Table 1 illustrates placement and replacement fragments, and fragment substitutions associated with TFC-MAT/*Controlled* airspace dependable-related variant. The acronyms in table columns respectively represent: variation point (*VP*), fragment substitution (*FS*), fragment type (*F*), and component failure data (*CFD*). An excerpt of mappings linking dependable-related variants to their realization in the dependability model, defined in the TFC-SPL variability model, is shown in Table 1. So, when TFC-MAT variant and its context are selected, as defined in a placement fragment, HARA results and component failure data associated with other TFC variants are removed from the dependability model. On the other hand, as specified in the replacement fragment, TFC-MAT related HARA results and component failure data are included in the final dependability model. Later, TFC-MAT related fragment substitution is created by combining both placement/replacement fragments. The final TFC-SPL variability model comprises 8 fragment substitutions, 2 placements, and 8 replace-ment fragments. Four fragments substitutions are associated with structural variability, and the other four are associated with variability in the dependability model.

Table 1. Pilot model/usage context variant and its realization in the dependability model.

VP	FS	F	HARA Results	CFD
Pilot mode/airspace	TFC-MAT/CONTROLLED	P	MAS-NoPilotCommands, MAS-ValuePilotCommands, MAP-NoPilotCommands, MAP-ValuePilotCommands, ALL-NoPilotCommands, ALL-ValuePilotCommands	ALL-BCP, MAS-BCP, MAS-PWD
		R	MAT-NoPilotCommands, MAT-ValuePilotCommands	MAT-BCP, MAT-MS, MAT-PWD

3.2   DEPendable-SPLE: Application Engineering

Product Requirements Analysis. *Input:* SPL feature model. *Purpose:* In this step, architectural and dependable-related variants, defined in the SPL feature model, which addresses product-specific requirements, are chosen. *Output:* product feature model.

Product Derivation. *Inputs:* SPL feature and augmented variability models, product feature model, and SPL assets, in this case, architecture, behavioral, and dependability models. *Purpose*: Variability specified in SPL architecture/dependability models are solved with the support of a variability management tool, and a product variant is then derived. Whereas the available variant management techniques do not provide native support for managing variability in the dependability model, in this paper, BVR toolset [34] was adapted to enable support for variability management in AADL Error Annex dependability models. The BVR adapter extends OSATE AADL model editor to enable BVR communicating with OSATE model editors to manage variability in AADL structural/behavioral/dependability models. Since BVR is built upon Eclipse Modeling Framework [9], the adapter was implemented as an Eclipse-based plugin. Due to page limitation, BVR AADL extension is not discussed in this paper. During TFC-SPL product derivation, for each product variant, the following artefacts were input to BVR: TFC-SPL feature model, an instance model, variability model, and SPL AADL/Error Annex structural/dependability models. *Outputs:* Variant-specific AADL/Error Annex models. Variability management in TFC-SPL enabled the systematic reuse of almost 100% of dependability information, produced during domain engineering, in the derivation of each TFC variant.

Variant-Specific Dependability Analysis. *Inputs:* product feature model, product architectural and behavioral models, analyst's domain knowledge. *Purpose:* After product derivation, variant-specific dependability analysis can be performed by following the steps defined in domain engineering. Such analysis focuses on identifying the impact of variant-specific system functions, added to the reused product architecture model, on the overall system safety. When variant-specific system functions are added to the SPL architecture, its corresponding dependability information should be added to the SPL repository. *Outputs:* Enhanced product architecture and dependability models, and in some cases, feedback to the SPL process, enhancing SPL architecture and dependability models.

Fault Trees and FMEA Synthesis. *Inputs:* The reused variant-specific architecture model, enhanced with specific dependability information, is the input for automatic synthesis of fault trees and FMEA, supported by compositional analysis techniques [6, 27, 30]. *Purpose:* Generating FTA and FMEA, which are evidence required by safety standards, e.g., ARP 4754A, to achieve safety certification, from the reused dependability information. The accuracy of the generated variant-specific fault trees and FMEA is dependent whether dependability analysis activities were performed aware of the impact of variation in the design and context. *Outputs:* FTA and FMEA are used to demonstrate that the system architecture addresses the safety requirements. Variant-specific TFC AADL structural and dependability models were input to generate fault trees for 8 variant-specific hazards, and FMEA results were synthesized from the fault trees. Figure 1f shows an excerpt of *no pilot commands* fault tree generated for TFC-ALL variant, which illustrates the impact of SPL variation on hazard causes (see Sect. 2.3). Such variation is further propagated throughout failure modes that indirectly contribute to the occurrence of this hazard. In FMEA, different component failures might directly/indirectly contribute to the occurrence of hazards in each TFC variant. Variation in fault trees and FMEA are further propagated throughout assurance cases, which can be generated from these assets with the support of model-based techniques [16]. The application of DEPendable-SPLE steps enabled the systematic analysis of the impact of variation in TFC-SPL product/context features in both SPL design and dependability analysis. Such analysis increased the precision of dependability analysis information produced in domain engineering, and enabled the systematic reuse of dependable-related information early on the SPL safety lifecycle, in comparison with conventional SPLE methods, which emphasize the analysis of the impact of product/context variation only on the SPL design, and reuse of development artefacts.

4 Related Work

Research on variability management in dependability assets is split into extensions of traditional safety analysis techniques, e.g., FTA and FMEA, to suite SPLE processes [5, 12, 26], and model-based techniques [7, 20, 21, 32]. The most notable work in the first category is the extension of software FTA (SFTA) to address the impact of SPL variation on dependability analysis [5, 12]. In such approach, each leaf node of a SFTA is labeled with the commonality or variability associated with that leaf node. This approach is built upon a technique for developing a product line SFTA in domain engineering, and a pruning technique for reusing SFTA in application engineering. Product Line SFTA was later extended to integrate SFTA results with state-based models [26]. Such extension allows mapping SFTA leaf nodes into components, and modeling the behavior of each component in a state chart. PL-SFTA and its extension consider FTA as a reusable asset. However, FTA can be automatically generated from dependability information produced in domain engineering, e.g., HARA and component failure modeling. Thus, variability management in dependability properties earlier on FTA and FMEA synthesis, as presented in this paper, enables the systematic reuse of dependability information, and traceability of dependable-related variation throughout SPL safety life-cycle. In the second category, Schulze *et al.* [32] have proposed an approach, by integrating commercial *Medini* ISO 26262 safety analysis and *pure::variants* tools, to support variability management in functional safety-related assets, which was evaluated in an automotive case study. Their approach is based on a referencing model, which maps problem-domain features with artefacts in the solution space, in this case, requirements, FTA, and safety goals. Schulze *et al.* approach was further extended with a process for model-based change impact analysis of variability into automotive functional safety [20]. This process combines variability management techniques with safety engineering and software configuration management activities to achieve a complete safety assessment. This process supports change impact analysis in the following scenarios: when a specific variant shows undesired behavior and it needs to be fixed, in cases where an innovative function requires an extension of an existing system function, and the function behavior is changed and it should be analyzed, and when a newer optional function is developed. In the same way as Schulze *et al.* approach and its extension, our approach is built upon a variability model, linking problem-domain context and product features with artefacts from the solution space, e.g., components and their failure data. Although Schulze *et al.* [32] approach provides support for variability management in functional safety, they didn't emphasize the management of the impact of contextual variation in architecture, HARA and component failure modeling, as presented in this paper. In addition, our approach is applicable to domains other than automotive, and it is independent from the underlying tooling support. Nevertheless, Schulze *et al.* approach [32] and its extension [20] also presented a good and efficient solution for variability/change management in functional safety. Kaßmeyer *et al.* [21] presented a systematic model-based approach integrated with the change impact analysis approach [20]. Kaßmeyer *et al.* approach combines requirements engineering and architectural design, safety analysis, and variant management tools, allowing seamless safety engineering across product variants by representing safety artefacts in a homogeneous UML-compliant model notation. In their approach, HARA and component fault modeling is performed by annotating the UML model in the same way as DEPendable-SPLE approach. As part of Kaßmeyer *et al.* *approach,* Domis *et al.* [7] have extended Component Integrated Component Fault Trees (C^2FT) with variation points and integrated it with UML via a profile into Enterprise Architect tool. Although Kaßmeyer *et al.* [21] approach and its extension [7] also provides a good solution for variant management in functional safety; it is dependent upon specific commercial tools. On the other hand, DEPendable-SPLE can be applied independently of the underlying tooling support.

5 Conclusion

This paper has presented DEPendable-SPLE model-based approach to support variant management in dependability analysis. Such approach enables the systematic reuse of SPL architecture and dependability models in application engineering. DEPendable-SPLE is applicable independently from the underlying variant management and dependability analysis techniques. In this paper, the approach was applied with the support of OSATE AADL & Error Annex architectural and error modeling tool, BVR toolset, and OSATE AADL BVR adapter. This adapter was developed by the authors to enable BVR managing variability in AADL architectural/error models. These tools were used to support dependability analysis and variant management steps for the TFC-SPL. DEPendable-SPLE supports the analysis of the impact of design and context variations on dependability analysis. Thus, Tiriba product/context variants were linked to their realization in architecture and dependability models. Further, multiple variant-specific architecture/dependability models were automatically generated during product derivation with the support of BVR tool. The systematic reuse of the dependability model is achieved early on SPL safety process. DEPendable-SPLE enabled the systematic reuse of almost 100% of TFC dependability information, produced in domain engineering, in the derivation of each one of the four TFC product variants. It contributed to reduce the effort and costs in performing dependability analysis for a specific product variant. With the support of compositional techniques, in this case, OSATE AADL, FTAs and FMEA were generated from the reused AADL architecture/dependability models. This paper also presented an analysis of the impact of design/context variations on architecture and dependability analysis. Further work on this topic is focused in detailing how variability in AADL architecture/error models is specified and managed. Further work also intends to investigate the impact of design/context variations on SIL allocation and development processes of safety-critical SPLs. Finally, we also intend to investigate the usage of model-driven techniques to generate variant-specific assurance cases, and the potential of SIL decomposition techniques in supporting SPL architectural decisions.

Acknowledgments. CNPq grant number: 152693-2011-4, and CAPES research agencies.

References

1. Big Lever: Gears (2016). http://www.biglever.com
2. Braga, R.T.V., Trindade Jr., O., Branco, K.R.L.J.C., Lee, J.: Incorporating certification in feature modelling of an unmanned aerial vehicle product line. In: Proceedings of the 16th SPLC, pp. 1–10 (2012)
3. Braga, R.T.V., Trindade Jr., O., Castelo Branco, K.R., Neris, L.D.O., Lee, J.: Adapting a software product line engineering process for certifying safety critical embedded systems. In: Ortmeier, F., Daniel, P. (eds.) SAFECOMP 2012. LNCS, vol. 7612, pp. 352–363. Springer, Heidelberg (2012). https://doi.org/10.1007/978-3-642-33678-2_30
4. Braga, R.T.V., Branco, K.R.L.J.C., Trindade Jr., O., Masiero, P.C.: The ProLiCES approach to develop product lines for safety-critical embedded system and its application to the unmanned aerial vehicles domain. CLEI Electron. J. **15**(2), 1–12 (2012)
5. Dehlinger, J., Lutz, R.: Software fault tree analysis for product lines. In: Proceedings of the 8th IEEE HASE, USA (2004)
6. Delange, J., Feiler, P.: Architecture fault modeling with the AADL error-model annex. In: Proceedings of the 40th EUROMICRO, Verona, pp. 361–368 (2014)
7. Domis, D., Adler, R. Becker, M.: Integrating variability and safety analysis models using commercial UML-based tools. In: Proceedings of the 19th SPLC, pp. 225–234. ACM, New York (2015)
8. Dordowsky, F., Bridges, R., Tschope, H.: Implementing a software product line for a complex avionics system. In: Proceedings of the 15th International SPLC, pp. 241–250. IEEE (2011)
9. ECLIPSE: Eclipse modeling framework project (2016). http://www.eclipse.org/modeling/emf
10. EUROCAE: ARP4754A - guidelines for development of civil aircraft and systems. EUROCAE (2010)
11. EUROCAE: Aircraft wheel braking system. https://github.com/osate/examples/tree/master/ARP4761
12. Feng, Q., Lutz, R.: Bi-directional safety analysis of product lines. J. Syst. Softw. **78**(2), 111–127 (2005)

13. Gómez, C., Liggesmeyer, P., Sutor, A.: Variability management of safety and reliability models: an intermediate model towards systematic reuse of component fault trees. In: Schoitsch, E. (ed.) SAFECOMP 2010. LNCS, vol. 6351, pp. 28–40. Springer, Heidelberg (2010). https://doi.org/10.1007/978-3-642-15651-9_3

14. Habli, I., Kelly, T., Hopkins, I.: Challenges of establishing a software product line for an aerospace engine monitoring system. In: Proceedings of the 11th SPLC, Japan, pp. 193–202. IEEE (2007)

15. Haugen, O., Moller-Pedersen, B., Oldevik, J., Olsen, G.K., Svendsen, A.: Adding standardized variability to domain specific languages. In: Proceedings of the 12th International Software Product Line Conference, pp. 139–148. IEEE (2008)

16. Hawkins, R., Habli, I., Kolovos, D., Paige, R., Kelly, T.: Weaving an assurance case from design: a model-based approach. In: Proceedings of the 16th HASE, Daytona Beach, pp. 110–117. IEEE (2015)

17. Heuer, A., Pohl, K.: Structuring variability in the context of embedded systems during software engineering. In: Proceedings of the 8th Workshop on Variability Modelling of Software-Intensive Systems. ACM (2014)

18. ISO: ISO 26262: road vehicles functional safety (2011)

19. Kang, K.C., Kim, S., Lee, J., Kim, K., Jounghyun Kim, G., Shin, E.: Form: a feature-oriented reuse method with domain-specific reference architectures. Ann. Softw. Eng. **5**, 143–168 (1998)

20. Käßmeyer, M., Schulze, M., Schurius, M.: A process to support a systematic change impact analysis of variability and safety in automotive functions. In: Proceedings of the 19th SPLC, pp. 235–244. ACM, New York (2015)

21. Käßmeyer, M., Moncada, D.S.V., Schurius, M.: Evaluation of a systematic approach in variant management for safety-critical systems development. In: Proceedings of the 13th International Conference Embedded and Ubiquitous Computing, pp. 35–43. IEEE (2015)

22. Kelly, T.P., McDermid, J.A.: Safety case construction and reuse using patterns. In: Daniel, P. (ed.) Safe Comp 97, pp. 55–69. Springer, London (1997). https://doi.org/10.1007/978-1-4471-0997-6_5

23. Krueger, C.: Variation management for software production lines. In: Proceedings of the 2nd SPLC, vol. 2379, pp. 37–48 (2002)

24. Lee, K., Kang, K.C.: Usage context as key driver for feature selection. In: Proceedings of the 14th SPLC, vol. 6287, pp. 32–46 (2010)

25. Leveson, N.: Door control system. https://github.com/osate/examples/tree/master/Train

26. Liu, J., Dehlinger, J., Lutz, R.: Safety analysis of software product lines using stated modeling. J. Syst. Softw. **80**(11), 1879–1892 (2007)

27. Mazzini, S., Favaro, J., Puri, S., Baracchi, L.: CHESS: an open source methodology and toolset for the development of critical systems. In: Join Proceedings of EduSymp, pp. 59–66 (2016)

28. Oliveira, A.L., Braga, R., Masiero, P.C., Papadopoulos, Y., Habli, I., Kelly, T.: Model-based safety analysis of software product lines. Int. J. Embed. Syst. **8**, 412–426 (2016)

29. Oliveira, A.L., Braga, R.T.B., Masiero, P.C., Papadopoulos, Y., Habli, I., Kelly, T.: A model-based approach to support the automatic safety analysis of multiple product line products. In: Proceedings of the 4th Brazilian Symposium on Computing Systems Engineering, Brazil, pp. 7–12. IEEE (2014)

30. Papadopoulos, Y., Walker, M., Parker, D., Rüde, E., Hamann, R.: Engineering failure analysis and design optimization with HIP-HOPS. J. Eng. Fail. Anal. **18**(2), 590–608 (2011)

31. RTCA: DO-178C software considerations in airborne systems and equipment certification (2012)

32. Schulze, M., Mauersberger, J., Beuche, D.: Functional safety and variability: can it be brought together? In: Proceedings of the 17th International SPLC, pp. 236–243. ACM, New York (2013)
33. Steiner, E.M., Masiero, P.C., Bonifácio, R.: Managing SPL variabilities in UAV Simulink models with Pure: variants and Hephaestus. CLEI Electron. J. **16**(1), 1–16 (2013)
34. Vasilevskiy, A., Haugen, Ø., Chauvel, F., Johansen, M.F., Shimbara, D.: The BVR tool bundle to support product line engineering. In: Proceedings of the 19th International Software Product Line Conference, pp. 380–384. ACM, New York (2015)

Towards Estimating and Predicting User Perception on Software Product Variants

Jabier Martinez[1](✉), Jean-Sébastien Sottet[2], Alfonso García Frey[4],
Tegawendé F. Bissyandé[3], Tewfik Ziadi[1], Jacques Klein[3], Paul Temple[5],
Mathieu Acher[5], and Yves le Traon[3]

[1] Sorbonne University, UPMC, Paris, France
{jabier.martinez,tewfik.ziadi}@lip6.fr
[2] Luxembourg Institute of Science and Technology, Esch-sur-Alzette, Luxembourg
jean-sebastien.sottet@list.lu
[3] University of Luxembourg, Luxembourg, Luxembourg
{tegawendef.bissyande,jacques.klein,yves.traon}@uni.lu
[4] Yotako, Luxembourg, Luxembourg
alfonsogarcia.frey@yotako.io
[5] Univ Rennes, Inria, CNRS, IRISA, Rennes, France
{paul.temple,mathieu.acher}@irisa.fr

Abstract. Estimating and predicting user subjective perceptions on
software products is a challenging, yet increasingly important, endeavour. As an extreme case study, we consider the problem of exploring
computer-generated art object combinations that will please the maximum number of people. Since it is not feasible to gather feedbacks for all
art products because of a combinatorial explosion of possible configurations as well as resource and time limitations, the challenging objective is
to rank and identify optimal art product variants that can be generated
based on their average likability. We present the use of Software Product
Line (SPL) techniques for gathering and leveraging user feedbacks within
the boundaries of a variability model. Our approach is developed in two
phases: (1) the creation of a data set using a genetic algorithm and real
feedback and (2) the application of a data mining technique on this data
set to create a ranking enriched with confidence metrics. We perform a
case study of a real-world computer-generated art system. The results
of our approach on the arts domain reveal interesting directions for the
analysis of user-specific qualities of SPLs.

Keywords: Software product lines · Quality attributes
Quality estimation · Computer-generated art · Product variants

1 Introduction

With the whole myriad of software alternatives that exist today, the adoption
of a software product is eventually dependent on users' subjective perception,

© Springer International Publishing AG, part of Springer Nature 2018
R. Capilla et al. (Eds.): ICSR 2018, LNCS 10826, pp. 23–40, 2018.
https://doi.org/10.1007/978-3-319-90421-4_2

beyond the offered functionalities. Being able to apprehend, estimate and predict this perception on the software as a whole will be an important step towards efficient software production. Unfortunately, subjective perception of a software product is hard to formalize. It cannot even be computed with a simple formula based on the perception of its components: melting good ingredients indeed does not necessarily produce a good recipe. Systematically predicting the subjective appreciation of software is therefore a research direction that is still at its early stages. An extreme case where appreciation is important, is when the intention of the product is just about "beauty": this is the case of computer-generated art. By studying computer-generated art we can infer insightful techniques for estimating the perception of other types of software involving user-specific quality aspects.

The practice of computer-generated art, also known as generative art, involves the use of an autonomous system that contributes to the creation of an art object, either in its whole, or in part by reusing pieces of art from a human artist, or using predefined algorithms or transformations [4]. This art genre is trending in the portfolio of many artists and designers in the fields of music, painting, sculpture, architecture or literature [4]. Apart from art installations, we consume computer-generated art systems in our daily life as in videogames, cinema effects, screen-savers or visual designs. A computer-generated art setup is driven at its core by a software system that implements the algorithms for "creating" the artworks. The development of such software presents the same challenges as any software development project. In general, the autonomous systems for computer-generated art rely to some degree to a randomization step in the generation algorithms. However, when no relevant stochastic component is introduced and the creation is not limited to a unique art object, computer-generated art allows one to derive different art objects in a predefined and deterministic fashion, giving rise to a *family of art products*. Usually, because of the combinatorial explosion of all possible art objects, not all of them will actually be created. Besides, a number of them may not reach the aesthetic quality desired by the users. Exploring the art product family to find the "best" products is thus challenging for computer-generated art practitioners.

We note that the challenges for exploring generative art products boil down to traditional Software Product Line Engineering (SPLE). It thus seems opportune to leverage SPL techniques for the design and implementation of generative art systems. Based on our experiments with a generative art case study, we devise an SPLE approach capable of dealing with subjective opinions and end-user concerns. SPLs are built following two main activities: variability modeling and product derivation. A given variability model defines a set of valid combinations of features, referred to as configurations. The product derivation step then assembles different assets related to the features of a specific configuration to yield a product instance. As an SPL can lead to high number of product variants, the challenge thus becomes to produce only those that are aligned with certain quality attributes. In our case study, this quality attribute is the appreciation of beauty which is not known a priori and difficult to formally define.

We propose a two-phase approach for leveraging user feedbacks and *ranking* all the possible art products based on the calculated estimations. Instead of continuously picking random products for requesting feedback, we rely on interactive genetic algorithms [22] in the first phase to explore the configuration space. The implemented fitness function, which is the genetic algorithm operator that drives the evolution, is not automatically calculated but provided interactively by users. This phase yields a subset that already tries to converge towards optimal or suboptimal products. In the second phase, we go beyond any other evolutionary art approach or analogue SPL technique, and we propose a method to infer the estimation on user perception for all art product variants applying data mining interpolation techniques based on a defined distance function between any pair of configurations.

As validation, we use real-world data from an artistic installation created in collaboration with a professional artist. We built a generative art system for landscape paintings, where each painting is generated by assembling visual components. To formalize the variability in the artist style, we rely on a feature model [14]. The derivation process is then performed using SPL techniques treating painting compositional elements as software reusable components.

The main contribution is to *empirically study whether we can predict the like/dislike user perception of a software, built by an SPL assembling perceivable components*. The related contributions are:

- We discuss how user feedback can be leveraged in the computer-generated art system derivation processes.
- We propose an approach for ranking all art products using user feedback on a relevant subset of products. This ranking is ordered by the score estimation. For each rank item we propose a confidence metric for the prediction.
- We propose a validation on the feasibility of the approach after applying it to a real-world installation for computer-generated art.
- We introduce SPLE formalisms as a computer-generated art technique.
- The approach is explained in detail so it can be employed in other software families where it is relevant to predict user-specific qualities.

This paper is an extension of a 2-page idea article [17] focused on genetic algorithms while this paper is more focused on the potential for assessing variants. The paper is structured as follows: Sect. 2 introduces related work and Sect. 3 presents our case study. Section 4 presents the motivation and Sect. 5 provides the details of our approach. Section 6 presents the results of the case study and its evaluation is presented in Sect. 7. Section 8 presents the threats to validity and Sect. 9 concludes and outlines future work.

2   Related Work

Leveraging user feedback to improve the results of the creation of software products is a challenging endeavour. This challenge has been already tackled both in the computer-generated art and SPLE community. Evolutionary computing applied to computer-generated art is the main technique used to leverage user feedback [19]. For evolution, the main aspect is the fitness function that represents the requirements to adapt to (it defines what improvement means). In our case, the evaluation function is based on user feedback in opposition to automatically calculated fitness functions. Some works already proposed to learn to predict user aesthetic preferences [12,15] but we focus on real user feedback and an SPL context in our approach. The relevant difference of our work compared with the evolutionary art approaches is that they only contain the evolution phase. Their assumption is that the better adapted products found at the end of the evolution should be the best ones. However, in a normal situation, not all the possible configurations were assessed given the time and resource limitations. In this paper we present a second phase to predict the user feedback of the non-assessed products. This phase was also missing in previous works in SPL-based User Interface (UI) design [18] or in other works dealing with SPL-based video configurations [7]. Regarding SPLE domain, only few works consider user feedback as driver for SPLE processes. In single-system development, user feedback has been already automatically leveraged for dealing with quality attributes related to software design (e.g., [2,8]). However, for SPLs, its importance was overlooked.

Many existing work can be found on selecting optimal SPL product variants based on some criteria. To achieve this, it is a common practice to enhance the FM by what is referred to as quality attribute annotations, which mainly specify non-functional properties [3,20,21,23]. Quality attribute annotations associated to the FM are then used to reason about the optimal selection of features. For instance, Benavides *et al.* [3] consider the selection problem as a Constraint Satisfaction Problem and solved it using CSP solvers, or Sayyad *et al.* [20] use Search-based algorithms. Also in the SPL testing community it is a well-known issue to select the best configurations to be tested guided by a set of predefined testing objectives [5,6,11,13] which can be considered as quality attributes. In comparison with approaches dealing with quality attributes, our work consider user feedback that presents two main peculiarities: The first one is that user appreciations are always based on a product as a whole while in these approaches quality attribute annotations are directly mapped to concrete features. The second peculiarity is that user feedback subjectivity requires feedback aggregation mechanisms while quality attribute annotations in these approaches are fixed independently of user feedback. For example, *cost* quality attribute annotations in [11,20] are defined as a fixed value per feature.

3   Introducing SPL-Based Generative Art

We collaborated with Gabriele Rossi, a professional art painter with whom we were able to conduct a large user study on computer-generated art built by composing portions of paintings. We developed this system using SPLE techniques.

Variability within a landscape painting: In the last years, Gabrielle has been drawing abstract representations of landscapes with quite a recognizable style of decomposing the canvas in different parts: a *sky* part, a *middle* part and the *ground*. This variability is further enhanced by the fact that the sky and ground are mandatory while the middle part is optional. For the realization of the computer-generated art system, he created different representative paintings for each part. For the sky part, he painted 10 concrete representative sky paintings hereafter noted S_i, with $i \in [1..10]$. Similarly, he painted 9 paintings of the middle part (noted M_i, where M_{10} means the absence of middle part), and 10 paintings of the ground part (noted G_i).

Another variability dimension identified by the artist concerns the perception of the composition. Indeed, this perception can change if any instance of any part is flipped horizontally, thus adding an optional property for configurations: For example, a given ground part may have more brightness in its left or right side, adding a compositional decision for where to place this brightness in the whole painting. The artist also stated that each of the parts could take more or less space in the canvas. We therefore included an optional property for extra size: For example, if a painting should have the sky visible in only a small section of the canvas, the middle and ground parts must be of extra size.

The variability in this domain can be expressed through Feature Modeling [14] which exposes the different configurations that can be selected to yield painting variants. It was thus easy to introduce the artist to different FM concepts and to discuss the different elements of paintings in terms of features. This led to the establishment of a FM (shown in Fig. 1) for his painting style.

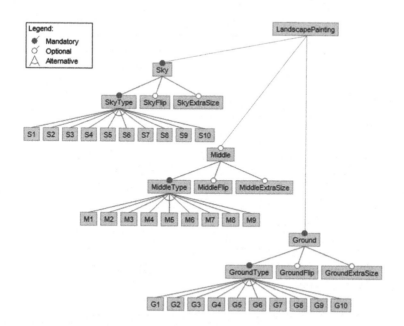

Fig. 1. Feature model of the landscape paintings

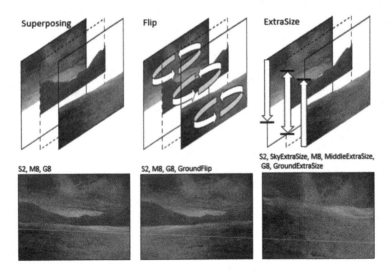

Fig. 2. Painting derivation process and examples

Deriving landscape paintings: Figure 2 illustrates the derivation process where a specific configuration, i.e., a given selection for sky, middle and ground, is assembled by superposition of the different visual components. We further illustrate how different paintings in the style of the artist can be obtained by flipping one or more painting parts or/and increasing the size of elements. We have implemented a tool which, given a configuration from the FM of Fig. 1, we can generate a landscape painting based on the reusable assets of painting parts provided by the artist.

4   Motivations and Problem Statement

Computer-generated art and SPLE yield product variants that users may like it or not. For computer-generated art, it is the beauty of the product that is appreciated while in SPLE, it can be the aesthetic quality of the user interface as well, but it can be other user-specific quality attributes such as usability aspects or, more broadly, human-computer interaction concerns [18]. In both cases, the user feedback is important for producing optimal products that are aligned with user expectations. The motivation behind our work is to explore how user feedback can be automatically leveraged in practice to rank SPL product variants. This ranking contain the estimations and predictions that serves as input for domain experts decision-making process to select the products that have more guarantees of collective acceptance.

The problem faced in this paper is **ranking computer-generated art product variants based on user feedback**. Specifically we deal with SPL-based computer-generated art where deriving all products and collecting user feedback on each of them is virtually impossible: with the relatively small FM presented in Fig. 1, the total number of possible configurations amounts to 59,200. Therefore, the first research question in this paper is:

– **RQ1:** Given the combinatorial explosion of configurations and the limited resources, how can one identify and select the optimal subset of products that are relevant for user assessment?

As we only consider a subset of products for user assessment, most of the products have not yet been assessed. In addition, user feedback are subjective by nature (different persons could assess the same product differently). Hence, the second research question for ranking product variants is:

– **RQ2:** Given a subset of assessed product variants, how can one infer the user feedback of the non assessed products? How can one aggregate user feedback to calculate new predictions even for the already assessed products?

5   Approach

We propose an enhanced method of collecting user feedback to create a relevant data set (first phase) which is processed to create a ranking (second phase).

5.1   Phase 1: Data Set Creation Through Evolution

The first phase of the approach aims at overcoming the challenge of selecting a relevant set of FM configurations to be presented to users for assessment. Indeed, to address the combinatorial explosion of possible configurations, we rely on an interactive genetic algorithm [22] which explore the possible configuration space trying to reach optimal or suboptimal solutions.

The genetic algorithm permits to create more data set instances in the regions that are more adapted to the fitness function. In our case study, the fitness function for the genetic algorithm is based on the user feedback captured using the device shown at the bottom of Fig. 3. This device implements a physical 5-point scale with values ranging from 1 (*strong dislike*) to 5 (*strong like*). When a user votes, the displayed painting (top of Fig. 3) vanishes and the next painting of the genetic algorithm population is displayed. When all paintings from the population have been

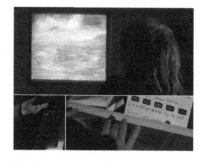

Fig. 3. Displayed painting and voting device with a five points scale

assessed, a new population is yielded based on the calculations of the genetic algorithm, and the exploration towards optimal paintings continues, until it is stopped manually at the end of the session.

Algorithm 1. Interactive genetic algorithm for data set creation

input: Population = 20 members, Genetic representation of a member = 9 positions: SkyType, SkyFlip, SkyExtraSize; MiddlePart, MiddleFlip, MiddleExtraSize, GroundType, GroundFlip, GroundExtraSize; Type value from 0 to 9, Flip and ExtraSize values 0 or 1; Example: 801510210

output: data set of user assessments

1: population ← initializePopulation()
2: **while** ManualStopNotPerformed **do**
3:    **for** $member_i \in \{population\}$ **do**
4:       $member_i.fitness$ ← getScore($member_i$)
5:       registerDataInstance($member_i$)
6:    **end for**
7:    parents ← parentSelection(population)
8:    offspring ← crossover(parents)
9:    offspring ← mutate(offspring)
10:   population ← offspring
11: **end while**

Algorithm 1 shows the panmictic, non-elitist, generational and interactive genetic algorithm that we implemented. The *input* section of the algorithm shows how the genotype of a landscape painting phenotype was designed. Sky type, middle and ground positions are assigned with values representing all possible parts. In the case of the middle part, which is optional, value 9 represents its absence in the composed painting. Further, for this special case, the flip and extra size features are not valid, and thus a special treatment is performed in the operators of the genetic algorithm.

We now describe the characteristics of the algorithm. At line 1, the *initialization operator* creates a pseudo-random initial population: actually, we force all sky, middle and ground parts to appear in the initial population. The evolution starts at line 2 until it is manually stopped. During the evolution, from line 3 to line 6 each member of the population is evaluated using an *evaluation operator* based on user feedback. In comparison with generic implementations where the fitness function is normally automatically computed, in our process we need the participation of users to set the fitness value. The *parent selection operator* is then based on a fitness proportionate selection (line 7). At line 8, the *crossover operator* is based on one-point crossover with the peculiarity that it is not possible to select the last two positions to force to crossover the sky, middle and ground parts. Then the *mutation operator* used at line 9 is uniform with $p = 0.1$. Such a high mutation factor is meant to prevent a loss of motivation from users by reducing the likelihood that they will keep assessing similar products from the population, while thus enabling us to explore new regions. Finally, at line 10, the *survivor selection operator* is based on a complete replacement of the previous generation with the new generation.

5.2   Phase 2: Ranking Computation

We make the assumption that when two products are similar in the way they were assembled they will be appreciated similarly. We describe how we compute the ranking of all products, including those which have not been directly assessed by users. First, we define a similarity measure for computing a *similarity distance* between two configurations in the domain (composed landscape paintings in our example). We then retrieve neighbors based on this similarity distance to compute a ranking of the configurations as well as confidence metrics.

Similarity Distance: Given two configurations C_i and C_j, we aim at formally computing a value for the similarity distance between them. The notion of similarity distance between configurations was already studied in the software engineering literature, specially by the SPL testing community [1,9,10]. Apart from the use of generic similarity distances (e.g., Jaccard distance in [10] or Hamming distance in [1]), other approaches can be based on ad hoc domain-specific similarity functions. In this work, we defined our own similarity function for the configurations of the FM presented in Fig. 1 as we considered that the results will be better than generic similarity distances. That means that the measure is ad hoc and defined based on artist's comments and our own expert judgement. To compare two configurations, we start by assuming that they are the same ($distance = 0$). The distance between them increases by 1 point for each painting part which is different. If a part is the same in both configurations, we check the flip feature and increase the distance by 0.2 in case of dissimilarities. Finally, and whether the parts are identical or not, we increase the distance by 0.2 if a part has an extra size in one configuration and not in the other: extra size is independent to the part as it has an impact on the whole composition. To account for the fact that the optional middle part may not be present, we always check that the part P is not null. The maximum distance between two configurations is 3.6 when the three parts are different and every part has extra size in one configuration and not in the other. Our intuition was that the fact that parts are different (1 point) is more important than the flip or extra size (we estimated it with 0.2 points). This definition of distance allows us to reason about the neighborhood of a configuration in the space.

Similarity Radius: To be part of the neighborhood of a given configuration, any configuration must be inside a *similarity radius*. Such a radius will allow to restrict the products that will be considered similar enough for inferring information from one to the other. For example, if we consider that two paintings are similar when only one of the parts is different (+1) and two transformations at most (flip +0.2 or extra size +0.2) should be performed to make them equal, then the radius value will amount to 1.4.

Weighted Mean Score Computation: To assess the collective agreement on the score of a given configuration, we consider its neighborhood and compute the mean score in a similarity radius. We also consider this computed score as the expected level of appreciation by users. For computing reliable mean values, a weight is assigned for each instance of the data set. This weight depends on their proximity with the configuration under study, C_c.

Equation 1 provides the formula for computing the weighted mean score $\bar{s}_c$ for configuration C_c where s_i and w_i represent respectively the score and the associated weight of each of the N configurations C_i, in the similarity radius, that were in the data set.

$$\bar{s}_c = \frac{\sum_{i=1}^{N} w_i \cdot s_i}{\sum_{i=1}^{N} w_i} \quad (1)$$

Figure 4 describes four approaches for assigning a weight to the scores of configurations in the similarity radius. In each weighting approach, we will consider that the weight of the score for any configuration outside the radius is null ($w_i = 0$ when $d_{c,i} > r$, where $d_{c,i}$ is the similarity distance between configurations C_c and C_i and r the value of the radius).

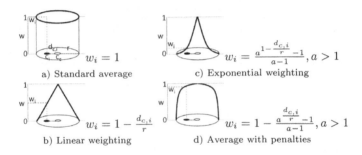

Fig. 4. Different options to calculate the weight

Empirical Selection of the Approach Settings: To select the radius and the weighting approach, we explore different combinations to identify the one that minimizes the error rate. The ideal experimental scenario would require to reconvene with all people who participated in the user study and ask them to assess some missing configurations for which we had previously inferred a score, and then evaluate the accuracy of the inference. However, this was not practically feasible, leading us to rely on a classical 10-fold cross-validation scenario.

The error rate is computed based on the difference between the expected value (the computed weighted mean score) and the actual user feedback score for each instance of the test set. The evaluation is a numeric prediction so we selected the *mean absolute error* (mae) as error rate metric as shown in Eq. 2, where T is the number of instances in the test set, $\bar{s}_i$ is the weighted mean score of C_i computed with the training set (which represents the expected score) and s_i is the score of C_i in this instance of the test set (the actual score).

$$mae = \frac{\sum_{i=1}^{T} |\bar{s}_i - s_i|}{T} \quad (2)$$

Figure 5 shows the performances of different combinations of radius values and weighting approaches. Besides the mean absolute error values, we also represent how the choice of radius values impacts the coverage of the test set: if the radius is small there is a possibility that for some configurations the neighboring will be empty, thus preventing the computation of a mean score. Because such instances are not taken into account for the computation of the mean absolute error, it is important to know the average proportion (i.e., percentage) of the test set that is covered. The graph reveals that we start covering all instances of the test set with a radius of 1.3.

Ranking Creation: After identifying empirically the most reliable radius value and weighting approach, we exhaustively compute the weighted mean for all possible configurations. In our case study, an exhaustive calculation for the 59,200 configurations is computationally feasible. In other cases where exhaustive calculation is not feasible, non-euclidean centroid calculations could be used to limit the configurations to analyze and make the approach scalable. In the possible cases where a configuration C_c has no neighbors within its similarity radius, no score is computed and it is ignored in the final ranking.

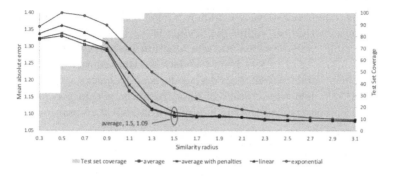

Fig. 5. Mean absolute error for different radius values and weight calculation approaches

Confidence Levels for Ranking Items: We define three main metrics for measuring the confidence levels.

Neighbors similarity confidence: The first metric explores the average distance with the neighbors. Figure 6a illustrates the importance of this metric. In both cases, the weighted mean is 5, however, intuitively, one is more confident about the accuracy of the mean score for the case on the left because the instance actually assessed is more similar.

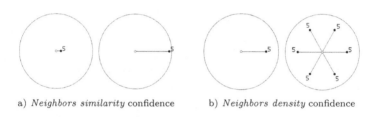

a) *Neighbors similarity* confidence   b) *Neighbors density* confidence

Fig. 6. Illustration of the importance of confidence levels for mean scores

We define a neighbors similarity confidence (*nsimc*) using Eq. 4 where N is the number of data instances (i.e., neighbors) within the radius of C_c. When $N = 0$, this metric is not applicable and

$$nsimc_c = \frac{\sum_{i=1}^{N} w_i}{N} \quad (3)$$

$nsimc_c = 1$ when all data instances are in the center, i.e., all configurations in the radius are identical to the configuration for which the score is inferred. For the calculations of *nsimc* in this paper we will use the linear weighting approach.

Neighbors density confidence: The second metric explores the density of neighbors in the similarity radius. Figure 6b illustrates the importance of this metric. In both cases, the weighted mean has a value of 5, but intuitively again, the confidence is greater for the second case. Equation 5 provides the formula for computing the neighbors density confidence where num represents the number of data instances within the radius of C_c, max is the highest value of num found in all the possible configurations and the function $instancesWithNeighbors(i)$ returns the number of instances from the data set that contain exactly i neighbors within their radius. We make a design decision to have a neighbors density confidence of 0.5 when the number of data instances within the radius of the configuration corresponds to the median of $instancesWithNeighbors(i)$.

$$ndenc_c = \frac{\sum_{i=1}^{num} instancesWithNeighbors(i)}{\sum_{i=1}^{max} instancesWithNeighbors(i)} \quad (4)$$

We describe in Fig. 7 the graph of neighbors density confidence for all possible configurations of our case study. The sum of all accumulated values is the total number of 59,200 possible configurations. For example, we can see that around 500 configurations in the data set have each a total of exactly 8 neighbors within their radius that corresponds to a $ndenc$ of the 8%. We also observe that the maximum of data instances within a similarity radius is 78 and was recorded for only one possible configuration. We highlight the Q1, Q2 and Q3 quartiles which divide the data set into four equal groups where Q2 corresponds to the median. In the example of our case study, Q1 = 16, Q2 = 23 and Q3 = 29 correspond to a neighbors density confidence values of 25%, 50% and 75% respectively.

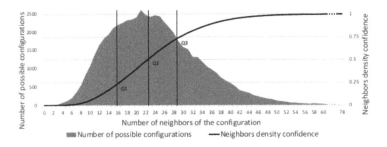

Fig. 7. Graph of neighbors density confidence

Global confidence: Finally we define a global confidence metric that takes into account the previous metrics. Equation 5 provides the formula for computing the global confidence. For our case study we decided to put more weight to $ndenc$. The rationale was to put an emphasis on the number of instances of user assessments used to compute the mean. We made the design decision of setting w_{ndenc} to 0.75 and w_{nsimc} to 0.25 in the computations presented in this paper.

$$gconf_c = w_{ndenc} \cdot ndenc + w_{nsimc} \cdot nsimc \quad (5)$$

6   Case Study Results

Phase 1 Results: Data Set Creation. The installation was available to the public as part of an art festival at Théâtre de Verre at Paris. The installation was operative for 4 h and 42 min and 1,620 votes were collected. The genetic algorithm and its exploration process towards optimal products led to 1,490 paintings being voted once, 62 paintings being voted twice and only 2 paintings being voted three times. No data was gathered to make distinctions about different user profiles nor any control mechanism was used to limit the number of votes per person. On average we were able to register 5.74 votes per minute from around 150 people of different ages and sociocultural backgrounds who voted for one or more paintings. Figure 8 shows the scores' distribution.

We applied data mining attribute selection algorithms in an attempt to discriminate between relevant and irrelevant features. Concretely, we evaluated the worth of each feature by computing the value of the chi-squared statistic with respect to the class (i.e., a score in the range of 1 to 5). The ranked features showed that ground, sky and

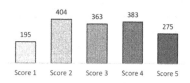

Fig. 8. Scores

middle parts were more relevant features than middleFlip, groundExtraSize, groundFlip, skyFlip, middleExtraSize, skyExtraSize. However, *a priori* association discovery algorithms and decision trees performed poorly (incorrect classification of 80% of instances in the 10-fold test sets).

Phase 2 Results: Ranking Creation. Based on the empirical investigation of the different radius and weighting approaches, we have tuned our ranking computation parameters to optimal values. We aimed at high coverage of configurations while minimizing mean absolute error rates. In Fig. 5, we marked with a circle our selected parameters. We set the radius to 1.5 and selected the standard average weighting approach for the weighted mean score computation. A radius of 1.5 further fits the artist's intuition of the minimum differences in paintings to be considered "similar".

We computed the weighted mean score for all 59,200 possible configurations and ranked them accordingly. Table 1 depicts the paintings that were derived from the top 10 configurations with highest weighted mean scores (wmean). The highest wmean was 4.75 for only one configuration. None of the configurations in the top 10 were part of the data set created in Phase 1 when collecting user feedback. For example, the third best configuration score was obtained based on the wmean of 11 different configurations with scores computed from actual user feedback. Table 2 depicts the bottom 5 configurations of the ranking. We observed that bottom configurations had in general less confidence given the effect of the genetic algorithm that tried to avoid these regions.

We also used the global confidence metric to filter and reorder at will the ranking items. The following examples aim to show the kind of analyses that are possible thanks to enriching the ranking with confidence metrics. Figure 9a shows the product that was derived for the configuration with the highest global confidence (82%). This configuration got a wmean of 3.27 and holds the rank 14,532. The configuration with the highest confidence level for configurations that are liked (i.e., *score* > 4) holds the position 102 within our ranking.

Table 1. Top 10. Each configuration is defined by: wmean {gconf% (*ndenc%, nsimc%*)}

4.75 {4% (≈ *0%,17%*)}	4.67 {5% (≈ *0%,20%*)}	4.64 {8% (*8%,10%*)}	4.54 {16% (*14%,23%*)}	4.5 {5% (*2%,13%*)}
4.42 {33% (*36%,32%*)}	4.41 {43% (*48%,27%*)}	4.4 {6% (≈ *0%,23%*)}	4.36 {48% (*56%,23%*)}	4.35 {37% (*40%,30%*)}

Table 2. Bottom 5 defined by: wmean {gconf% (*ndenc%, nsimc%*)}

1.5 {4% (*2%,8%*)}	1.5 {3% (*1%,11%*)}	1.33 {5% (≈ *0%,20%*)}	1.33 {3% (≈ *0%,11%*)}	1 {3% (≈ *0%,13%*)}

The corresponding product is illustrated in Fig. 9b. Similarly, we identify the configuration with the highest confidence level for configurations that are disliked (i.e., *score* < 2). It holds the rank 59,145 and it is shown in Fig. 9c.

a) $gconf = 82\%$	b) $gconf = 63\%$	c) $gconf = 21\%$
Rank 15,532	Rank 102 - liked	Rank 59,145 - disliked

Fig. 9. Key paintings with high confidence levels (overall, liked only, disliked only)

7   Evaluation

To respond to RQ1 and RQ2 we evaluated our approach from different angles:

Controlled Assessment: The objective of the controlled assessment is to quantitatively study the error rates in how the scores were estimated in the presented case study. In Sect. 5.2, we had already performed a 10-fold cross-validation to empirically select an optimal value for the similarity radius and the weighting approach. Now we also estimate the error rates using the whole data set with real user feedback to draw both training and test sets. The goal is to predict the score of a configuration and assess against the actual scores provided by users. The computed *resubstitution error* is an optimistic case for evaluating classification approaches. The mean absolute error in the case of resubstitution is 1.0523 and the mean absolute error using 10-Folds average is 1.0913. These results suggest that any prediction has a margin of error around 1. This means that if the actual score of the painting is 4 (*like*), the margin of error is between 3 (*normal*) and 5 (*strong like*). We consider the mean absolute error values, in conjunction with the confidence metrics of the rankings, to be a good performance when attempting to capture collective understanding of beauty within the boundaries of our landscape paintings SPL.

Artist Perspective: The artist obtained and analyzed the ranking and the confidence metrics using the approach providing the following qualitative discussion. He claimed that the collective as a whole stated their scores in a very coherent fashion according to the parameters of traditional and classical painting principles of perspective and contrast. For example in Fig. 9b, the brightness in the sky found its counterpart in the brightness of the sea but only in the left side because of the mountain on the right. People understood that they were dealing with landscapes and they disliked the ones that tended to be flat or that they did not respect some of these principles. The objective of the installation was to explore his painting style in a feasible way to leverage user feedback. The resulting ranking was very interesting to understand people sensibility about the possible configurations. The ranking showed him liked configurations with high global confidence that he never considered and that he liked them too. The results of the approach exposed him to novelty that, as added value, he considered that they have some guaranties of success when exposing them to the public. For example, before this exercise, whether he put mountains or sea but never together in the same composition. He considered that he has learned about his own painting style as well as about the perception of the people about it.

Individualized Evaluation: Using the previous controlled assessment it was not feasible to bring the whole collective back for evaluating the created ranking. However, by conducting the experiment with only one person we can create a ranking with his or her own feedback and then evaluate the validity of our estimations with the person on site. The objective was to evaluate if the ranking successfully discriminate between the liked and disliked for the perception of each user. We selected 10 persons for this evaluation which had not seen the paintings before. Each user was voting in a session of 20 min. In average this duration corresponded to a data set of 16 populations (320 paintings). Once the ranking was created we took 10 liked and 10 disliked that they were not shown during the evolutionary phase. In concrete, we took the first 10 paintings with a weighted mean score from 4.5 to 5 that had the highest global confidence. In the same way, we took the first 10 with a weighted mean score from 1 to 1.5 that had the highest global confidence. After randomly shuffling these 20 paintings, we obtained an average of 91% accuracy in the prediction between like and dislike. The results suggest that the predictions in the extremes of the ranking are accurate in the case of individualized estimation.

8   Threats to Validity

Despite of the promising findings of our study, the approach presents threats to validity as we have made several design choices, which may introduce biases in our results. In Phase 1 we should investigate different genetic algorithm operators for the same case study to try to find the optimal operators and compare it to other approaches not relying on genetic algorithms. In Phase 2, the main threat in validity lies in the approach for computing the similarity distance between two paintings. We chose to implement the presented distance function algorithm while we could have relied upon more complex algorithms based on image difference metrics or on distance matrices for each of the features. In addition, the methods for empirically selecting the similarity radius as well as the approaches for weighting the scores could be further improved.

The principles and techniques of the presented approach are repeatable for any case study dealing with user feedback on SPL product variants. However, as discussed during the paper, this approach will not scale in phase 2 for FMs that can produce large number of possible configurations. In this case it is not feasible to compute and create ranking for all configurations. To solve this, instead of calculating the weighted mean score for all the possible configurations as we have done in the case study, we will investigate on non-euclidean centroid-based approaches or filtering mechanisms to restrict the calculation to a feasible amount of configurations.

Given that we deal with subjective assessments, the inherent subjectivity of ratings is an important threat. Also, our approach considers the rates as numbers in order to summarize the variant assessments for calculating the score means. In rating scales, for example from one to five, depending on the person, the distance from one to two may not be the same as the distance from two to three. This non-linearity of the scores scale is related to personal and cultural factors. The conversion of numerical values to nominal values [16] is an alternative for the ranking creation phase that is worthy to explore and compare.

9   Conclusion

Leveraging user feedbacks in the context of SPLE is an emerging problem that addresses an important aspect of products success: user expectations on product variants. This paper presents an approach for estimating and predicting user perception through the creation of a ranking of all the possible configurations based on user feedbacks. We use computer-generated art as an extreme case of subjective perception of a software product. This ranking, that we enhance with confidence metrics for each ranking item, has the objective to serve as input for the decision making process to select the products that have more guarantees of collective acceptance by users. The approach contains two phases at which we use (1) an interactive genetic algorithm for the initial data set creation and (2) a tailored data mining interpolation technique for reasoning about the data set to infer the ranking and the confidence metrics. We apply and validate the approach on an SPL-based computer-generated art system dealing with landscape paintings. This case study exhibits the same challenges than other assessment scenarios on user-specific qualities of a family of products: combinatorial explosion of possible configurations and limitation of resources for getting user feedback. The results of the case study are promising and enhanced versions of the approach will be applied to other case studies on SPLs where exploiting user feedbacks is of special importance.

Acknowledgments. Martinez and Tewfik's work is supported by the ITEA3 15010 REVaMP² project: FUI the Île-de-France region and BPI in France.

References

1. Al-Hajjaji, M.: Scalable sampling and prioritization for product-line testing. In: Software Engineering & Management 2015, Dresden, Germany, pp. 295–298 (2015)
2. Bavota, G., Carnevale, F., De Lucia, A., Di Penta, M., Oliveto, R.: Putting the developer in-the-loop: an interactive GA for software re-modularization. In: Fraser, G., Teixeira de Souza, J. (eds.) SSBSE 2012. LNCS, vol. 7515, pp. 75–89. Springer, Heidelberg (2012). https://doi.org/10.1007/978-3-642-33119-0_7
3. Benavides, D., Trinidad, P., Ruiz-Cortés, A.: Automated reasoning on feature models. In: Pastor, O., Falcão e Cunha, J. (eds.) CAiSE 2005. LNCS, vol. 3520, pp. 491–503. Springer, Heidelberg (2005). https://doi.org/10.1007/11431855_34
4. Boden, M.A., Edmonds, E.A.: What is generative art? Digit. Creat. **20**(1–2), 21–46 (2009)
5. do Carmo Machado, I., McGregor, J.D., de Almeida, E.S.: Strategies for testing products in software product lines. ACM SIGSOFT SE Notes **37**(6), 1–8 (2012)
6. Cohen, D.M., Dalal, S.R., Fredman, M.L., Patton, G.C.: The AETG system: an approach to testing based on combinatiorial design. IEEE TSE **23**(7), 437–444 (1997)
7. Galindo, J.A., Alférez, M., Acher, M., Baudry, B., Benavides, D.: A variability-based testing approach for synthesizing video sequences. In: ISSTA (2014)
8. Ghannem, A., El Boussaidi, G., Kessentini, M.: Model refactoring using interactive genetic algorithm. In: Ruhe, G., Zhang, Y. (eds.) SSBSE 2013. LNCS, vol. 8084, pp. 96–110. Springer, Heidelberg (2013). https://doi.org/10.1007/978-3-642-39742-4_9
9. Hemmati, H., Arcuri, A., Briand, L.C.: Achieving scalable model-based testing through test case diversity. ACM Trans. Softw. Eng. Methodol. **22**(1), 6 (2013)
10. Henard, C., Papadakis, M., Perrouin, G., Klein, J., Heymans, P., Traon, Y.L.: Bypassing the combinatorial explosion: using similarity to generate and prioritize t-wise test configurations for software product lines. IEEE TSE **40**(7), 650–670 (2014)
11. Henard, C., Papadakis, M., Perrouin, G., Klein, J., Traon, Y.L.: Multi-objective test generation for software product lines. In: SPLC, pp. 62–71 (2013)
12. Hornby, G.S., Bongard, J.C.: Accelerating human-computer collaborative search through learning comparative and predictive user models. In: GECCO (2012)

13. Johansen, M.F., Haugen, Ø., Fleurey, F., Eldegard, A.G., Syversen, T.: Generating better partial covering arrays by modeling weights on sub-product lines. In: France, R.B., Kazmeier, J., Breu, R., Atkinson, C. (eds.) MODELS 2012. LNCS, vol. 7590, pp. 269–284. Springer, Heidelberg (2012). https://doi.org/10.1007/978-3-642-33666-9_18

14. Kang, K.C., Cohen, S.G., Hess, J.A., Novak, W.E., Peterson, A.S.: Feature-oriented domain analysis (FODA) feasibility study. Technical report, DTIC Document (1990)

15. Li, Y.: Adaptive learning evaluation model for evolutionary art. In: CEC (2012)

16. Martínez, H.P., Yannakakis, G.N., Hallam, J.: Don't classify ratings of affect; rank them!. Trans. Affect. Comput. **5**(3), 314–326 (2014)

17. Martinez, J., Rossi, G., Ziadi, T., Bissyandé, T.F.D.A., Klein, J., Traon, Y.L.: Estimating and predicting average likability on computer-generated artwork variants. In: GECCO (Companion), pp. 1431–1432. ACM (2015)

18. Martinez, J., Sottet, J.-S., Frey, A.G., Ziadi, T., Bissyandé, T., Vanderdonckt, J., Klein, J., Le Traon, Y.: Variability management and assessment for user interface design. In: Sottet, J.-S., García Frey, A., Vanderdonckt, J. (eds.) Human Centered Software Product Lines. HIS, pp. 81–106. Springer, Cham (2017). https://doi.org/10.1007/978-3-319-60947-8_3

19. Romero, J., Machado, P. (eds.): The Art of Artificial Evolution: A Handbook on Evolutionary Art and Music. Natural Computing Series. Springer, Heidelberg (2008). https://doi.org/10.1007/978-3-540-72877-1

20. Sayyad, A.S., Menzies, T., Ammar, H.: On the value of user preferences in search-based software engineering: a case study in software product lines. In: ICSE (2013)

21. Siegmund, N., Rosenmüller, M., Kästner, C., Giarrusso, P.G., Apel, S., Kolesnikov, S.S.: Scalable prediction of non-functional properties in software product lines: footprint and memory consumption. IST **55**(3), 491–507 (2013)

22. Takagi, H.: Interactive evolutionary computation: fusion of the capabilities of EC optimization and human evaluation. IEEE **89**(9), 1275–1296 (2001)

23. White, J., Benavides, D., Schmidt, D.C., Trinidad, P., Dougherty, B., Cortés, A.R.: Automated diagnosis of feature model configurations. JSS **83**(7), 1094–1107 (2010)

Hierarchies and Reuse Measures

Reusability Index: A Measure for Assessing Software Assets Reusability

Apostolos Ampatzoglou[1]($\boxtimes$), Stamatia Bibi[2],
Alexander Chatzigeorgiou[3], Paris Avgeriou[4], and Ioannis Stamelos[1]

[1] Department of Informatics, Aristotle University of Thessaloniki,
Thessaloniki, Greece
apostolos.ampatzoglou@gmail.com,
stamelos@csd.auth.gr
[2] Department of Informatics and Telecommunications,
University of Western Macedonia, Kozani, Greece
sbibi@uowm.gr
[3] Department of Applied Informatics, University of Macedonia,
Thessaloniki, Greece
achat@uom.gr
[4] Department of Mathematics and Computer Science,
University of Groningen, Groningen, Netherlands
paris@cs.rug.nl

Abstract. The reusability of assets is usually measured through reusability indices. However, these indices either do not synthesize their constituent metrics into an aggregate or they do not capture all facets of reusability, such as structural characteristics, external qualities, and their documentation. To alleviate these shortcomings, we introduce a reusability index (REI) as a synthesis of various software metrics that cover a number of related reusability aspects. Furthermore, we evaluate its ability to quantify reuse, by comparing it to existing indices through a case study on 15 reusable open-source assets (i.e., libraries and frameworks). The results of the study suggest that the proposed index presents the highest predictive and discriminative power, it is the most consistent in ranking reusable assets, and the most strongly correlated to their levels of reuse.

Keywords: Reusability · Quality model · Metrics · Validation

1 Introduction

Assessing the reusability of a software asset (i.e., the degree to which it can be reused in other systems) is an important step towards successfully applying reuse practices. To this end, a wide range of reusability models have been proposed [4]; these models usually determine high level quality attributes affecting reusability and each such attribute is quantified by a set of metrics. However, existing reusability models (see Sect. 2 for a detailed description) suffer from either of two limitations: (a) they only deal with the quality attributes that affect reusability (e.g., coupling and cohesion, etc.) and not reusability per se, i.e. they do not provide an aggregated reusability measure or

© Springer International Publishing AG, part of Springer Nature 2018
R. Capilla et al. (Eds.): ICSR 2018, LNCS 10826, pp. 43–58, 2018.
https://doi.org/10.1007/978-3-319-90421-4_3

index, or (b) they only consider structural aspects of the software asset, ignoring aspects such as documentation, external quality, etc.

In this study we propose Reusability Index (REI), an index that overcomes said limitations by: synthesizing various metrics that influence reusability—related to limitation (a); and considering multiple aspects of reusability, such as structural quality, external quality, documentation, availability, etc.—related to limitation (b). In particular, REI is calculated by synthesizing seven metrics that correspond to both structural (e.g., complexity, maintainability, etc.) and non-structural (e.g., documentation, bugs, etc.) quality characteristics. To validate the accuracy of the developed index, we have performed a case study on 15 well-known open source assets (i.e., libraries and frameworks). In particular, we first assess the reusability of the assets, based on the proposed index and other indices from the literature and subsequently contrast them to the actual reuse of those assets (the assessment of actual reuse in a particular context is further discussed in Sect. 3.3).

In Sect. 2 we present related work and in Sect. 3 we describe the proposed REusability Index (REI). In Sect. 4, we present the study design that was used for evaluation purposes (i.e., comparing the assessing power of REI and existing indices from the literature to the actual reuse). The evaluation results are presented and discussed in Sects. 5 and 6. We present threats to validity in Sect. 7, and conclude the paper in Sect. 8.

2   Related Work

In this section, we present the reusability models/indices that have been identified by a recent mapping study [4]. For each reusability model/index, we present: (a) the aspects of the software that are considered (e.g., structural quality, documentation, etc.), (b) the way of synthesizing these aspects, and (c) the validation setup.

Bansiya and Davis [5] proposed a hierarchical quality model, named QMOOD, for assessing the quality of object-oriented artifacts and relied on human evaluators to assess its validity. The model provides functions that relate structural properties (e.g., encapsulation, coupling and cohesion) to high-level quality attributes, one of which is reusability. Furthermore, Nair et al. [14] examine the reusability of a certain class based on the values of three metrics defined in the Chidamber and Kemerer suite [7]. Multifunctional regression was performed across metrics to define the Reusability Index which was evaluated in two medium-sized java projects. Additionally, Kakarontzas et al. [12] proposed an index for assessing the reuse potential of object-oriented software modules. The authors used the metrics introduced by Chidamber and Kemerer [7] and developed a reuse index (named FWBR) based on the results of a logistic regression performed on 29 OSS projects. Their validation compared FWBR with the two aforementioned indices (from [5, 14]). As a proxy of reusability, the authors used classes D-layer [12].

From another perspective, Sharma et al. utilized Artificial Neural Networks (AAN) to estimate the reusability of software components [16]. The rationale of their model is that structural metrics cannot be the sole predictors of components reusability, in the sense that reusability can be performed at other levels of granularity as well. Thus, they proposed four factors and several metrics affecting component reusability, namely: (a) customizability, measured as the number of setter methods per total number of properties, (b) interface complexity measured in scale from low to high, (c) understandability, depending on the appropriateness of the documentation (demos, manuals, etc.), and (d) portability measured in scale from low to high. The authors developed a network from 40 Java components and tested their results in 12 components presenting promising results. Finally, Washizak [17] suggested a metric-suite capturing the reusability of components, decomposed to understandability, adaptability, and portability. The validity of the model was evaluated with 125 components against expert estimations.

The metrics used in the aforementioned studies are summarized in Table 1. Based on Table 1, we can observe that the proposed models are either depending upon only structural characteristics, or they do not provide a way to aggregate the proposed metrics into a single reusability index. In this paper, we overcome this limitation, by synthesizing metrics that consider multiple aspects of software reusability, into a quantifiable reusability index (which is shown in the last column of Table 1).

Table 1. Metrics associated with reusability

	Metrics	[5]	[12]	[14]	[16]	[17]	REI
Complexity - Structural quality	*Direct Class Coupling*	X					
	Coupling between objects			X			
	Lack of cohesion between methods			X			X
	Cohesion among methods of class	X					
	Class interface size	X					
	Response for a class		X	X			
	Weighted methods for class		X	X			X
	Design size in classes	X					
	Number of Classes			X			X
	Depth of inheritance		X	X			
	Number of properties				X		
	Setter methods				X		
Adaptability	*Interface Complexity*				X		
	Number of External dependencies					X	X
External quality	*Documentation quality*				X		X
	Existence of meta information					X	
	Observability					X	
	Portability				X	X	
	Number of open bugs						X
Availabilty	*Number of Components*						X
	Aggregation of Metrics	YES	YES	YES	NO	NO	YES

3 Proposed Reusability Index

In this section we present the proposed Reusability Index (**REI**), which is calculated as
a function of a set of metrics, each one weighted with a specific value. To select these
metrics we consider the reusability model of Hristov et al. [11] that consists of eight
main factors. Subsequently, we select metrics for each factor (see Fig. 1).

3.1 Reuse Factors

According to Hristov et al. [11]
reusability can be assessed by
quantifying eight main factors:
incurred reuse, maintainability,
adaptability, price, external quality, availability, documentation,
and complexity. As this model
consists of both structural and
non-structural qualities, we consider it a fitting starting point, as
we do not want to limit the proposed reusability index only to
structural quality characteristics.

Incurred Reuse indicates the
extent to which a software asset
is built upon reused components.
Adaptability is reflecting the ease
of asset adaptation, when reused

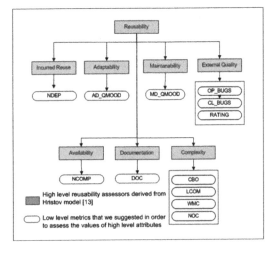

Fig. 1. Reusability measurement model

in a new system. *Price* indicates how expensive or cheap an asset is. *Maintainability*
represents the extent to which an asset can be extended after delivery. *External Quality*
describes the fulfillment of the asset's requirements and could be quantified by two
different aspects: (a) bugs of the asset, and (b) rating from its users. *Availability*
describes how easy it is to find an asset (e.g., instantly, after search, unavailable, etc.).
Documentation reflects the provision of documents related to an asset. The existence
of such documents makes the asset easier to understand and reuse. *Complexity* reflects
the structure of the asset, and is depicted into many aspects of quality (e.g., the easiness
to understand and adapt in a new context). Component/System complexity is measured
through size, coupling, cohesion, and method complexity. We note that the relationship
between reusability and these factors is not always positive. For example, the higher the
complexity, the lower the reusability. Additionally, from the aforementioned factors,
we do not consider price, since both in-house (assets developed by the same company)
and OSS reuse, are usually not associated with a cost model (but not always).

3.2 Reuse Metrics

In this section we present the metrics that are used for quantifying the reusability
factors. We note that the selected metrics are only few of the potential candidates.

Therefore, we acknowledge the existence of alternative metrics, and we do not claim that the set we selected consists of optimal reusability predictors. In total, 12 metrics have been addressed for the scope of this study in an attempt to avoid missing important attributes. The metrics are described in Table 2.

Table 2. Proposed metrics

Reuse factor	Metric	Description/Calculation method
Incurred reuse	NDEP	The number of reused libraries in the project. It can be measured through the number of files in lib folder, or dependencies in the pom.xml (in case of Maven)
Adaptability	AD_QMOOD	As a proxy of adaptability, we use an index defined by Bansiya and Davies [5], as the ability of an asset to be easily adapted from the source systems that it has been developed for, to a target system (i.e., adaptation to the new context) **= -0.25 DCC + 0.25 CAM + 0.5 CIS + 0.5 DSC** DCC is calculated as the number of different classes that a class is related to. CAM is calculated using the summation of intersection of parameters of a method with the maximum independent set of all parameter types in the class. CIS is calculated as the number of public methods in a class. DSC is the total number of classes
Maintainability	MD_QMOOD	As a way to quantify maintainability, we use the metric for extendibility, as defined by Bansiya and Davies [5]. **= 0.25*ANA – 0.5*DCC + 0.5*NOH + 0.5*NOP** ANA is calculated as the average number of classes from which a class inherits information. NOH is the number of class hierarchies in the design. NOP is derived as a count of methods that can exhibit polymorphic behavior
External quality	OP_BUGS	The number of Open Bugs reported in the Issue Tracker of each asset
	CL_BUGS	The number of Closed bugs as reported in the Issue Tracker of each asset
	RATING	The average rating by the users of the software is a proxy for independent rating
Documentation	DOC	To assess the amount, completeness, and quality of documentation, we suggest a manual inspection of the asset's website. We suggest a scale defined as follows: H—complete, rich, and easily accessible documentation M—one of the aforementioned characteristics is not at a satisfactory level L—two of the previous characteristics are not at a satisfactory level
Availability	NCOMP	Number of Components. The number of independent components that have been identified for the specific asset. This is used as an indicator of how many concrete

(continued)

Table 2. (*continued*)

Reuse factor	Metric	Description/Calculation method
		functionalities can be found into the asset. The methodology that is used to identify components from open source projects and populate the repository has been proposed by Ampatzoglou et al. [3] is based on the identification of reusable sets of classes, by applying a path-based strong component algorithm
Complexity	CBO	Coupling between Objects. CBO measures the number of classes that the class is connected to, in terms of method calls, field accesses, inheritance, arguments, return types and exceptions. High coupling is related to low maintainability
	LCOM	Lack of Cohesion of Methods. LCOM measures the dissimilarity of pairs of methods, in terms of the attributes being accessed. High Lack of Cohesion is an indicator of violating the Single Responsibility Principle [13], which suggests that each class should provide the system with only one functionality
	WMC	Weighted Method per Class. WMC is calculated as the average Cyclomatic Complexity (CC) among methods of a class
	NOC	Number of Classes provides an estimation of the amount of functionality offered by the asset. The size of the asset needs to be considered, since smaller systems are expected to be less coupled, less complex

3.3 Calculation of REI

REI is calculated as an aggregation of the values of independent metrics of the model, by performing Backwards Linear Regression on 15 Open-Source Software projects (OSS)[1]. The response (dependent) variable is the actual reusability according to Maven downloads[2]. The number of Maven downloads is an accurate measure of actual reuse, since each download from Maven corresponds to one case in which the asset has been reused in practice. That is because declaring the dependency to a Maven library in the POM file of a sample project, automatically downloads the library and puts it in the local Maven repository when the project is built (i.e. a download corresponds to an actual project having a dependency to that library). We note that even though we employed Maven downloads as an accurate reuse metric for our validation, our

---

[1] Due to space limitations we present the 15 OSS projects that are used as a training set for the Backwards Linear Regression, together with the test set of the validation in Sect. 4.

[2] The number of downloads is retrieved from https://mvnrepository.com. The value is obtained by the "used by" artifacts tag which is expected to be more accurate.

proposed index is not limited to open source reusable assets already stored in Maven. It can be equally useful for assessing the reusability of assets that: (a) are open-source but not deployed on Maven, or (b) are developed in-house, or (c) are of different levels of granularity (e.g., classes, packages, etc.) for which no actual reuse data can be found.

Regression is applied by initially including all predictor variables (see metrics on Table 2) and then by removing predictors, in a stepwise fashion, until there is no justifiable reason to remove any other predictor variable. The decision to apply backward regression was based on our intention to develop an index that is based on as few variables as possible. This reduction is expected to be beneficial regarding its applicability in the sense that: (a) it will be easier to calculate, and (b) it will depend upon fewer tools for automatic calculation. The end outcome of Backwards Linear Regression is a function, in which independent variables contribute towards the prediction of the dependent variable, with a specific weight, as follows:

$$REI = Constant + \sum_{i=0}^{i < num\_metrics} B(i) * metric(i)$$

To calculate REI we ended-up with a function of seven variables (i.e., metrics). The variables of the function accompanied with their weights and the standard beta coefficient are presented in Table 3, respectively. The standardized Beta of each factor can be used for comparing the importance of each metric in the calculation of REI. Finally, the sign of Beta denotes if the factor is positively or negatively correlated to the reusability of the asset. The accuracy of the index is presented in Sect. 5.2, since it corresponds to the predictive power of the REI index. The coefficients of the model as presented in Table 3 can be used to assess the reusability of assets whose actual levels of reuse are not available (e.g., OSS assets not deployed in Maven repository, or in-house developed assets, or assets of lower level of granularity—e.g., classes, or packages).

Based on Table 3, *components availability (NCOMP)* and *size (NOC)* of the software asset are the most important metrics that influence its reusability, followed by *number of dependencies (NDEP)* and *quality of documentation (DOC)*. From these metrics, size and number of dependencies are inversely proportional to reusability, whereas components availability and quality of documentation are proportional. A more detailed discussion of the relationship among these factors and reusability is provided in Sect. 5.1.

Table 3. REI metric calculation coefficients

Metric (i)	B(i)	Std. beta	Metric (i)	B(i)	Std. beta
Constant	1.267,909		DOC	2.547,738	0,410
NDEP	–316,791	–0,524	LCOM	7,477	0,280
OP_BUGS	2,661	0,202	WMC	–1.081,78	–0,212
NCOMP	5,858	0,736	NOC	–11,295	–0,827

4 Case Study Design

To empirically investigate the validity of the proposed reusability index, we performed a case study on 15 open source reusable assets (i.e., libraries and frameworks), that are of course different from those that are used for developing the regression model (see Sect. 3.3). The study aims at comparing the validity of the obtained index (REI) to the validity of the two indices that produce a quantified assessment of reusability: (a) the QMOOD reusability index [5] and (b) the FWBM index proposed by Kakarontzas et al. [12]. The reusability obtained by each index is contrasted to the actual reuse frequency of the asset, as obtained by the Maven repository. QMOOD_R and FWBR have been selected for this comparison, since they provide clear calculation instructions, as well as a numerical assessment of reusability (similarly to REI), and their calculations can be easily automated with tools. The case study has been designed and reported according to the guidelines of Runeson et al. [15].

To investigate the validity of the proposed reusability index (REI) and compare it with two other reusability indices, we employ the properties described in the 1061 IEEE Standard for Software Quality Metrics [1]. The standard defines six metric validation criteria (namely: correlation, consistency, predictability, discriminative power, and reliability) and suggests the statistical test that shall be used for evaluating every criterion. We note that although the IEEE 1061 Standard introduces a sixth criterion, i.e., tracking, it has not been considered in this study since it would require to record the values of all metrics along the evolution of the software which is a heavy-weight process for an after-the-fact analysis. Therefore, we decided to omit this analysis from this study and propose it as a standalone research effort that would complementarily study the evolution of the levels of reusability for software assets.

Research Objectives and Research Questions. The aim of this study, based on GQM, is to *analyze* REI and other reusability indices (namely FWBM and QMOOD) for the purpose of evaluation *with respect to* their validity when assessing the reusability of software assets, *from the point of view of* software engineers *in the context of* open-source software reuse. Driven by this goal, two research questions have been set:

RQ$_1$: What is the correlation, consistency, predictability and discriminative power of REI compared to existing reusability indices?

RQ$_2$: What is the reliability of REI as an assessor of assets reusability, compared to existing reusability indices?

The first research question aims to investigate the validity of REI in comparison to the other indices, with respect to the first four validity criteria (i.e. correlation, consistency, predictability and discriminative power). For the first research question, we employ a single dataset comprising of all examined projects belonging to the test set of the case study. The second research question aims to investigate validity in terms of the fifth criterion: Reliability is examined separately since, according to its definition, each of the other four validation criteria should be tested on different projects.

Cases and Units of Analysis. This study is a holistic multiple-case study, i.e. each case comprises a unit of analysis. Specifically, the cases of the study are open source reusable assets (i.e., open source software libraries and development frameworks) found in the widely-known Maven repository. Thirty of the most reused software assets were selected based on their reuse potential [8] (see Table 4). Out of these assets, 15 were used as a training set to calculate REI (see Sect. 3.3) and the rest 15 as a test set for this case study. Each software asset can be categorized either as framework or library (see parenthesis in Table 4), which are the standardized methods for reusing third-party code. To classify an asset as a library or framework, we used its level of offered functionalities. Thus, we consider that a library performs specific, well-defined operations; whereas a framework is a skeleton through which the application defines operations[3].

Table 4. Selected projects for training and test set

Test set project		Training set project	
GeoToolKit (L)	Apache Axis (F)	jDom (L)	jFree (L)
ASM (L)	Plexus (F)	Commons-lang (L)	Commons-io (L)
Commons-cli (L)	POI (L)	Spring Framework (F)	slf4j (L)
Struts (F)	Slick 2D (L)	Joda-time (L)	Apache wicket (F)
Guava (F)	Wiring (F)	Jopt Simple (L)	Groovy (F)
WiQuery (L)	Wro4j (L)	scala xml (L)	iText (L)
ImageJ(L)	Xstream (L)	Lucene (L)	Superfly (L)
JavaX XML/saaj (F)		Apache Log4j (L)	

Data Collection. For each case (i.e., software asset), we have recorded seventeen variables, as follows: **_Demographics_**: 2 variables (i.e., project, type). **_Metrics for REI Calculation_**: 12 variables (i.e., the variables presented in Table 1). These variables are going to be used as the independent variables for testing correlation, consistency predictability and discriminative power. **_Actual Reuse_**: We used Maven Reuse (MR), as presented in Sect. 3.3, as the variable that captures the actual reuse of the software asset. This variable is going to be used as the dependent variable in all tests. **_Compared Indices_**: We compare the validity of the proposed index against two existing reusability indices, namely FWBR [12] and QMOOD [5] (see Sect. 2). Therefore, we recorded two variables, each one capturing the score of these indices for the assets under evaluation. The metrics have been collected in multiple ways: (a) the actual reuse metrics has been manually recorded based on the statistics provided by the Maven Repository website; (b) opened and closed bugs have been recorded based on the issue tracker data of projects; (c) rating has been recorded from the stars that each project has been assigned by the users in GitHub; (d) documentation was manually evaluated, based on the projects' webpages; and (e) the rest of the structural metrics, have been calculated using the Percerons Client tool. Percerons is an online platform [2] created to facilitate empirical studies.

---

[3] See https://martinfowler.com/bliki/InversionOfControl.html.

Data Analysis. To answer each RQ we will use three variables as candidate assessors of actual reuse: REI, QMOOD_R, and FWBR. The reporting of the empirical results will be performed, based on the performed analysis, using the Candidate Assessors as *Independent Variable*, and Actual reuse as the *Dependent Variable*:

- ***Predictability:*** We present the level of statistical significance of the effect (sig.) of the independent variable on the dependent (how important is the predictor in the model), and the accuracy of the model (i.e., mean standard error). While investigating predictability, we produced a separate linear regression model for each assessor (univariate analysis).
- ***Correlation*** and ***Consistency:*** We use the correlation coefficients (coeff.) and the levels of statistical significance (sig.) of Pearson and Spearman Correlation, respectively. The value of the coefficient denotes the degree to which the value (or ranking for Consistency) of the actual reuse is in analogy to the value (or rank) of the assessor.
- ***Discriminative Power:*** Represents the ability of the independent variable to classify an asset into meaningful groups (as defined by the values of the dependent variables). The values of the dependent variable have been classified into 3 mutually exclusive categories (representing low, medium and high metric values) adopting equal frequency binning [6]. Then Bayesian classifiers [10] are applied in order to derive estimates regarding the discrete values of the dependent variables. The positive predictive power of the model is then calculated (precision) along with the sensitivity of the model (recall) and the models accuracy (f-measure).
- ***Reliability:*** We present the results of all the aforementioned tests, separately for the two types of reusable software types (i.e., libraries and development frame-works). The extent to which the results on the projects are in agreement (e.g., is the same metric the most valid assessor asset reusability for both types?) represents the reliability of REI.

5   Results

In this section, we present the results of the empirical validation of the proposed reusability index. The section is divided into two parts: In Sect. 5.1, the results of RQ_1 regarding the correlation, consistency, predictive and discriminative power of the REI are presented. In Sect. 5.2 we summarize the results of RQ_2, i.e., the assessment of REI reliability. We note that Sect. 5 only presents the raw results of our analysis and answers the research questions. Any interpretation of results and implications to researchers and practitioners are collectively discussed in Sect. 6.

5.1   RQ₁ — Correlation, Consistency, Predictive and Discriminative Power of REI Cases and Units of Analysis

In this section we answer RQ_1 by comparing the relation of REI, QMOOD_R, and FWBR to actual reuse, in terms of correlation, consistency, predictive and discriminative power. The results are cumulatively presented in Table 5. The rows of Table 5

Table 5. Correlation, consistency and predictive power

Validity criterion	Success indicator	REI	QMOOD_R	FWBR	Validity criterion	Success indicator	REI	QMOOD_R	FWBR
Predictive power	R-square	40.1%	4.0%	2.5%	Discriminative power	Precision	53%	33%	33%
	Std. error	4698.11	5270.36	5311.23		Recall	66%	33%	16%
	Significance	*0.08*	0.28	0.40		F-measure	60%	33%	22%
Correlation	Coefficient	0.633	0.200	−0.158	Consistency	Coefficient	0.587	0.330	−0.075
	Significance	*0.00*	0.28	0.40		Significance	*0.01*	*0.07*	0.69

are organized/grouped by validity criterion. In particular, for every group of rows (i.e., criterion) we present a set of success indicators. For example, regarding predictive power we present three success indicators, i.e., R-square, standard error, and significance of the model [9]. Statistically significant results are denoted with italic fonts.

Based on the results presented in Table 5, REI is the optimal assessor of software asset reusability, since: (a) it offers prediction significant at the 0.10 level, (b) it is strongly correlated to the actual value of the reuse (Pearson correlation coefficient > 0.6), and (c) it ranks software assets most consistently with respect to their reuse (Spearman correlation coefficient = 0.587). The second most valid assessor is QMOOD_R. Finally, we note that the only index that produces statistically significant results for all criteria at the 0.10 level is REI. QMOOD_R is able to provide a statistically significant ranking of software assets, however, with a moderate correlation.

To assess the discriminative power of the three indices, we employed Bayesian classifiers [10]. Through Bayesian classifiers we tested the ability of REI to correctly classify software assets in three classes (low, medium, and high reusability), with respect to their reuse (see Sect. 4). The accuracy of the classification is presented in Table 5, through three well-known success indicators: namely precision, recall, and F-measure [9]. Precision quantifies the positive predictive power of the model (i.e., TP/(TP + FP), and recall evaluates the extent to which the model captures all correctly classified artifacts (i.e., TP/(TP + FN). F-measure is a way to synthesize precision and recall in a single measure, since in the majority of cases there are trade-offs between the two indicators. To calculate these measures we split the dataset in a training and a test group in a random manner, using a 2-fold cross validation [10]. By interpreting the results presented in Table 5 we can suggest that REI is the index with the highest discriminative power. In particular, REI has shown the highest precision, recall, and f-measure. Therefore it has the ability to most accurately classify software assets into reuse categories.

> *REI has proven to be the most valid assessor of software asset reusability, when compared to the QMOOD reusability index and FWBR. In particular, REI excels in all criteria (namely correlation, consistency, predictive and discriminative power) being the only one providing statistically significant assessments.*

5.2   RQ$_2$ — Reliability of the REI

In this section we present the results of evaluating the reliability of the three indices. To assess reliability, we split our test set into two subsets: frameworks and utility libraries.

Table 6. Reliability

Validity criterion	Asset type	Success indicator	REI	QMOOD	FWBR	Validity criterion	Asset type	Success indicator	REI	QMOOD	FWBR
Predictive power	L	R-square	35.0%	4.3%	5.6%	Consistency	L	Coeff.	0.570	0.270	−0.142
		Std. error	4600.10	5581.19	5543.38			Sig.	0.00	0.22	0.52
		Sig.	0.00	0.35	0.29		F	Coeff.	0.476	0.071	0.143
	F	R-square	64.9%	13.4%	0.4%			Sig.	0.23	0.86	0.73
		Std. error	3016.44	4734.91	5077.62	Discriminative power	L	Precision	50%	25%	13%
		Sig.	0.01	0.37	0.87			Recall	50%	25%	25%
Correlation	L	Coeff.	0.591	0.206	-0.236			F-measure	50%	25%	17%
		Sig.	0.00	0.35	0.29		F	Precision	85%	28%	31%
	F	Coeff	0.805	0.366	0.06			Recall	75%	38%	38%
		Sig.	0.01	0.37	0.87			F-measure	75%	31%	34%

All the tests discussed in Sect. 5.1 are replicated for both sets and the results are compared. The outcome of this analysis is outlined in Table 6.

For each validity criterion we present all success indicators for both libraries (L) and frameworks (F). With italics we denote statistically significant results. The results of Table 6 suggest that in most of the cases, the reusability index is more accurate in the group of frameworks rather than the libraries. The fact that the Frameworks dataset is of small size and still produces statistically significant results, further highlights the fitness of REI. Concerning reliability, REI has been validated as a reliable metric regarding correlation, predictive and discriminative power, but not regarding consistency. In particular, REI was not able to accurately rank the eight frameworks of the dataset. Nevertheless, compared to the other indices, REI achieves the highest levels of reliability.

> *The reliability analysis suggested that REI is consistently the most valid assessor of software asset reuse, regardless of the dataset. However, the ranking ability of the proposed index needs further investigation. Nevertheless, REI is the most reliable assessor of reusability, compared to the other indices.*

6   Discussion

In this section we interpret the results obtained by our case study and provide some interesting implications for researchers and practitioners.

Interpretation of Results. The validation of the proposed reusability index on 15 open assets, suggested that REI is capable of providing accurate reusability assessments. REI outperforms the other examined indices (i.e., QMOOD_R and FWBR) and presents significant improvement in terms of estimation accuracy and classification efficiency. We believe that the main advantage of REI, compared to state-of-the-art indices is the fact that it synthesizes both structural aspects of quality (e.g., source code complexity metrics) and non-structural quality aspects (e.g., documentation, correctness, etc.). This finding can be considered intuitive in the sense that nowadays, software development produces a large data foot-print (e.g. bug trackers, issue trackers), and taking the diversity of the collected data into account provides a more holistic and accurate evaluation of software quality. Although the majority of reusability models and indices emphasize on low-level structural quality attributes (e.g., cohesion, complexity, etc.— quantified through source code structural metrics) the results of this study highlight the importance of evaluating non-structural artifacts. The contribution of the different types of characteristics is explained as follows:

- **Low-level structural characteristics** (complexity, cohesion, and size in classes). These are very important when assessing software assets reusability, in the sense that they highly affect the understandability of the reusable asset along its adaptation and maintenance. Although size can be related to reusability into two ways (i.e., as the amount of code that you need to understand before reuse or as the amount of offered functionality), we can observe that size is negatively affecting reuse (i.e., smaller assets are more probable to be reused). Therefore, the first interpretation of the relationship appears to be stronger than the second.
- **High-level structural characteristics** (number of dependencies and available components). First, the number of dependencies to other assets (i.e., an architectural level metric) seems to outperform low-level coupling metrics in terms of importance when assessing component reusability. This observation can be considered intuitive since while reusing a software asset developers are usually not interfering with structural asset dependencies, they are forced to "inherit" the external dependencies of the asset. Specifically, assets, whose reuse imply importing multiple external libraries (and thus require more configuration time), seem to be less re-used in practice by developers. Second, the number of available components, as quantified in this study, provides an assessment of modularity, which denotes how well a software asset can be decomposed to sub-components. This information is important while assessing reuse in the sense that a modular software is easier to understand and modify.
- **Non-structural characteristics** (quality of documentation and number of open bugs). First, documentation is an important factor that indicates the level of help and guidance that a reuser may receive during the adoption of a component. As expected, assets with a lot of documentation, are more likely to be reused. Second, open bugs suggest the number of pending corrections for a particular asset. Although this finding might be considered as unexpected, in the sense that assets with less bugs should be more attractive for reuse, we found that this number essentially acts as an indicator of the maturity of the asset. The results show that average and high values of OP_BUGS metric are indicators of higher reusability.

The multiple perspectives from which the REI index assesses reusability are further highlighted by the fact that from the seven factors that affect reusability (according to Hristov et al. [11] —see Sect. 3), only two are not directly participating in the calculation of REI (i.e., maintainability and adaptability). Although we did not originally expect this, we can interpret it as follows: either (a) the metrics that we have used for assessing these parameters, i.e., by borrowing equations from the QMOOD model, were sub-optimal, or (b) the metrics are subsumed by the other structural quality metrics that participate in the calculation of REI. Based on the literature LCOM, WMC, NOC have a strong influence on maintainability and extendibility. Therefore a synthesized index (like REI) does not seem to benefit from including extra metrics in its calculation that are correlated to other metrics that participate in the calculation.

Implications to researchers and practitioners. The major findings of this study show that reusability indices need to further focus on the inclusion of non-structural factors.

We encourage *researchers* to introduce formal metrics and procedures for quantifying quality aspects that till now are evaluated by adopting ad-hoc procedures. Attributes like Documentation, External Quality and Availability are underexplored and usually assessed subjectively. More formal definitions of these factors could further increase the accuracy and adoption of reusability metrics. Additionally, we believe that researchers should evaluate the proposed reusability model on inner source development ([17]). From such a study, it would be interesting to observe differences in the parameters and the weight that will participate in the calculation of REI. A possible reason for deviation, is the belief that reusable assets that have been developed inside a single company might present similarities in terms of some factors (e.g., documentation, open bugs, etc.). In that case it might it be interesting to investigate the introduction of new metrics customized to the specificities of each software company. This is particularly important, since for in-house components it is not possible to obtain an external, objective reusability measure such as Maven Reusability (MR). Finally, we suggest to further validate REI, based on the effort required to adopt the asset in a fully operating mode in a new software. Clearly it is important to select the right asset that will require less time, effort, cost and modifications while being reused. Similarly to any empirical endeavor, we encourage the replication of REI validation in larger samples of reusable assets, examining different types of applications, in order to further refine its accuracy.

Regarding practitioners, the proposed reusability index will be a useful tool for aiding practitioners to select the most important factors (and the associated metrics) to be used when assessing in-house reusable assets, or OSS assets that are not deployed on the Maven repository. The fact that the majority of metrics that are used for quantifying REI can be automatically calculated from available tools, in conjunction with its straightforward calculation, is expected to boost the adoption of the index, and its practical benefits. The two-fold analysis that we adopt in this paper (i.e., prediction and classification) enables practitioners to select the most fitting one for their purposes. In particular, the classification of assets to low, medium, and highly reusable, provides a coarse-grained, but more accurate approach. Such an approach can be useful when software engineers are not interested in quantifying the actual value of reusability, but when they are just interested in characterization purposes.

7   Threats to Validity

In this section we discuss the threats to validity, based on the classification schema of Runeson et al. [15]. **Construct Validity** in our case refers to whether all the relevant reusability metrics have been explored in the proposed index. To mitigate this risk we considered in the calculation of the index a plethora of reusability aspects representing both structural and non-structural qualities such as, adaptability, maintainability, quality, availability, documentation, reusability and complexity each of which synthesized by the values of 12 metrics as depicted in Table 2. Furthermore, as already mentioned in Sect. 3 the selected metrics are established metrics for the respective factors, although we do not claim they are the most optimal ones. Additionally although the number of downloads from Maven is considered an accurate assessor of reuse (see Sect. 3.3) we need to acknowledge the selection of this metric as a possible threat to construct validity. **Internal Validity** is related to the examination of causal relations. Our results pinpoint particular metrics that affect significantly the reuse potential of a certain project but still we do not infer causal relationships.

Concerning generalizability of results, known as **External Validity** we should mention that different data sets could cause differentiations in the results. Still this risk is mitigated by the fact that the analysis was performed selecting a pool of projects that are well-known and popular in the practitioners community [8] forming a representative sample for analysis. However, a replication of this study in a larger project set and in an industrial setting would be valuable in verifying the current findings. Regarding the reproducibility of the study known as **Reliability**, we believe that the research process documented thoroughly in Sect. 4 ensures the safe replication of our study by any interested researcher. However, researcher bias could have been introduced in the data collection phase, while quantifying the metric value of the level of documentation provided for each project. In that case, the first two authors gathered data on the documentation variable, adopting a manual recording process. The results were further validated by the third and fourth author.

8 Conclusions

The selection of the most fitting and adaptable asset is one of the main challenges of the software reuse process as it depends on the assessment of a variety of quality aspects characterizing the candidate assets. In this study we presented and validated the Reusability Index (REI), which decomposes reusability to seven quality factors quantifying each one of them with certain metrics. Non-structural metrics along with low- and high-level structural metrics synthesize the proposed reusability index. Based on this model, REI is derived by applying backward regression. To investigate the validity of REI we have employed a two-step evaluation process that validates the proposed index against: (a) well-known reusability indices found in literature, and (b) the metric validation criteria defined in the 1061-1998 IEEE Standard for a Software Quality Metrics [1]. The results from the holistic multiple-case study on 15 OSS projects suggested that REI is capable of providing accurate reusability assessments. REI outperforms the other examined indices (i.e., QMOOD_R and FWBR) and presents significant improvement in terms of estimation accuracy and classification efficiency. Based on these results, we provide implications for researchers and practitioners.

Acknowledgement. This work was financially supported by the action "Strengthening Human Resources Research Potential via Doctorate Research" of the Operational Program "Human Resources Development Program, Education and Lifelong Learning, 2014–2020", implemented from State Scholarship Foundation (IKY) and co-financed by the European Social Fund and the Greek public (National Strategic Reference Framework (NSRF) 2014–2020).

References

1. 1061-1998: IEEE Standard for a Software Quality Metrics Methodology, IEEE Standards, IEEE Computer Society, 31 December 1998. Reaffirmed 9 December 2009
2. Ampatzoglou, A., Stamelos, I., Gkortzis, A., Deligiannis, I.: Methodology on extracting reusable software candidate components from open source games. In: Proceedings of the 16th International Academic MindTrek Conference, pp. 93–100. ACM, Finland (2012)
3. Ampatzoglou, A., Gkortzis, A., Charalampidou, S., Avgeriou, P.: An embedded multiple-case study on OSS design quality assessment across domains. In: 7th International Symposium on Empirical Software Engineering and Measurement (ESEM 2013), pp. 255–258. ACM/IEEE Computer Society, Baltimore, October 2013
4. Arvanitou, E.M., Ampatzoglou, A., Chatzigeorgiou, A., Galster, M., Avgeriou, P.: A mapping study on design-time quality attributes and metrics. J. Syst. Softw. **127**, 52–77 (2017)
5. Bansiya, J., Davis, C.G.: A hierarchical model for object-oriented design quality assessment. IEEE Trans. Softw. Eng. **28**(1), 4–17 (2002)
6. Bibi, S., Ampatzoglou, A., Stamelos, I.: A Bayesian belief network for modeling open source software maintenance productivity. In: Crowston, K., Hammouda, I., Lundell, B., Robles, G., Gamalielsson, J., Lindman, J. (eds.) OSS 2016. IAICT, vol. 472, pp. 32–44. Springer, Cham (2016). https://doi.org/10.1007/978-3-319-39225-7_3
7. Chidamber, S.R., Kemerer, C.F.: A metrics suite for object oriented design. IEEE Trans. Softw. Eng. **20**(6), 476–493 (1994)
8. Constantinou, E., Ampatzoglou, A., Stamelos, I.: Quantifying reuse in OSS: a large-scale empirical study. Int. J. Open Source Softw. Process. (IJOSSP) **5**, 1–19 (2014)
9. Field, A.: Discovering Statistics Using IBM SPSS Statistics. SAGE Publications Ltd., Thousand Oaks (2013)
10. Hall, M., Frank, E., Holmes, G., Pfahringer, B., Reutemann, P., Witten, I.: The WEKA data mining software: an update. ACM SIGKDD Explor. Newsl. **11**(1), 10–18 (2009)
11. Hristov, D.: Structuring software reusability metrics for component-based software development. In: 7th International Conference on Software Engineering Advances (2012)
12. Kakarontzas, G., Constantinou, E., Ampatzoglou, A., Stamelos, I.: Layer assessment of object-oriented software: a metric facilitating white-box reuse. J. Syst. Softw. **86**(2), 349–366 (2013)
13. Martin, R.C.: Agile Software Development: Principles, Patterns and Practices. Prentice Hall, New Jersey (2003)
14. Nair, T.R.G., Selvarani, R.: Estimation of software reusability: an engineering approach. SIGSOFT Softw. Eng. Notes **35**(1), 1–6 (2010)
15. Runeson, P., Höst, M., Rainer, A., Regnell, B.: Case Study Research in Software Engineering: Guidelines and Examples. John Wiley & Sons, New York (2012)
16. Sharma, A., Grover, P.S., Kumar, R.: Reusability assessment for software components. SIGSOFT Softw. Eng. Notes **34**(2), 1–6 (2009)
17. Washizaki, H., Yamamoto, H., Fukazawa, Y.: A metrics suite for measuring reusability of software components. In: 9th International Software Metrics Symposium. IEEE (2003)

A Hybrid Approach for Tag Hierarchy Construction

Shangwen Wang[(⊠)], Tao Wang[(⊠)], Xiaoguang Mao[(⊠)],
Gang Yin, and Yue Yu

National University of Defense Technology, Changsha, China
shang_wen_wang@163.com,
{taowang2005,xgmao,yingang,yuyue}@nudt.edu.cn

Abstract. Open source resources are playing a more and more important role in software engineering for reuse. However, the dramatically increasing scale of these resources brings great challenges for their management and location. In this study, we propose a hybrid approach for automatic tag hierarchy construction, which combines the tag co-occurrence relations and domain knowledge to build and optimize the hierarchy. We firstly calculate the generality of each tag in accordance with the co-occurrence relationship with others, and construct the hierarchy based on the generality. Then we leverage the domain knowledge of existing hierarchical categories to perform an optimization and promote the final hierarchy. We select 8064 projects in *Openhub* community and 10703 posts in *StackOverflow* community as the original data and use the information of the *SourceForge* community as the domain knowledge. We conduct extensive experiments and evaluate our approach by utilizing *Wordnet* and *F-measure* method. The results show that our approach exhibits better performance than others with accuracy rate and recall that exceed 90%.

Keywords: Open source community · Tag hierarchy construction
Domain knowledge · Optimization

1 Introduction

Open source software is a computer program of freely available source code and has been favored by the majority of developers since its release. The rise in the number of open source software brings together the creativity and wisdom of the entire society to promote software updates and bug fixes, thereby providing much attention to software development and increasing the types of producers participating in the development. Different types of producers come together to form two different open source communities: collaborative development community and knowledge sharing community. Software reuse technology [1], which utilizes others' code to perfect one's own program, is developed by this open source movement.

However, the increasing number of open source software has brought difficulty for traditional methods in organizing and managing large amounts of software resources. Organizing and locating open source software effectively and improving the efficiency of software reuse have become major challenges. Begelman et al. [2] proposed a

© Springer International Publishing AG, part of Springer Nature 2018
R. Capilla et al. (Eds.): ICSR 2018, LNCS 10826, pp. 59–75, 2018.
https://doi.org/10.1007/978-3-319-90421-4_4

method to automate the construction of taxonomy by using a tagging mechanism. Since then, this approach has been extensively studied since a reasonable and comprehensive tag hierarchy can organize open source resources well and provide convenience for software reuse. In 2012, Wang et al. [3] inferred term taxonomy by leveraging collaborative tagging. At the same time, an approach that can automatically derive a domain-dependent taxonomy from a set of keyword phrases was proposed by Liu [4].

This study presents a method for automatically constructing a tag hierarchy and optimizing it with domain knowledge. First, we calculate the generality of each tag on the basis of the co-occurrence relationships between tags. We then construct hierarchy in accordance with the generalities by selecting the most suitable father node for each tag except the one with largest generality. For each tag p, its father node q must satisfy two conditions: (1) q possesses a larger generality than p; (2) among the tags of generality larger than p, q possesses the largest degree of correlation with p.

Domain knowledge refers to some existing human-created hierarchies. In the last step, we take the construction of the tag hierarchy into the domain knowledge for testing. The proposed algorithm uses the "reverse" idea. In particular, the hierarchy construction of manual construction is compared with the result of previously automated construction, the incorrect side of the automatic construction result is corrected, and the relationship that exists in the domain knowledge but does not exist in the automated hierarchy construction is added to the results. After these steps, we finally obtain our results.

Our experimental dataset is taken from one open source community, Openhub, and a programming knowledge sharing community, Stackoverflow, to avoid the error caused by a single data source. After calculating tag generalities, we choose 342 tags to build hierarchy, and all the tag generalities are greater than 1,000. SourceForge open source community hosts more than 600,000 projects and has established a software taxonomy hierarchy by hand. Thus, its classification is plausible. In our experiment, we use the taxonomy hierarchy in SourceForge as the domain knowledge for optimization. Experimental results show that our method can construct tag hierarchy efficiently and accurately, and the optimized hierarchical structure accuracy can reach more than 90%, which surpasses that of the previous methods. The main contributions of this study are described as follows:

- We take advantage of the co-occurrence relationship between tags, calculate the software tag generalities by digging the inherent relationship between them, and build tag hierarchy in an unsupervised mode.
- We propose an optimization algorithm based on domain knowledge to optimize the results of automated building by using the manually established taxonomic hierarchies in some communities. We obtain improved taxonomy results by merging the information from two different hierarchies.
- We conduct extensive experiments. We select 342 tags at the top of the generality ranking, all of which possess a generality greater than 1,000. We conduct various types of experiments to prove the superiority of our approach.

The rest of the paper is organized as follows. Section 2 introduces some works related to tag hierarchy construction. We describe our method in detail in Sect. 3.

We introduce the design of our experiments in Sect. 4 and provide results and discussions in Sect. 5. Section 6 elaborates the conclusions and comes up with a plan for our future work.

2 Related Work

Taxonomies constructed with general tags have been widely investigated. A key step in the existing methods of taxonomy construction is to calculate the generality for each tag. This step can be achieved by two types of technology as follows.

One is to use set theory techniques. Among these works, each resource is considered a distinct data item with their textual contents ignored, and each tag presents the collection of items it annotates. For example, Heymann et al. [5] came up with a simple but effective way to learn a tag taxonomy. Heymann modeled each tag as m-d vector with m documents it annotates and used the cosine similarities between tag vectors to generate the tag similarity graph. He then demonstrated that the social network notion of graph centrality seems to be a valid way to calculate generality. Sanderson and Croft [6] compared the size of image collection in which two tags occur to determine the affiliation relation between them. Schmitz [7] developed Heymann's model to control highly idiosyncratic vocabulary frequency limits to improve the quality of the results. Liu et al. [8] used association rule mining. This method takes each tagged resource as a transaction and tags as items. The method is governed by the following rule: "for a specific unknown resource X, if tag A appears, then tag B will probably appear," that is, "tag B subsumes tag A." The natural possibility of inclusion is naturally modeled on the confidence and support of the corresponding rules. On the basis of the inclusion probabilities between each pair of tags, they calculated the overall general rating of each tag by using a random walk. Finally, they built taxonomies in a top-down fashion. The two methods exhibit a common flaw, that is, they only distinguish one resource from another but do not exploit tagged web documents.

Another way is based on *LDA (Latent Dirichlet Allocation)* model [9]. Tang et al. [10] designed a tag–topic model based on this classic model. They assumed each tag possesses multiple submeanings, which are also called topics. Tags with similar high distributions on multiple topics indicate a high probability that the tag is a normal tag, whereas a tag with a high distribution on only one specific topic indicates that the tag may possess a specific meaning. Wang [11] suggested that a document annotated by the same tag can be considered the interpretation of this tag. He said we can combine these documents into a new document, learn the subject distribution of standard LDA models from the basic corpus, and measure the generality on the basis of "surprise" theory [12] plus an intuitive law that, "given an anticipated tag A, the appearance of a document on a more general tag B will cause less 'surprise' than if A and B are switched." This theory is a slight modification of LDA.

Hierarchy construction can be done in several ways. Liu et al. [4] argued that building taxonomy on the basis of keywords is difficult. They obtained knowledge using short context conceptualization and a general-purpose knowledge base called Probase to distinguish the relation between tags. They retrieved the excerpts by submitting the query to a commercial search engine and then calculated the generality by combining knowledge and context to obtain the context. Wang et al. [3] measured similarity on the basis of open source community labeling system by combining document collection and text similarity. Brooks and Montanez [17] avoided computing tag generality. They adopted a method that only relies on the similarity or distance between two tags in building a hierarchy. However, their obtained hierarchy lacks supertype–subtype relationships. Li et al. [13] referred to this model, proposed an approach based on agglomerative hierarchical clustering by skipping the error prone step of calculating each tag generality, and called this model *AHCTC (Agglomerative Hierarchical Clustering for Taxonomy Construction)*.

Gu et al. [14] suggested utilizing domain knowledge for optimization. In this method, they introduced the construction into domain knowledge for testing. This work is similar to ours but presents two weak points. First, the above-mentioned authors did not add the tags contained in the domain knowledge but not contained in the construction to be optimized to the final results. Second, they considered the tags contained in the construction to be optimized but not contained in the domain knowledge as incorrect relations and deleted them, thereby possibly affecting the diversity of tags. Fahad et al. [19] suggested another idea for optimization. They ordered tags in descending order by generality and then added them into the hierarchy by choosing the tag of the most co-occurrence frequency and the tag already in the hierarchy to be its father node. They then checked the correctness of the direction of this edge. This method is limited because it simply checks the edge relation rather than finding another suitable father node.

Construction of taxonomy generally has two types: tree and *DAG (Directed Acyclic Graph)*. The author in [15] proposed a tree-based label hierarchy research method, used the Jaccard coefficient to measure the label similarity, and proposed the label hierarchy algorithm of the maximum spanning tree. Marszalek et al. [16] found through observation that finding a suitable segmentation of feature space increasingly becomes difficult with the increase in the number of categories. Therefore, they proposed the idea that the unspecified classification can be extended to classification when the classification boundaries are clear. Accordingly, assigning of each son node can be postponed, thereby resulting in a DAG chart. Finally, a relaxed classification level can be obtained.

3   Hybrid Hierarchy Construction Method

In this section, we introduce our approach from two aspects. We provide an overview of the framework first and then describe each part in detail.

Our goal is to build a reasonable hierarchy for tags which means we need to consider the relationship between tags and the scope of tag to be used. We define two terms as follows:

Definition 1. **Co-occurrence frequency:** For a tag pair (p, q), its co-occurrence frequency is the sum of times it occurs in the tag list of a project.

Definition 2. **Tag generality:** Tag generality is an indicator to measure the limited scope of the tag to be used. Tags of large generality generally possess a large scope to be used.

3.1   Overview of Our Approach

Co-occurrence frequency shows the relevance of two tags and generality reflects the degree of acceptance of the tag. These two characteristics have good use of value for our goal and thus are utilized. Some errors may be contained in the construction for a defect may exist in our approach. We choose to optimize the construction with the guidance from domain knowledge in that it possesses high reliability.

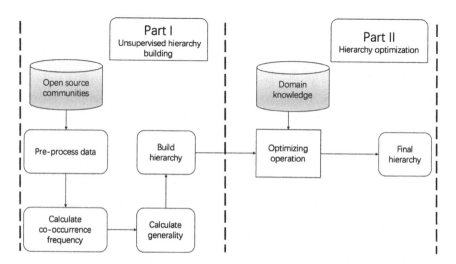

Fig. 1. Framework of our method

Our approach to build tag hierarchy consists of two parts, namely, unsupervised hierarchy building and hierarchy optimization. The framework of our method is shown in Fig. 1.

The figure shows our approach is a two-phase hybrid model. It combines unsupervised hierarchy building through tag co-occurrence relation information with optimization utilizing domain knowledge. These two main phases are as follows:

Unsupervised hierarchy building: The first phase involves four steps, most of which are related to mathematical calculation. First, we extract data from several open source communities and pre-process the original data. Second, we calculate co-occurrence frequency for tag pairs. Third, we calculate generality for each tag. Fourth, we can build this hierarchy using the data calculated from the previous steps. All these steps except the first one are automatically completed.

Hierarchy optimization: In the second phase, we introduce domain knowledge. We combine it with the hierarchy we have built into an algorithm for optimization. The algorithm checks whether the construction possesses incorrect edges by comparing with domain knowledge and fixing the errors if any exists.

3.2 Unsupervised Hierarchy Building

According to [13], one tag can only be connected with the tag that is most relevant to it, and tags with large generalities should be at the upper levels in an ideal hierarchy. Thus, we should calculate co-occurrence frequency for tag pairs and generality for each tag before building. We design our approach for unsupervised hierarchy building on the basis of this idea. Our approach involves the following steps:

Pre-process data: The information we need to construct the hierarchy are the project number and the tags it contains. We obtain a great deal of unpractical information in the detail page from the communities. We pre-process them in the database and retain only two columns, namely, project id and tags, to minimize the size of the data space and ensure efficient data query.

Calculate co-occurrence frequency: In a collaborative development community, each project is tagged with multiple tags that are related to its content as a basis of recommendation to developers. Similarly, in a knowledge sharing community, each post is associated with multiple tags. Co-occurrence between two tags indicates that both tags appear in the tag list of the same project. We define a helper function $P(t_1, t_2)$ to judge whether the two tags, namely, t_1 and t_2, are in the tag list of project P.

$$P(t_1, t_2) = \begin{cases} 1 & \text{if } t_1 \text{ and } t_2 \text{ are both tags of } P \\ 0 & \text{if } t_1 \text{ or } t_2 \text{ is not the tag of } P \end{cases} \tag{1}$$

In Eq. (1), t_1 and t_2 denote two specific tags. We calculate the co-occurrence frequency of two tags by Eq. (2) as follows:

$$Co(t_i, t_j) = \sum_{x=1}^{n} P_x(t_i, t_j). \tag{2}$$

In Eq. (2), t_i and t_j denote the tags we are calculating. P denotes a project in the project set. We obtain the co-occurrence frequency of each of the two tags by applying the equation to every tag pair.

Calculate generality: The generality of a tag is not only related to the number of tag it co-occurrences. The co-occurrence frequency of this tag to the other tags is important as well. We define Eq. (3) to calculate tag generality as follows:

$$G(t) = \sum_{i=1}^{n} Co(t, t_i). \tag{3}$$

In Eq. (3), t denotes the tag we are calculating, and t_i denotes another tag in the tag set. We calculate tag generality through this circulation.

Build hierarchy: The generality of tag reflects the commonality of this tag. On this basis, we consider that a tag with a large generality should be located at a high place in the hierarchy construction. We introduce our method to build tag hierarchy in Algorithm 1.

We construct the hierarchy in accordance with the generalities by selecting a most suitable father node for each tag except the one with largest generality. For each tag p, its father node q must satisfy two conditions: (1) q possesses a larger generality than p; (2) among the tags of generality larger than p, q possesses the largest degree of correlation with p.

Algorithm 1. Tag Hierarchy Construction

Input: T: Set of tags
       G: Set of generality for each tag
       Co-occurrence: Set of co-occurrence frequency for each two tags
Output: R: Tag hierarchy construction

1: **for** tag t in T **do**
2:     set $tmp \leftarrow 0$
3:     **for** tag e in T-{t} **do**
4:         **if** G(e) > G(t) **then**
5:             **if** Co-occurrence (e, t) > tmp **then**
6:                 update $tmp \leftarrow$ Co-occurrence(e, t)
7:                 record this key-value (tmp, e)
8:             **end if**
9:         **end if**
10:    **end for**
11:    get tag f which is correspond to current tmp
12:    add edge relation f → t to R
13: **end for**

We first traverse the tags on line 1. Line 2 defines a variable tmp to record the largest co-occurrence frequency between t and one of the other tags. We then traverse the other tags and compare the generality of the selected tag e with t on line 4. If its generality is larger than that of t, we then check if the co-occurrence frequency between e and t is larger than tmp. If this condition is satisfied, we then regard e as a candidate father node for tag t. We modify the value of tmp and record this candidate tag similar to lines 6–7. When the inner loop is finished, we obtain tag f that corresponds to current tmp in accordance with our records in line 11. For the tag pair (f, t), we add direction from f to t. Finally, we obtain the full hierarchy after the outer loop is completed.

3.3 Hierarchy Optimization

Our construction algorithm presents the following defect. For two tags of great relevance, the one with large generality can be the father node of the other during our building procedure, but they should be on the same level in terms of their semantics (e.g., dvd → cd). As a result, fixing incorrect edges is important. Domain knowledge refers to some existing hierarchy, its artificially built character gives it high reliability. We can use it to trim some unreasonable edges and add some reasonable edges. We obtain these data from open source community and utilize them for optimization.

We design an optimization algorithm based on the "reverse" thinking, that is, the domain knowledge is introduced into the hierarchy construction to be optimized for testing. In accordance with different test results, we conduct different operations on the construction to achieve optimization.

For each tag pair in the domain knowledge, we consider the following conditions:

Algorithm 2. Optimizing Tag Hierarchy

Input: Tagpair1: tag pairs in the domain knowledge
Tagpair2: tag pairs in the construction to be optimized
Tags: all tags that are in the construction to be optimized
Output: R: hierarchy construction after optimizing

1: Initialize set Changed ← Φ
2: **for** tag pair (p, q) in Tagpair1 **do**
3:    **if** p not in Tags ∨ q not in Tags **then**
4:       add edge relation p → q to R
5:    **else**
6:       **if** p and q satisfy function isfather (p, q) **then**
7:          continue
8:       **else**
9:          add edge relation p → q to R
10:         add q to Changed
11:      **end if**
12:   **end if**
13: **end for**
14: **for** tag pair (m, n) in Tagpair2 **do**
15:    **if** n ∈ Changed **then**
16:       continue
17:    **else**
18:       add edge relation m → n to R
19:    **end if**
20: **end for**

---

(1) If the domain knowledge contains tags that do not appear in the construction to be optimized, we then add this relation to the result directly.
(2) If both tags are already in the construction, we then place this tag pair into the construction for checking.

We use function *isfather* to conduct this check. Its parameters are two tags, namely, p and q, and it returns a Boolean value. It uses a recursive method to search if a structure such as p → ... → q exists in the construction to be optimized. There are two conditions when the returned value is true: One is tag pair (p, q) is included in the construction to be optimized. Another is the construction to be optimized contains structure like: p → ... → t → ... → q. The results are described in two conditions:

(1) If the result returns true, then this relation is correct. We do nothing under this condition.
(2) If the result returns false, then the construction possesses a fault. Thus, tag q must be optimized. We change q's father node to p and record q into a set named *Changed*. In other words, this tag has changed its father node.

Finally, we traverse the construction to be optimized. For each child node in the tag pairs, we check if it has been recorded.

(1) If it has not been recorded, then this tap pair possesses a right relation. We then place this relation into the final results.
(2) If it has been recorded, then this tag's father node has been changed. Thus, we do not need to do any operation here.

The pseudo-codes of our algorithm are shown in Algorithm 2.

4 Experiment Design

In this section, we describe the research questions, experiment setting, and evaluation metrics in detail.

4.1 Research Questions

In order to check the performance of our optimization algorithm as well as to make a comprehensive evaluation for our approach, we focus on the following research questions:

- **RQ1:** Does domain knowledge promote the tag hierarchy?
- **RQ2:** Does our approach work more accurately than others'?

For RQ1, we compare the hierarchies before and after optimization to observe the differences and make evaluation. For RQ2, we reproduce others' work and make comparison with ours to evaluate the performance.

4.2 Experimental Setting

Data and storage: We collect 8,064 projects from Openhub and 10,703 posts from StackOverflow. The sum of the tags they include is over 40,000. After pre-processing, we only retain two columns of information, namely, id and tags.

Procedure: We use the information previously extracted from open source communities to conduct our experiment. We calculate co-occurrence frequency for tag pairs first and then calculate tag generality for each tag. Next, we select 342 tags of generalities larger than 1,000 to build hierarchy and thus constrain the time consumption of our experiment. We select out some tags that are commonly used in the open source communities and display their generality values in Table 1.

Table 1. Some important tags and their generality values

Tags	Generality value
html	9,469
javascript	26,059
mysql	17,876
python	42,914
linux	35,700

SourceForge open source community hosts more than 600,000 projects and has established a software taxonomy hierarchy by hand. Thus, its taxonomy presents a high reliability. In our experiment, we choose hierarchy information from SourceForge community as our domain knowledge for optimization. We obtain the final results by conducting optimization operations.

Experimental environment: All our experiments are conducted under Window7 operation system, with Eclipse programming environment and mysql database for data storage.

4.3   Evaluation Metrics

For the proposed research questions, we use two methodologies for evaluation.

One is to use the WordNet [18] tool. This tool has been widely considered as a gold standard for testing hyponym/hypernym relations between tags. We can find synonyms, vocabularies in the sub-categories, and vocabularies in the higher level for a specific tag. We use this tool to check each edge relation in our hierarchy and record the total number of edges in the hierarchy(t), the number of edges found in WordNet(f), and the number of correct edges checked by WordNet(c). The two evaluation factors, *Edge coverage* and *Agreement with WordNet*, equal to f divided by t and c divided by f, respectively.

Another is to apply F-measure, which was introduced by Mario et al. [20], to compare accuracy and recall. The formulas are as follows:

$$PRC_i = \frac{TP_i}{TP_i + FP_i}; \quad REC_i = \frac{TP_i}{TP_i + FN_i}; \quad F_i = \frac{2 * PRC_i * REC_i}{PRC_i + REC_i} \quad (4)$$

For a specific subtree, we manually check each edge relation by comparing with WordNet and record terms should have belonged to this subtree but not by searching synonyms and vocabularies in the sub-categories for tags in this subtree traversely.

We calculate three parameters: TP_i is the number of true positives (edge relations that are correct), FP_i is the number of false positives (edge relations that are incorrect, for example, *ftp* is a false positive in http → ftp), and FN_i is the number of false negatives (edge relations that do not belong to this tree but should have belonged, for example, *dns* is a false negative if it is not belong to *web*). Implementing this method to all the subtrees in hierarchy construction will result in Formula (5) as follows:

$$PRC = \frac{\sum_i TP_i}{\sum_i TP_i + FP_i}; \ REC = \frac{\sum_i TP_i}{\sum_i TP_i + FN_i}; \ F = \frac{2 * PRC * REC}{PRC + REC} \quad (5)$$

where PRC represents the average precision; REC represents recall; and F, which is a harmonic mean of PRC and REC, provides a way to combine precision and recall in a unique metric. We use this theory to calculate the values of F-measure for each hierarchy to check its performance.

5 Results and Discussions

In this section, we present the experimental results for the research questions we have proposed. We also use a case study to show the superiority of our approach and discuss the threats to validity in detail.

5.1 RQ1: Does Domain Knowledge Promote the Tag Hierarchy?

In this section, we conduct qualitative and quantitative analyses for hierarchies before and after optimization to check whether domain knowledge promotes the tag hierarchy from content and evaluation metrics.

Hierarchies before and after optimization have 317 and 429 edges respectively, indicating that the content in the hierarchy after optimization is much richer than before. Some errors are corrected and some new tags are added. We choose the subtree of *web* as a case to evaluate this question in detail. Subtrees of *web* before and after optimization are shown in Figs. 2 and 3, respectively.

Qualitative analysis: The subtree of *web* before optimization possesses four incorrect relation edges, namely, http → ftp, web → statistics, web → publishing (we consider that the father node of *publishing* should be *tomcat*), and web → templating (we consider that the father node of *templating* should be a programming language, such as *jquery*). *Web* is a tag about some terms and technologies about net. Four nodes should appear in this subtree: *html*, *xhtml*, *ssh*, and *dns*.

During the optimization, we modify the incorrect edge http → ftp, add tags *dns* and *ssh* into the hierarchy construction, and enlarge the number of the nodes in the tree, which can be construed as enriching the contents of the tree.

Quantitative analysis: We check each edge in the constructions with the help of Wordnet, and the results are illustrated in Table 2.

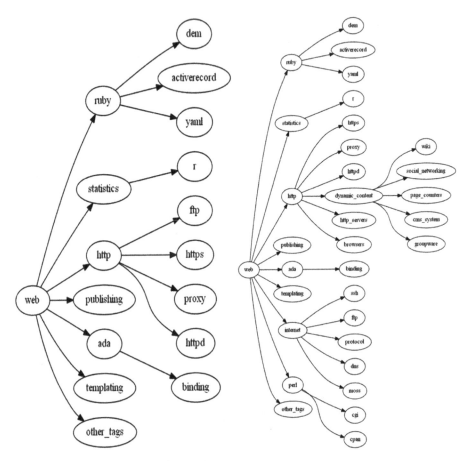

Fig. 2. Subtree of *web* before optimization   **Fig. 3.** Subtree of *web* after optimization

Table 2. Edges evaluation against WordNet

	Number of edges found in WordNet	Edge coverage (%)	Agreement with WordNet (%)
Before optimization	317	92.96	82.20
After optimization	429	95.76	91.93

The results show that we obtain a large number of edges in the hierarchy after optimization, indicating that optimization enriches the content of hierarchy. The percentages of edge cover and agreement with WordNet are increased. We then calculate the values of F-measure for the two hierarchies, and the results are illustrated in Table 3.

Table 3. Values of F-measure for hierarchies before and after optimization

	PRC	REC	F-measure
Before optimization	87.10%	79.41%	83.08%
After optimization	95.90%	98.08%	96.98%

The results show that accuracy and recall rate significantly differ before and after optimization. Our optimization improves the accuracy and recall rate for domain knowledge brings new information to this hierarchy, thereby increasing the value of F-measure to a large extent.

The above-mentioned analysis shows that the optimization based on domain knowledge exerts a satisfactory effect. Domain knowledge not only enriches the content of the tag hierarchy but also improves the accuracy. It promotes the tag hierarchy to a large extent.

5.2   RQ2: Does Our Approach Work More Accurately Than Others'?

In this section, we choose Fahad's work [19] and Gu's work [14] for comparison with ours in that both of them have an optimization step as we have mentioned in Sect. 2. Using our dataset, we reproduce their works. For Fahad's method, we set the values of *occurrence* to 1,000, *generality* to 2,000, and *min_sim* to 10. For Gu's method, we select tags of generality greater than 5,000 to build construction and use information from SourceForge to optimize. The subtrees containing tag "xml" built by their methods are shown in Fig. 4.

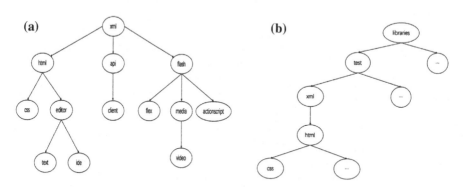

Fig. 4. (a) "xml" in Fahad's. (b) "xml" in Gu's

We check each edge in the hierarchies by Wordnet for comparison with ours. The results are listed in Table 4.

The results show that our hierarchy possesses far more information than others. Our hierarchy possesses more than 400 edges found in Wordnet whereas others possess around 50. In addition, our edge coverage and agreement with Wordnet are both the highest. We calculate F-measure values for the three hierarchies to further verify our conclusion, and the results are shown in Table 5.

Table 4. Edge comparison results against Wordnet

	Number of edges found in WordNet	Edge coverage (%)	Agreement with WordNet (%)
Fahad's	55	93.22	83.64
Gu's	40	86.96	90.00
Ours	429	95.76	91.93

Table 5. Results of applying F-measure to three methods

	PRC	REC	F-measure
Fahad's method	79.60%	71.43%	74.06%
Gu's method	83.33%	66.67%	74.07%
Ours	95.90%	98.08%	96.98%

The results prove the superiority of our approach with accuracy and recall rate reaching approximately 95% whereas others reach only around 80%. As mentioned in Sect. 2, Gu's optimization reduces many tags from the original construction, and its recall is low as a result. Fahad's optimization plays a little role in finding a suitable parent node for tags. Thus, this method presents a low accuracy rate. Our method presents no apparent flaw, and our F-measure is thus far larger than that of others.

This experiment proves the validity and rationality of our method. Widely used tool and theoretical calculation show that our approach exhibits better performance than others in terms of accuracy.

5.3   Case Study

In this section, we provide a case study to show the superiority of our approach. *Multimedia* is widely used in tag hierarchy as a classification symbol and subtree of *multimedia* in our approach is shown in Fig. 5.

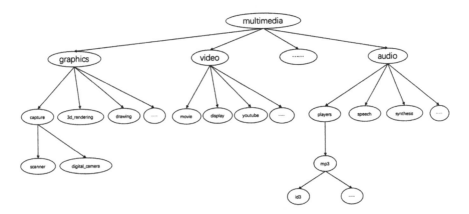

Fig. 5. A case study: subtree of *multimedia*

The subtree contains 52 edges in total, which is a large number, and the paths in this hierarchy contain 5 layers at most. *Graphics*, *video*, and *audio* are all commonly used sub-category under *multimedia*, proving that our classification is reasonable. Terminologies widely used under *graphics* (e.g., *capture*, *3d_rendering*, and *drawing*), *video* (e.g., *movie*, *display*, and *youtube*), and *audio* (e.g., *players*, *speech*, and *synthesis*) are all in this construction, indicating that our approach provides a high recall rate with abundant content of tags.

Some errors are noted in this construction (e.g., dvd → cd, mp3 → mp4). These errors may be caused by the defect of our algorithm. For two tags of great relevance, the one with large generality can be the father node of the other during our building procedure, but they should be on the same level in terms of their semantics. We check our domain knowledge dataset and find that those tags in the incorrect edge are excluded in it. Accordingly, we cannot fix them during optimization.

We reach the conclusion that our approach can build a reasonable and comprehensive hierarchy. We can fix all the errors if we obtain a domain knowledge containing sufficient information.

5.4   Threats to Validity

Some threats to the validity of our experiment may affect the results. First, we only choose tags of generality larger than 1,000 to build hierarchy to limit the time consumption of our experiment. As a result, some key tags may be dropped, thereby influencing our result. Second, we assume domain knowledge is absolutely right in the optimization procedure. Although domain knowledge is artificially established, it may still possess some defects. Thus, the process of enriching the contents of our hierarchy may introduce some errors.

6   Conclusion and Future Work

The increasing amount of information in the open source community has introduced the need for effective information management. In this study, we put forward a hybrid approach to build tag hierarchy. First, we extract data from StackOverflow and the Openhub community, define concepts and computational methods for tag co-occurrence frequency and tag generalization, and propose an unsupervised hierarchical building algorithm based on tag generalization. Next, we design a new set of reverse complementation optimization algorithms that takes the existing taxonomic levels in SourceForge as domain knowledge into the established hierarchy and tests it to arrive at an optimized, accurate hierarchy. We conduct extensive experiments. We compare the hierarchy constructions before and after optimization to show that our optimization exerts great effect. We also compare our work with others to verify its superior performance by utilizing the Wordnet tool and F-measures method.

However, some limitations exist. First, we do not have operations for synonyms. In the subtree of *multimedia*, *movie* and *movies* are son nodes of *video*, but they have the same meaning in semantic. We can merge the two tags into one. The study for plurals and stems has been going on for a long time and several achievements have been realized. If we introduce some relative methods into our approach, we will obtain an accurate result. Second, we simply compare our approach with two state-of-the-art methods to verify the superior performance of our approach. There are many other ways to resolve this problem as this topic has been studied for a long time. In the future, we plan to make a comprehensive comparison with other methods to further verify the performance of our approach.

Acknowledgement. Our approach is publicly-available to support further research on tag hierarchy construction and provide convenience for others to reproduce our experiment: https://github.com/Kaka727/Tag_Hierarchy_Construction_WSW.

References

1. Tao, W., Huaimin, W., Gang, Y.I.N., et al.: Hierarchical categorization of open source software by online profiles. IEICE Trans. Inf. Syst. **97**(9), 2386–2397 (2014)
2. Begelman, G.; Keller, P., Smadja, F.: Automated tag clustering: improving search and exploration in the tag space. In: Collaborative Web Tagging Workshop at WWW 2006, Edinburgh, Scotland (2006)
3. Wang, S., Lo, D., Jiang, L.: Inferring semantically related software terms and their taxonomy by leveraging collaborative tagging. In: Proceedings of the 2012 IEEE International Conference on Software Maintenance (ICSM) (ICSM 2012), pp. 604–607. IEEE Computer Society, Washington, DC (2012)
4. Liu, X., Song, Y., Liu, S., Wang, H.: Automatic taxonomy construction from keywords. In: Proceedings of the 18th ACM SIGKDD International Conference on Knowledge Discovery and Data Mining (KDD 2012), pp. 1433–1441. ACM (2012)
5. Heymann, P., Garcia-Molina, H.: Collaborative creation of communal hierarchical taxonomies in social tagging systems. Technical report, Computer Science Department, Standford University, April 2006
6. Sanderson, M., Croft, B.: Deriving concept hierarchies from text. In: Proceedings of the 22nd Annual International ACM SIGIR Conference on Research and Development in Information Retrieval, pp. 206–213. ACM (1999)
7. Schmitz, P.: Inducing ontology from flickr tags. In: Collaborative Web Tagging Workshop at WWW 2006, Edinburgh, Scotland, vol. 50 (2006)
8. Liu, K., Fang, B., Zhang, W.: Ontology emergence from folksonomies. In: Huang, J., Koudas, N., Jones, G.J.F., Wu, X., Collins-Thompson, K., An, A. (eds.) CIKM, pp. 1109–1118. ACM (2010)
9. Blei, D.M., Ng, A.Y., Jordan, M.I.: Latent dirichlet allocation. J. Mach. Learn. Res. **3**, 993–1022 (2003)
10. Tang, J., Leung, H.-f., Luo, Q., Chen, D., Gong, J.: Towards ontology learning from folksonomies. In: Boutilier, C. (ed.) IJCAI, pp. 2089–2094 (2009)
11. Wang, W., Barnaghi, P.M., Bargiela, A.: Probabilistic topic models for learning terminological ontologies. IEEE Trans. Knowl. Data Eng. **22**(7), 1028–1040 (2010)
12. Itti, L., Baldi, P.: Bayesian surprise attracts human attention. In: NIPS (2005)
13. Li, X., Wang, H., Yin, G., Wang, T., Yang, C., Yu, Y., Tang, D.: Inducing taxonomy from tags: an agglomerative hierarchical clustering framework. In: Zhou, S., Zhang, S., Karypis, G. (eds.) ADMA 2012. LNCS (LNAI), vol. 7713, pp. 64–77. Springer, Heidelberg (2012). https://doi.org/10.1007/978-3-642-35527-1_6

14. Gu, C., Yin, G., Wang, T., Yang, C., Wang, H.: A supervised approach for tag hierarchy construction in open source communities. In: Asia-Pacific Symposium on Internetware, pp. 148–152 (2015)
15. De Meo, P., Quattrone, G., Ursino, D.: Exploitation of semantic relationships and hierarchical data structures to support a user in his annotation and browsing activities in folksonomies. Inf. Syst. **34**(6), 511–535 (2009)
16. Marszałek, M., Schmid, C.: Constructing category hierarchies for visual recognition. In: Forsyth, D., Torr, P., Zisserman, A. (eds.) ECCV 2008. LNCS, vol. 5305, pp. 479–491. Springer, Heidelberg (2008). https://doi.org/10.1007/978-3-540-88693-8_35
17. Brooks, C.H., Montanez, N.: Improved annotation of the blogosphere via auto-tagging and hierarchical clustering. In: Carr, L., Roure, D.D., Iyengar, A., Goble, C.A., Dahlin, M. (eds.) WWW, pp. 625–632. ACM (2006)
18. Miller, G.: WordNet: a lexical database for English. Commun. ACM **38**(11), 39–41 (1995)
19. Almoqhim, F., Millard, D.E., Shadbolt, N.: Improving on popularity as a proxy for generality when building tag hierarchies from folksonomies. In: Aiello, L.M., McFarland, D. (eds.) SocInfo 2014. LNCS, vol. 8851, pp. 95–111. Springer, Cham (2014). https://doi.org/10.1007/978-3-319-13734-6_7
20. Linares-Vásquez, M., McMillan, C., Poshyvanyk, D., Grechanik, M.: On using machine learning to automatically classify software applications into domain categories. Empirical Softw. Eng. **19**(3), 582–618 (2014)

Top-Down Evaluation of Reusable Goal Models

Mustafa Berk Duran$^{(\boxtimes)}$ and Gunter Mussbacher

Department of Electrical and Computer Engineering, McGill University,
Montréal, Canada
berk.duran@mail.mcgill.ca, gunter.mussbacher@mcgill.ca

Abstract. Top-down evaluation of goal models allows designers to find
the optimal set of solutions that would satisfy the stakeholders of their
system and their goals. However, the computational complexity of top-
down evaluation increases with the growing size of goal models and goal
model reuse hierarchies, when goal models are used in collaboration with
other modeling formalisms that may impose some external constraints
on them (e.g., feature models). This paper (i) introduces novel modeling
constructs and goal prioritization methods into the existing bottom-up
evaluation algorithm for its adaptation to top-down evaluation of goal
models, (ii) introduces an algorithm to propagate top-level importance
values down the reuse hierarchy to benefit from reuse boundaries and
allow the goal model of each reuse level to be evaluated individually for
the top-down evaluation in the whole reuse hierarchy (i.e., without having to backtrack through the entire reuse hierarchy), and (iii) shows the
feasibility of this novel evaluation via its proof-of-concept implementation in the TouchCORE reuse tool.

Keywords: Goal model · Reuse · Top-down evaluation
Trade-off analysis · Constraints
Model-driven requirements engineering

1 Introduction

Goal models provide the capability to represent the hierarchy and relationships
among the requirements of a system, objectives of the stakeholders, and the
potential solutions to satisfy those requirements. Goal-oriented modeling is considered as a useful approach for requirements engineering due to the benefits of
using goals for elicitation, elaboration, and clarification of requirements as well as
handling conflicts and driving the design and implementation of systems [20,27].

In the early requirements phase, they are used to help stakeholders com-
municate their needs and expectations, better understand the requirements and
their solutions along with the impacts that alternative solutions may have on
stakeholder goals. Having multiple stakeholders often results in having conflicting goals and requires designers to deal with those conflicts and make trade-offs
among requirements [9]. Analysis and reasoning capabilities that are associated
with goal modeling help designers in this decision making process.

© Springer International Publishing AG, part of Springer Nature 2018
R. Capilla et al. (Eds.): ICSR 2018, LNCS 10826, pp. 76–92, 2018.
https://doi.org/10.1007/978-3-319-90421-4_5

Reuse of software artifacts allows designers to build software of higher quality with increased productivity [7, 22]. Similar to any software artifact created during the software development process, potential benefits of reuse also apply to model reuse. For goal models, as each goal model encapsulates its modelers' knowledge and expertise, it is essential to establish the means to reuse a goal model and still benefit from its capabilities for trade-off analysis and reasoning.

While bottom-up evaluation of a goal model shows the impact of solutions on goals [3], top-down evaluation aims to find the optimal set of solutions (typically leaf-level tasks) that would satisfy the stakeholders of the system (i.e., actors) and their goals [17, 23]. However, running a top-down evaluation in a goal model can be a computationally complex task especially when the size of the goal model grows (i.e., the number of possible solution sets increases) and when goal models are used in collaboration with other modeling formalisms such as feature models that may impose some external constraints on them (i.e., constraints can limit the possible solution sets for the goal model and make it more difficult to find the optimal set of solutions).

In this work, we introduce a novel top-down evaluation algorithm for reusable goal model hierarchies. For this purpose, *(i)* the previously implemented lazy recursive goal model evaluation algorithm for bottom-up evaluation [14] is modified to handle additional constraints that may be introduced by stakeholders (i.e., goal importance values and threshold satisfactions), *(ii)* a new algorithm propagates the importance values defined by the application designers (i.e., at the top level of a goal model reuse hierarchy) down to the reused goal models to benefit from the reuse boundaries between goal models and to avoid evaluating a large flattened goal model that represents the entire reuse hierarchy, *and (iii)* a proof-of-concept implementation examines the feasibility of this novel evaluation algorithm in the TouchCORE reuse tool [25].

The remainder of this paper gives a brief background on goal modeling and the use of relative contribution values in reusable goal models in Sect. 2, followed by the explanation of the first contribution of this work (i.e., the modifications and concepts introduced into the prior evaluation algorithm) and how it is used for the top-down evaluation of a single goal model in Sect. 3. Our novel importance propagation algorithm (i.e., the second contribution of this work) for the top-down evaluation of reusable goal model hierarchies is introduced in Sect. 4. Section 5 then presents the proof-of-concept implementation (i.e., the third contribution of this work) and discusses the feasibility of the algorithm with measured performance results. A brief overview of related work is given in Sect. 6 and Sect. 7 concludes the paper and presents future work.

2   Background on Goal Modeling

Several different notations are used in practice for the design of goal models. Despite their differences, many commonalities exist among the most commonly used formalisms for goal-oriented modeling, namely, the Goal-oriented Requirement Language (GRL) [19], i* [28], KAOS [11], NFR framework [10], and Tropos [8]. All languages introduce the concept of a goal in their own way. GRL and i* classify a goal as an intentional element and extend the scope of intentional elements with the addition of softgoals (i.e., goals whose satisfaction cannot be measured in an objective manner), tasks, and resources. In GRL, i*, and Tropos, intentional elements are contained in an actor which may represent a stakeholder of a system or the system itself. Actors, being holders of intentions, want tasks to be performed and resources to be available for their goals to be satisfied. The NFR framework, on the other hand, only uses softgoals. Links that are used to represent the relationships among intentional elements may take the form of contribution links or decomposition links (i.e., AND and OR). While all languages cover decomposition links, KAOS uses different means to express contributions.

Trade-off analysis through goal model evaluation is one of the biggest strengths of goal modeling as it allows modelers to reason about high-level goals (e.g., system qualities and non-functional requirements) and potential solutions. Bottom-up evaluation propagates the satisfaction values of leaf elements up to their parent elements based on the type and value of the link between them, hence demonstrating the impact of selecting one solution over another on high-level stakeholder goals [3]. On the other hand, top-down evaluation mechanisms aim to find optimal sets of solutions given the desired satisfaction values of stakeholder goals. Even though the two evaluation mechanisms serve different purposes, contribution values and how they are assigned are integral parts of goal model evaluation in both cases.

Qualitative, quantitative, and real-life values are different types of contribution values known for GRL, i*, and the NFR Framework. For reusable goal models, we advocate the use of either real-life values (if they are available) or relative values for contribution links [14]. For non-relative contribution values, a global agreement among modelers on what contribution values mean is needed. However, global agreements are unlikely to be reached for vague goals such as security or user convenience. Relative contribution values eliminate the need for such global agreements since the reusable artifact designer differentiates competing solutions locally within the reusable artifact.

The use of relative contributions leads to relative satisfaction values and these relative satisfactions need to be normalized for composability reasons. Normalization ensures that each satisfaction value is in the same range (i.e., $[0, 100]$), indicating the worst and best case values for their corresponding goals (0 and 100, respectively). This normalization is required to be able to compose goal model elements with relative satisfaction values. To normalize the satisfactions, it is necessary to determine an element's actual minimum and maximum satisfaction values. For this purpose, a lazy recursive algorithm that calculates the actual minimum and maximum satisfaction values to normalize the satisfactions (i.e., through scaling and offsetting) has been implemented in previous work [14].

While goal models can be used in isolation, they can also be used in collaboration with other modeling formalisms that may impose additional constraints on some goal model elements, typically tasks in a goal model. For example, tasks in the goal model may represent features in a feature model, which may dictate which tasks can be used together in a system [14]. Furthermore, a workflow model may express causal relationships between tasks (e.g., via describing the possible scenarios where some tasks are on alternative paths and cannot occur in the same scenario execution) [12]. When conducting trade-off analysis with goal models, ignoring these constraints may result in an incorrect evaluation. For instance, if the feature model expresses that two tasks that cannot be selected together, they should not be evaluated together in the goal model. As a result, it is required to take the constraints imposed by other modeling notations into account for trade-off analysis.

The lazy recursive goal model evaluation algorithm introduced in our previous work for bottom-up evaluation enables the use of relative contribution values in reusable goal models in the presence of external constraints [14] and delayed decisions (i.e., the decisions that are postponed to the designers of higher level goal models in the reuse hierarchy) [13]. In the following section, the lazy recursive algorithm is explained with the novel modifications and concepts introduced into it for top-down evaluation of goal models.

3 Top-Down Evaluation of Goal Models

In the lower and intermediate levels of reuse hierarchies, reusable goal models represent the local impacts of alternative solutions provided by a reusable artifact on different qualities and non-functional requirements. When an application is built at the top of the reuse hierarchy with the help of goal modeling, trade-off analysis helps decision making among different reusable solutions that are available to build the application. To drive the decision making process, it is necessary to provide guidelines for questions such as *"Which goals are more important for the stakeholders of the application?"* or *"How much of a goal's satisfaction can we sacrifice to improve on another goal's satisfaction?"*.

In the remainder of this section, our proposed method for goal prioritization in support of trade-off analysis at the application level is introduced, followed by the description of how top-down evaluation is achieved with our novel algorithm, both for a single-level goal model (in this section) and through the entire hierarchy of reusable goal models (in Sect. 4).

3.1 Goal Prioritization with Thresholds

First, let us consider prioritization of goals for decision making via trade-off analysis in goal models. When the application consists of several top-level goals, it is necessary to determine what these goals mean for the application. For this purpose, our approach uses percentage *importance* values that are assigned by the application designers at the top level in the reuse hierarchy to express the priority of a goal.

Application designers may introduce an *actor* into the goal model and assign importance values to top-level goals to represent the overall prioritization of goals. For some goals such as cost and performance, *importance* values may be based on quantified, real life measurements. However, for the cases when those measurements are not available, and for non-functional requirements (i.e., *softgoals*) such as user convenience, security, and privacy, for which it is hard to define measurement units, application designers shall assign importance values through discussions with stakeholders as well as using their expertise. Using percentage importance values for goal prioritization allows us to address both cases and figure out the best solutions for an application using goal models.

Having decided on how the satisfaction of some high-level goals may influence the satisfaction of their stakeholders, designers can, in turn, limit the variability among the possible solutions to a desired, smaller set of solutions that complies with those decisions. In other words, with the help of goal models and trade-off analysis, designers can decide on the most suitable set of solutions (i.e., *tasks*) to be included in the application based on their impacts on the high-level goals that are prioritized by stakeholders.

In addition to the prioritization through importance values, our approach takes into account *threshold* values that may be assigned by application designers. Setting a threshold on a goal complements the goal prioritization with importances and allows application designers to specify their desired worst-case satisfaction value for that goal so that the algorithm can work to find the solutions sets that do not have the goal's satisfaction drop below the threshold.

3.2 The Lazy Recursive Algorithm in Top-Down Evaluation

As explained in Sect. 2, the lazy recursive algorithm is initially designed to determine the possible minimal and maximal satisfaction values for goals and to use those values in the normalization of goal satisfactions in reusable goal models with constraints [14]. The lazy recursive algorithm avoids combinatorial explosion as it only takes a possible solution set into consideration when necessary (i.e., only when a constraint is violated by a solution set, the next best solution sets are evaluated). Even though in the worst case (i.e., where all possible solution sets violate a constraint) 2^n combinations have to be examined, where n stands for the number of solutions (i.e., typically *tasks* in the goal model), the actual calculation time is reduced significantly [14]. Consequently, as the first contribution of this work, we propose to reuse and adapt this lazy recursive algorithm to handle additional constraints that may be introduced by stakeholders (i.e., goal importances and threshold satisfactions as explained in Sect. 3.1) and conduct the top-down evaluation.

An *actor* (i.e., stakeholder) is represented as a hidden top-level goal (i.e., dashed ellipse at the top of Fig. 1) with incoming contribution links from the goals for which an importance value is defined. An *importance value* that is defined for an actor-goal tuple is represented as the contribution value for its corresponding contribution link (i.e., values labeled "Importance" on dashed arrows at the top of Fig. 1). Finally, a *threshold value* is defined for a top-level goal to represent the desired worst-case satisfaction value for that goal (i.e., values labeled "Threshold" on top-level goals in Fig. 1).

The desired result of the top-down evaluation is one of two possible outcomes:

- Find all combinations of solutions that do not violate any constraints, including the defined threshold values, and that correspond to the same, best possible evaluation result for the actor.

– If it is not possible to satisfy all of the thresholds at the same time, suggest all solution combinations that violate the least amount of threshold constraints and that correspond to the best possible evaluation result for the actor.

To calculate the maximal solution for a goal, the algorithm *(i)* asks the goal's children (i.e., nodes that have outgoing contribution links with positive/negative contribution values to the goal) for the next highest/lowest solution combinations they can provide, *(ii)* calculates the potential satisfaction values for received combinations, *(iii)* checks the combined solution set for constraint violations, and if there are constraint violations, repeats from step *(i)*, or else, *(iv)* records this solution set and the best result achieved for it and repeats steps *(i)* to *(iv)* until the calculated satisfaction value drops below the recorded best result.

An explanatory model depicting the top-down evaluation process is shown in Fig. 1. To keep readers' focus on the description of the algorithm iterations, the model size is kept minimal. The goal model contains two goals (i.e., *Goal X* and *Goal Y*) and 5 tasks (i.e., *Solution1–5*) that contribute to them. Since this goal model is reusable, contribution values are defined relatively and goal satisfaction

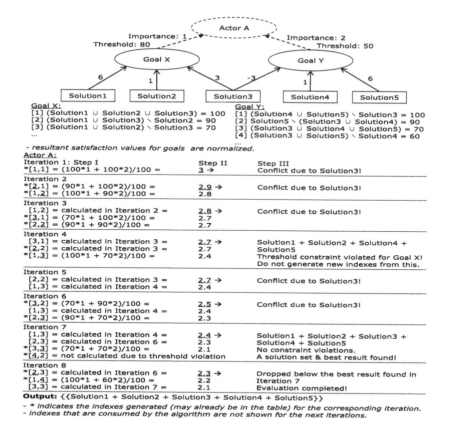

Fig. 1. Top-down evaluation on a single level reusable goal model

values must be normalized by scaling factor and offset values calculated for each goal [14]. For the sake of simplicity, no external constraints are defined among the five tasks. However, as explained in Sect. 2, it is possible to introduce external constraints for the tasks when using them as features in a feature model. In such scenario, two or more solutions may be conflicting due to numerous reasons (e.g., being XOR children of the same parent feature, having an *excludes* constraint between them, etc.). Those potential conflicts are handled in *Step III* of the algorithm with the constraint checker.

When the application designer decides to find the optimal result for the goal model, they define an actor (e.g., *Actor A*) and set the importance and threshold values for high-level goals. The designer may also choose to include or exclude some solutions (i.e., tasks) from the result as a precondition to the top-down evaluation (e.g., select or unselect a feature that represents a task in the goal model to be in the feature configuration). In that case, the decisions made by the designer as preconditions are reflected on the initializations of the tasks. Setting preconditions reduces the size of the possible solution set for a task from 2 (i.e., task will be either included or excluded in the result) to 1. In Fig. 1, to not oversimplify the example, no preconditions are set on *Solution1–5*.

The top-down evaluation is done per root element in the goal model (i.e., an actor) with the importance values defined for them. The example in Fig. 1 illustrates that the algorithm begins with *Actor A*, and examines combination $[1, 1]$ in *Step I* of the first iteration (i.e., the combination with the highest satisfaction value of each of *Actor A*'s contributors (*Solution1*, *Solution2*, *Solution3* for *Goal X*, and *Solution4* and *Solution5* excluding *Solution3* for *Goal Y*)). The potential actor satisfaction for this combination is calculated as 3 in *Step II* of the same iteration, but because the solution set of *Goal Y* excludes *Solution3*, the constraint check fails in *Step III* and this result is considered invalid.

Therefore, the algorithm moves on to the second iteration to examine the next best combinations where the index of each child is incremented individually. Having classified $[1, 1]$ as invalid in the previous iteration, the combinations $[2, 1]$ and $[1, 2]$ are taken into consideration for the next (Step I of the second iteration), because any other remaining combination cannot result in a higher satisfaction value. This results in the satisfaction values of 2.9 and 2.8, respectively, in *Step II* of the second iteration, indicating that the combination $[2, 1]$ is the next best option. While the algorithm takes the combination $[2, 1]$ into account (i.e., consumes it in *Step III*), it still keeps the combination $[1, 2]$ in the table. However, the same conflict due to *Solution3* reappears for combination $[2, 1]$ and hence it is again found to be invalid.

In the third iteration, the next best combinations are again brought to the table (i.e., since $[2, 1]$ is found invalid in the previous iteration, $[3, 1]$ and $[2, 2]$ are added). The next highest valued combination that has not been examined in the table is $[1, 2]$. Up until *Step III* of the fourth iteration, the algorithm behaves the same way as it does for its previous application to find the maximal solution to calculate the scale factor and offset values for normalization [14].

Upon the evaluation of the combination $[1, 2]$ at the last step of the third iteration, the algorithm adds $[2, 2]$ and $[1, 3]$ with their corresponding values 2.7 and 2.4, respectively, to the table. At this point, the already calculated (in third iteration) $[3, 1]$ is now at the top of the table and is examined in *Step III*. The constraint check finds out that, while this combination satisfies all other constraints, the threshold constraint for *Goal X* is violated (i.e., the satisfaction of *Goal X* for its third best combination yields 70, whereas its threshold is 80).

Considering a single level goal model only, the change to the existing lazy recursive algorithm for its adaptation to top-down evaluation is that it does not generate new indexes from those that violate a threshold constraint for a goal (e.g., at *Iteration 5* in Fig. 1, $[4, 1]$ and $[3, 2]$ are not generated), because all remaining indexes also violate the threshold. Furthermore, the goal whose index caused the threshold violation (e.g., at *Iteration 4*, *Goal X* drops below its threshold for index value 3) is not asked for any index values greater than that (e.g., at *Iteration 7* in Fig. 1, the combination for index $[4, 2]$ is not calculated).

The algorithm keeps going through the next combinations (i.e., iterations 5–7) and at *Step III* of the seventh iteration, it discovers a solution set with no constraint violations (i.e., *Solution1*, *Solution2*, *Solution3*, *Solution4*, and *Solution5* together results in an evaluation of 2.4 for *Actor A*). At this point, it is important to note that there can still be other valid solution sets with the same evaluation result for the actor (i.e., 2.4). As described in the first possible outcome of the top-down evaluation, it is desired to find not one but all of the possible solutions that do not violate any constraints and comply with the importances set by the application designer. Therefore, after finding a best case solution, the algorithm still continues until the result examined in *Step III* drops below the best result that was previously found. As the next best evaluation result of 2.3 for the combination $[2, 3]$ in *Step III* of *Iteration 8* drops below the previously found best result of 2.4, the output of the top-down evaluation in Fig. 1 is a single solution: *Solution1*, *Solution2*, *Solution3*, *Solution4*, and *Solution5*.

Note that the first index that causes the evaluation to drop below a threshold is still kept in the table (e.g., 3 for *Goal X*) and only the next index is not kept (e.g., 4 for *Goal X*). The reasoning behind this is being able to provide the application designer the second possible outcome of the top-down evaluation. If the algorithm finds out that there are no possible combinations to satisfy all of the thresholds at the same time, it must find and suggest solution combinations with the highest evaluation result that violate the least amount of threshold constraints. If this is the case, the algorithm goes through the table starting from the top, looks for and returns all combinations with the lowest number of threshold violations, no other constraint violations, and the highest evaluation.

4   Top-Down Evaluation in Reuse Hierarchies

When reusable goal models are used to build a hierarchy of reusable artifacts, new challenges arise for the top-down evaluation.

In previous work, in addition to the use of relative contribution values with normalization, we introduced two new modeling constructs (i.e., *reuse link* and *feature impact element*) that allows us to clearly define the reuse interface for goal models [15]. In this context, goal models and feature models are used in collaboration and tasks in the goal model represent features in the feature model. For its realization, a feature may reuse other artifacts that also make use of reusable goal models and the impacts of reused goals are reflected on the goal model at the higher level through the feature impact elements. Each reused goal in a feature impact element is assigned a weight along with the feature itself (e.g., reused goal *Authorization - Increase Performance* is assigned a weight of 4 whereas the feature *Transfer Funds* is assigned a weight of 1 in the *Bank Goal Model* in Fig. 2). The feature impact element is evaluated internally based on *(i)* the satisfaction values of its reused goals, and *(ii)* whether or not the feature itself has been selected. The reuse link only becomes active if the feature is selected and included in the solution. Hence, the feature impact element's own satisfaction is evaluated only if the feature is selected and is set to 0 otherwise.

The reuse boundary introduced by the feature impact element enables the evaluation of individual levels and prevents backtracking across levels since the normalization algorithm [14] knows that each reused goal will evaluate to 100 for its best-case solution and 0 for its worst, regardless of what their corresponding

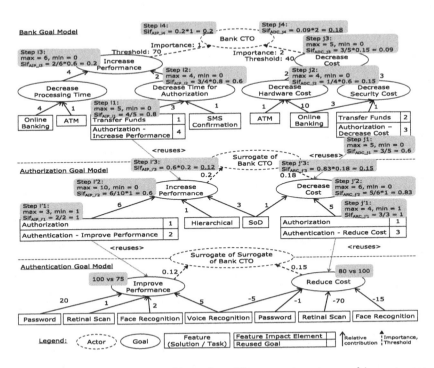

Fig. 2. Bank application reuse hierarchy with surrogate actors and importances

solution sets are (i.e., it is not possible to have conflicts across levels as constraints are defined internally for the models at the same level [15]).

A three-level reuse hierarchy built with the help of reuse links and feature impact elements is illustrated in Fig. 2. At the top level (i.e., *Bank Goal Model*), two feature impact elements (i.e., *Transfer Funds, Authorization - Increase Performance* and *Transfer Funds, Authorization - Decrease Cost*) represent that the feature *Transfer Funds* reuses the *Authorization* artifact and separately reflects the impacts of *Increase Performance* and *Decrease Cost* goals of the *Authorization* on the *Bank Goal Model*. Similarly, at the intermediate level (i.e., *Authorization Goal Model*), the feature *Authorization* reuses the *Authentication* artifact and separately reflects the impacts of *Improve Performance* and *Reduce Cost* goals of the *Authentication* on the *Authorization Goal Model*.

At the top level of the reuse hierarchy, the application designer introduces the actor (i.e., *Bank CTO*) and sets the importance and threshold values for the two high-level goals (i.e., *Increase Performance* and *Decrease Cost*) to conduct the top-down evaluation.

The main difference in running the top-down evaluation in a reuse hierarchy instead of a single level goal model is that it is possible to have conflicting solution sets for different reused goals of the same reused goal model. Consequently, when the algorithm asks a feature impact element for its next best combinations, it needs to go into the lower level reused goal model and find the possible solution sets there. Furthermore, when it is time to evaluate a combination (i.e., *Step III* of an iteration in Fig. 1) for the actor (i.e., *Bank CTO* in Fig. 2), the algorithm also needs to combine the solutions provided by those reused goals (i.e., *Increase Performance* and *Decrease Cost* goals of the *Authorization*) and check for the constraint violations in the lower level artifact (i.e., feature model of the *Authorization* artifact).

The trivial way to handle the reuses of a goal model is to disregard the goal model reuse hierarchy and treat it as one big flattened goal model to run the top-down evaluation on it. However, the computational complexity of the top-down evaluation increases as the goal model grows bigger. A better approach considers the reuse boundaries between reusable goal models that are already defined, taking advantage of this modular structure to reduce computational complexity. For this purpose, we introduce a pre-processing algorithm that creates a surrogate actor for the lower level (i.e., reused) goal model and derives the importance values between reused goals and this surrogate actor. Derivation of the importance values for the surrogate actor is done via calculating the *comparative self-impact factors* of the reused goals (i.e., *Increase Performance* and *Decrease Cost* goals of the *Authorization*) on the actual actor in the goal model doing the reuse (i.e., *Bank CTO* in Fig. 2). The derivation starts at the feature impact elements that represent the impact of the reused goal (i.e., *Transfer Funds*) and the calculated self-impact factor of the reused goal on the feature impact element is propagated upwards through the contribution links until the self-impact factor of the reused goal on the actor is obtained.

The self-impact factor calculation is illustrated in Fig. 2. First, the derived importance values for *Surrogate of Bank CTO* is calculated. In the first step (i.e., *Step i1*), the self-impact factor of the reused goal *Increase Performance* on the feature impact model element is calculated as 0.8 since the possible range (max - min) for the feature impact element is 5 and the weight of the reused goal is 4 (i.e., $Sif_{AIPi1} = 4/5 = 0.8$). In the second step (i.e., *Step i2*), the self-impact factor of the feature impact model element on the goal *Decrease Time for Authorization* is calculated as 0.6 since the possible range (max - min) for the goal is 4 and the contribution of the feature impact element is 3 (i.e., $Sif_{AIPi2} = 3/4 * 0.8 = 0.6$). Similarly, in the third step (i.e., *Step i3*), the self-impact factor of the goal *Decrease Time for Authorization* on *Increase Performance* is calculated as 0.2 (i.e., $Sif_{AIPi3} = 2/6*0.6 = 0.2$) and propagated to the actor (i.e., *Bank CTO*) as 0.2 (i.e., $Sif_{AIPi4} = 0.2 * 1 = 0.2$) in *Step i4*. When the same process is repeated for the reused goal *Decrease Cost* (shown in steps j1–4 in Fig. 2), its self-impact factor is calculated as 0.18.

Using the derived comparative importance values (0.2 and 0.18) in the reused *Authorization Goal Model*, the same algorithm then calculates the derived importance values (i.e., 0.12 and 0.15 for goals *Improve Performance* and *Reduce Cost*, respectively) for *Surrogate of Surrogate of Bank CTO* at the bottom level (shown in steps i'1–3 and j'1–3 in Fig. 2).

Derived comparative importance values of 0.12 and 0.15 for goals *Improve Performance* and *Reduce Cost* in *Authentication Goal Model* imply that regardless of the initialization of the features in the reuse hierarchy, the two example cases shown in Fig. 2 (i.e., when the satisfaction values of *Improve Performance* and *Reduce Cost* are 100 and 80, respectively, and when the satisfaction values are 75 and 100, respectively) would yield the same satisfaction result for the top actor (i.e., *Bank CTO*) when everything else is kept the same.

Calculating the derived importance values for surrogate actors allows the use of the same lazy recursive top-down evaluation algorithm on the reused goal model. The top-down evaluation starts at the application level, finds all reused goal models and if different goals from the same reused goal model are used in the reusing goal model, derives the importance values for the surrogate and moves on to the evaluation of the reused goal model. This process recursively repeats until a goal model with no reuses (i.e., no active feature impact elements) is found. Then, the top-down evaluation is executed at the bottom level and the algorithm starts going back up while collecting the valid, best case solution sets at each lower level goal model.

At higher levels, to calculate the best case solution sets, the algorithm uses the resultant satisfaction values for the reused goals that are already calculated during the recursion. At the application level, when the top-down evaluation is completed, all the solution sets (i.e., the solution sets for both the lower level models and the top-level goal model) are combined and presented to the application designer. At this point it is important to note that it is not possible to have a conflict across different levels of the reuse hierarchy as the feature selections are independent (i.e., each goal model has their own, distinct feature model that is used by the conflict checker). Consequently, propagating the importance values down and recursively using the same top-down evaluation algorithm for each level individually allows the top-down evaluation algorithm to benefit from the modularity granted by the reuse boundaries and prevents backtracking through the entire goal model reuse hierarchy for this evaluation. However, threshold values defined at the top level are not considered for the evaluation of lower level goal models. As a consequence, a solution set from a reused goal may violate threshold constraints. Hence, this algorithm may determine an approximate solution with the best overall actor satisfaction but violated threshold constraints. It does not attempt to find other solutions with lower overall actor satisfactions that satisfy the thresholds.

A major issue with the evaluation of reusable goal models is the increased computational complexity with increasing model size. Rather than running the top-down evaluation on a large, flattened goal model in a sizable reuse hierarchy, our novel approach takes advantage of the reuse boundaries and individually evaluates reusable goal models of smaller size. This makes the top down evaluation feasible as is demonstrated in the next section.

5 Proof-of-Concept Implementation

A proof-of-concept implementation of the novel top-down evaluation algorithm for goal model reuse hierarchies as described in Sect. 4 has been implemented in the TouchCORE reuse tool [25], which uses feature and goal modeling in collaboration to build reusable artifacts called *concerns* in support of Concern-oriented Reuse (CORE) [1] and provides support for evaluation of goal models in reuse hierarchies [2].

To argue the feasibility of our algorithm in comparison to other possible ways to conduct a top-down evaluation, we additionally implemented two alternative algorithms. As explained in Sect. 4, our algorithm (labeled *"with thresholds"* in Table 1) finds all of the (potentially approximate) best-case solutions, taking the threshold values into account. The algorithm goes through the complete set of solutions from a reused goal model and if any of those solutions satisfies the thresholds at the top level, it finds all of the best-case solutions (not approximations in this case); if not, it offers all of them as approximations. A first alternative algorithm (labeled *"without thresholds"* in Table 1) finds all of the best-case solutions, without allowing threshold values. In this case, the complete set of solutions from a reused goal model still needs to be considered for the evaluation of the reusing goal model, however, since thresholds do not exist, this algorithm does find all of the best-case solutions. The second alternative algorithm (labeled *"without surrogates [with thresholds]"* in Table 1) treats the entire goal model reuse hierarchy as one flat goal model, and consequently it is able to find all of the best-case solutions even with thresholds taken into account.

As the complexity of the problem depends on both the size of the solution set (i.e., possible combinations of leaf level tasks) and how the models are structured (e.g., how external constraints are defined, how contribution links are added, and how contribution values are assigned), for the performance evaluation, 5 different 3-level reuse hierarchies are prepared (i.e., H1–5 in Table 1) via randomly

Table 1. Performance results

	Execution time per reuse hierarchy (s)				
	H1	H2	H3	H4	H5
With thresholds	**9.22**	**222.47**	**2.19**	**5.88**	**1.58**
Without thresholds	14.99	421.64	2.20	5.86	1.64
Without surrogates [with thresholds]	>30 min	>30 min	>30 min	>30 min	>30 min

selecting 3 different concerns (each with 50 features and 8 cross-tree constraints (i.e., includes or excludes relationships between features) in their feature model and 30 nodes in their goal model) out of the 7 test cases with feature model constraints generated for previous work [12]. Since the goal models of those test cases had a single top-level goal with 3 intermediate goals contributing to it, those top-level goals are removed from the test cases, hence resulting in 3 new top-level goals. At the top of each reuse hierarchy, an actor is added to the goal model with randomly generated importance values (i.e., a value in the range [1, 10]) for each of the 3 top goals. Threshold values used are also determined at random (i.e., a multiple of 10 in the range [0, 100]). For the reusing goal models (i.e., goal models at the top and middle levels of the hierarchies), a feature represented as a leaf level task in the goal model is picked at random to represent the impact of a reused goal (i.e., to become a feature impact element) and added once again to the goal model with a different reused goal (in the end, reusing goal models contained 30 nodes, excluding the actor at the top level). The reused goals are also picked at random, but with one constraint that at each reuse boundary both reuse links are active (i.e., each of the two goals from the bottom level has an impact on the actor at the top level). In other words, 2 out of 3 top-level goals from each reused goal model always have an impact on the reusing goal model. To not decrease the size of the possible solution sets by ruling out some of the possibilities, no preconditions were added to the hierarchies under evaluation (i.e., none of the features were selected or unselected initially).

Table 1 reports the results of the performance evaluation on a computer with a 2.5 GHz processor and 16 GB, 1600 MHz, DDR3 memory. The execution time is given in seconds and is calculated as the average of 20 runs to discount for program startup time. An algorithm is interrupted manually after exceeding 30 min for an evaluation. The performance results show that our proposed approach (i.e., *with thresholds*) makes the top down evaluation feasible compared to the *without surrogates [with thresholds]* algorithm, which does not complete in all five cases. Furthermore, comparing the *without thresholds* algorithm shows that use of threshold values may help the algorithm execute faster, which is the case for reuse hierarchies *H1* and *H2*. This result is expected since the use of a threshold value may stop the algorithm from exploring a subset of solutions further (e.g., possible solutions for *Goal X* are not explored further upon reaching its threshold in Fig. 1) and, in return, can make it simpler to find the best-case solutions. For the goal model reuse hierarchies where this simplification is not the case (i.e., *H3*, *H4*, and *H5* where threshold values do not affect the evaluation), observed execution times for the *with thresholds* and *without thresholds* algorithms are similar as the execution of the algorithms become similar as well.

The chosen size of feature and goal models used at each level of the reuse hierarchies built for this performance evaluation go beyond the common and typical models we have encountered in the context of CORE (the largest feature and goal models in the "reusable concern library" of TouchCORE contain 26 nodes). Consequently, the results indicate that the proposed top-down evaluation mechanism is feasible in realistic settings. The possibility of the algorithm providing approximations when the thresholds cannot be met with the best-case solutions from reused goal models is a trade-off for having higher performance in some cases.

6   Related Work

To the best of our knowledge, no other approach in the literature addresses the top-down evaluation of reusable goal models. However, there are approaches for the top down evaluation of goal models without external constraints, and with other types of contribution values (i.e., without using relative contributions).

The declarative semantics introduced for GRL [23] enables both top-down and bottom-up evaluation of goal models via translating them into constraint satisfaction problems. This approach also considers actors and actor importances assigned to goals, the decomposition (i.e., AND and OR) and dependency links in GRL, in addition to the possible additional constraints. However, reuse hierarchies of goal models, and hence the requirement for using relative contribution values are not considered by this approach.

A survey of Goal-Oriented Requirements Engineering (GORE) analysis techniques [18] provides a comprehensive set of top-down satisfaction analysis approaches that will be discussed for the remainder of this section.

The backwards search of the possible input values leading to a desired final value [24] aims to find the minimum cost assignments for leaf elements to satisfy root goals under desired constraints and is later used for diagnosing of run-time failures [26]. While this approach allows for the addition of analysis constraints, it uses qualitative labels for the evaluation.

The framework for top-down reasoning with Tropos [16] enables the analysis of Tropos models also with qualitative values. Extending Tropos goal model to analyze risk to help risk mitigation [5,6] introduces quantitative analysis of acceptable levels of risks as well as costs.

For i* models, the interactive backward reasoning approach [17] introduces an evaluation procedure to find solutions. This approach uses qualitative labels for contributions and requires human intervention for conflict resolution.

The approach that extends KAOS goal models with probabilities [21] provides quantitative analysis using the probabilities of goals being satisfied or denied, without addressing reusability or possible external constraints that may be imposed by other modeling formalisms.

While all aforementioned approaches provide means to evaluate and analyze goal models in a top-down fashion, they either use qualitative or quantitative contribution values, hence hindering their applicability in the context of goal model reuse [14]. Our approach aims to overcome this problem and deals with potential performance issues with the use of relative contributions and percentage importance values, while benefitting from the reuse boundaries via surrogate actors and derived importance values in a lazy, recursive algorithm.

7   Conclusions and Future Work

At the top level of a goal model reuse hierarchy, application designers aim to find the optimal set of solutions to satisfy the stakeholders of their system and their goals. The novel top-down evaluation algorithm for reusable goal models introduced here allows designers to find such solution sets even when reuse hierarchies grow larger and external constraints are imposed on the goal models.

The contributions of this work are threefold. First, for goal prioritization and the adaptation of the existing bottom-up evaluation algorithm to top-down evaluation of goal model reuse hierarchies, we introduce three modeling constructs (i.e., *actor*, *importance*, and *threshold*). Secondly, to benefit from reuse boundaries and allow the goal model of each reuse level to be evaluated individually in the top-down evaluation, we introduce an algorithm that propagates top-level importance values down the reuse hierarchy to *surrogate actors* and finds the derived importance values for reused goals at the lower level goal models. Finally, we show the feasibility of this novel top-down evaluation with a proof-of-concept implementation in the TouchCORE reuse tool.

In future work, we plan to look at alternative ways for goal prioritization (e.g., goal rankings) and how those could be handled with our approach. While this paper discusses one actor, the algorithm can be trivially extended to multiple actors by adding another layer of importance links from actors to the system [4]. This paper evaluates the goal model reuse hierarchy only in the presence of feature model constraints. In future, we will also investigate external constraints imposed by other modeling formalisms such as workflow models [12]. Furthermore, we will look into possible optimizations for the algorithm, which includes processing the set of solutions resulting in the same satisfaction value at the same time instead of one after the other.

References

1. Alam, O., Kienzle, J., Mussbacher, G.: Concern-oriented software design. In: Moreira, A., Schätz, B., Gray, J., Vallecillo, A., Clarke, P. (eds.) MODELS 2013. LNCS, vol. 8107, pp. 604–621. Springer, Heidelberg (2013). https://doi.org/10.1007/978-3-642-41533-3_37
2. Alexandre, R., Camillieri, C., Berk Duran, M., Navea Pina, A., Schöttle, M., Kienzle, J., Mussbacher, G.: Support for evaluation of impact models in reuse hierarchies with jUCMNav and TouchCORE. In: Demonstration Paper at MODELS 2015, vol. 1554, pp. 28–31. CEUR, September 2015

3. Amyot, D., Ghanavati, S., Horkoff, J., Mussbacher, G., Peyton, L., Yu, E.: Evaluating goal models within the goal-oriented requirement language. Int. J. Intell. Syst. **25**(8), 841–877 (2010)

4. Aprajita: TimedGRL: specifying goal models over time. Master's thesis, Department of Electrical and Computer Engineering, McGill University, Canada (2017)

5. Asnar, Y., Bryl, V., Giorgini, P.: Using risk analysis to evaluate design alternatives. In: Padgham, L., Zambonelli, F. (eds.) AOSE 2006. LNCS, vol. 4405, pp. 140–155. Springer, Heidelberg (2007). https://doi.org/10.1007/978-3-540-70945-9_9

6. Asnar, Y., Giorgini, P.: Modelling risk and identifying countermeasure in organizations. In: Lopez, J. (ed.) CRITIS 2006. LNCS, vol. 4347, pp. 55–66. Springer, Heidelberg (2006). https://doi.org/10.1007/11962977_5

7. Basili, V.R., Briand, L.C., Melo, W.L.: How reuse influences productivity in object-oriented systems. Commun. ACM **39**(10), 104–116 (1996)

8. Bresciani, P., Perini, A., Giorgini, P., Giunchiglia, F., Mylopoulos, J.: Tropos: an agent-oriented software development methodology. Auton. Agent. Multi-Agent Syst. **8**(3), 203–236 (2004)

9. Chung, K.L.: Representing and using non-functional requirements: a process-oriented Approach. Ph.D. thesis, Canada (1993)

10. Chung, L., Nixon, B.A., Yu, E., Mylopoulos, J.: Non-Functional Requirements in Software Engineering. SOFT, vol. 5. Springer, Boston (2000). https://doi.org/10.1007/978-1-4615-5269-7

11. Dardenne, A., van Lamsweerde, A., Fickas, S.: Goal-directed requirements acquisition. Sci. Comput. Program. **20**(1–2), 3–50 (1993)

12. Duran, M.B., Mussbacher, G.: Investigation of feature run-time conflicts on goal model-based reuse. Inf. Syst. Front. **18**(5), 855–875 (2016)

13. Duran, M.B., Mussbacher, G.: Evaluation of goal models in reuse hierarchies with delayed decisions. In: IEEE 25th International Requirements Engineering Conference Workshops, RE 2017 Workshops, Portugal, pp. 6–15 (2017)

14. Duran, M.B., Mussbacher, G., Thimmegowda, N., Kienzle, J.: On the reuse of goal models. In: Fischer, J., Scheidgen, M., Schieferdecker, I., Reed, R. (eds.) SDL 2015. LNCS, vol. 9369, pp. 141–158. Springer, Cham (2015). https://doi.org/10.1007/978-3-319-24912-4_11

15. Duran, M.B., Pina, A.N., Mussbacher, G.: Evaluation of reusable concern-oriented goal models. In: MoDRE Workshop 2015, Canada, pp. 53–62 (2015)

16. Giorgini, P., Mylopoulos, J., Sebastiani, R.: Goal-oriented requirements analysis and reasoning in the tropos methodology. Eng. Appl. Artif. Intell. **18**(2), 159–171 (2005)

17. Horkoff, J., Yu, E.: Finding solutions in goal models: an interactive backward reasoning approach. In: Parsons, J., Saeki, M., Shoval, P., Woo, C., Wand, Y. (eds.) ER 2010. LNCS, vol. 6412, pp. 59–75. Springer, Heidelberg (2010). https://doi.org/10.1007/978-3-642-16373-9_5

18. Horkoff, J., Yu, E.S.K.: Analyzing goal models: different approaches and how to choose among them. In: 2011 ACM Symposium on Applied Computing (SAC), Taiwan, pp. 675–682 (2011)

19. International Telecommunication Union (ITU-T): Recommendation Z.151 (10/12): User Requirements Notation (URN) - Language Definition (approved October 2012)

20. van Lamsweerde, A.: Requirements engineering in the year 00: a research perspective. In: 22nd International Conference on Software Engineering, pp. 5–19. ACM, USA (2000)

21. Letier, E., van Lamsweerde, A.: Reasoning about partial goal satisfaction for requirements and design engineering. In: 12th ACM SIGSOFT International Symposium on Foundations of Software Engineering, USA, pp. 53–62 (2004)
22. Lim, W.C.: Effects of reuse on quality, productivity, and economics. IEEE Softw. **11**(5), 23–30 (1994)
23. Luo, H., Amyot, D.: Towards a declarative, constraint-oriented semantics with a generic evaluation algorithm for GRL. In: 5th International i* Workshop, Italy, pp. 26–31 (2011)
24. Sebastiani, R., Giorgini, P., Mylopoulos, J.: Simple and minimum-cost satisfiability for goal models. In: Persson, A., Stirna, J. (eds.) CAiSE 2004. LNCS, vol. 3084, pp. 20–35. Springer, Heidelberg (2004). https://doi.org/10.1007/978-3-540-25975-6_4
25. TouchCORE tool: (version 7.0.1) (2017). http://touchcore.cs.mcgill.ca
26. Wang, Y., McIlraith, S.A., Yu, Y., Mylopoulos, J.: An automated approach to monitoring and diagnosing requirements. In: 22nd IEEE/ACM International Conference on Automated Software Engineering, ASE 2007, pp. 293–302. ACM (2007)
27. Yu, E.S.K., Mylopoulos, J.: Why goal-oriented requirements engineering. In: Proceedings of the 4th International Workshop on Requirements Engineering: Foundation for Software Quality, REFSQ 1998, Italy, pp. 15–22 (1998)
28. Yu, E.S.K.: Modelling strategic relationships for process reengineering. Ph.D. thesis, Canada (1996). uMI Order No. GAXNN-02887 (Canadian dissertation)

Dependencies and Traceability

An Empirical Analysis of Technical Lag in npm Package Dependencies

Ahmed Zerouali[1]([✉]) [iD], Eleni Constantinou[1] [iD], Tom Mens[1] [iD],
Gregorio Robles[2] [iD], and Jesús González-Barahona[2] [iD]

[1] Software Engineering Lab, Université de Mons, 7000 Mons, Belgium
{ahmed.zerouali,eleni.constantinou,tom.mens}@umons.ac.be
[2] GSyC/LibreSoft, Universidad Rey Juan Carlos, Madrid, Spain
{grex,jgb}@gsyc.urjc.es

Abstract. Software library packages are constantly evolving and increasing in number. Not updating to the latest available release of dependent libraries may negatively affect software development by not benefiting from new functionality, vulnerability and bug fixes available in more recent versions. On the other hand, automatically updating to the latest release may introduce incompatibility issues. We introduce a technical lag metric for dependencies in package networks, in order to assess how outdated a software package is compared to the latest available releases of its dependencies. We empirically analyse the package update practices and technical lag for the npm distribution of JavaScript packages. Our results show a strong presence of technical lag caused by the specific use of dependency constraints, indicating a reluctance to update dependencies to avoid backward incompatible changes.

Keywords: Software library · Technical lag
Package dependency · npm

1 Introduction

Today's (open source) software systems are increasingly relying on reusable libraries stored in online package distributions for specific programming languages (e.g., npm, RubyGems, Maven) or operating systems (e.g., Debian and Ubuntu). The availability of such a huge amount of reusable packages facilitates software development and evolution. However, it can also cause problems, such as software becoming out of date with respect to more recent package releases. This implies that bug fixes and new functionality are not utilized by applications using such library packages [11]. A possible reason for this may be the mechanisms used to specify, track and maintain dependencies, that are often observed to induce a latency when updating a library [12].

Gonzalez-Barahona et al. [10] refer to this problem as "technical lag", indicating the increasing difference between deployed software packages and the upstream packages that they reuse. Technical lag captures the delay between versions of software deployed in production and more recent compatible versions

© Springer International Publishing AG, part of Springer Nature 2018
R. Capilla et al. (Eds.): ICSR 2018, LNCS 10826, pp. 95–110, 2018.
https://doi.org/10.1007/978-3-319-90421-4_6

available upstream. Reusable software packages may also suffer from technical lag, because they may depend on (i.e., reuse) other packages of which more recent releases are available. Depending on an outdated release of a reusable package may not be a problem in itself ("if it ain't broke, don't fix it"), but it comes at a price of not being able to benefit from new functionalities, or patches that fix known bugs and security issues [11].

While assessing the problem of technical lag is important at the level of individual packages, it becomes even more relevant at the level of large distributions of software packages where packages depend, directly or indirectly, on a large number of other packages [6,7]. If a package imposes too strict version constraints on its dependencies, it may become outdated. As a direct consequence of this, all packages that directly or indirectly depend on such packages may suffer from technical lag. This may affect a large portion of the entire ecosystem. On the other hand, updating even a single package to address technical lag may be quite challenging, since the changes of the updated package may cause a ripple effect through the ecosystem, potentially causing many other packages to break and requiring significant portions of the ecosystem to be tested.

To advance the body of knowledge on how software systems are reusing packages through dependencies and how this induces technical lag, we carry out a large-scale empirical study on the npm package distribution. We focus on five research questions: RQ_0 How do packages manage their dependencies?; RQ_1 How often do packages release new versions?; RQ_2 What is the technical lag induced by outdated dependencies?; RQ_3 How often do dependencies inducing technical lag release new versions?; and RQ_4 What is the appropriate moment to update dependencies? To answer these questions, we measured technical lag based on dependencies between package releases in the npm registry. As a result of our study, we found a high potential of technical lag. One of the causes of technical lag appears to be the use of too strict package dependency constraints, disallowing packages to benefit from more recent releases of their dependencies.

2   Dataset and Background

There is a large variety of package managers for different programming languages (CRAN for R, RubyGems for Ruby, npm for JavaScript, etc.) and datasets providing their historical evolution. For example, the libraries.io dataset monitors $2.5M$ packages across 34 package managers. For our study, we selected the npm package manager because: (1) npm is a popular and growing package manager, allowing us to exploit a variety of ways that dependency-based reuse and updates occur, and limiting bias in our study; (2) npm has a large and active developer community [4], making our results relevant for a large number of developers; and (3) JavaScript is the most popular programming language on GitHub, the world's leading software development platform [3].

Our empirical study uses the libraries.io[1] dataset, an open source package tracker and repository containing metadata of package versions and their

---

[1] http://www.libraries.io/

dependencies [14], available as open access under the CC Share-Alike 4.0 license. Package information includes the version number, date of publication and dependency information, i.e., used packages, constraints and dependency types. The used timeframe for our analysis was between *09-11-2010* (i.e., the first package release found in the dataset) and *02-11-2017*. Our dataset comprises $610K$ packages with more than $4.2M$ releases and $44.9M$ dependencies among them.

In npm, there are three different types of dependencies. *Runtime* dependencies are required to install and execute the package. *Development* dependencies are used during package development (e.g., for testing). *Optional* dependencies will not hamper the package from being installed if the dependency is not found or cannot be installed. Our analysis includes all three types of dependencies and the dataset contains 43% runtime dependencies, 56% development dependencies, and only 1% (133 in total) optional dependencies.

All code and data required to reproduce the analysis in this paper are available on https://github.com/neglectos/techlag_icsr/.

2.1   Semantic Versioning and Dependency Constraints

With many software packages being created and updated every day, it is important to standardize the way of versioning and keeping track of package releases and dependencies. *Semantic Versioning* (semver.org, referred as *semver*) has become a popular policy for communicating the kinds of changes made to a software package. It allows dependent software packages to be informed about possible "breaking changes" [2]. A *semver*-compatible version is a version number composed of a *major*, *minor* and *patch* number. The version numbers allow to order package releases. For example, *1.2.3* occurs before *1.2.10* (higher patch version), which occurs before *1.3.0* (higher minor version), which occurs before *2.1.0* (higher major version). Backward incompatible updates should increment the major version, updates respecting the API but adding new functionalities should increment the minor version, while simple bug fixes should increment the patch version. Unfortunately, the semantic versioning policy is not always respected by package maintainers, as an empirical study on Java packages in the maven package manager has revealed [15].

Like maven and many other package managers, npm recommends software packages to follow a specific flavor of semantic versioning[2]. Package releases specify their version number in the metadata (stored in a *json* file[3]), and use dependency constraints to specify the version ranges of other packages they depend upon. These constraints are built from a set of comparators that specify versions that satisfy the range. Table 1 summarizes the types of dependency constraints for npm, their interpretation and an illustrative example of each constraint type.

---

[2] https://docs.npmjs.com/misc/semver.

[3] https://docs.npmjs.com/files/package.json.

Table 1. Types of dependency constraints for npm package dependencies.

Constraint	Interpretation	Example	Satisfied versions
Fixed	Exact version required	=2.3.1	2.3.1
Minimal	Only use releases above the declared version	>=2.3.0	$\geq$2.3.0
Maximal	Only use releases below the declared version	<2.3.0	<2.3.0
Latest	Use latest available release	Latest	$\geq$0.0.0
Hyphen ranges	Only use releases between two versions	1.2.3–2.3.4	$\geq$=1.2.3 $\wedge$ <=2.3.4
x ranges	Only update where "x" or "*" is	1.2.x	$\geq$=1.2.0 $\wedge$ <1.3.0
Tilde ($\sim$)	Only update patches	$\sim$2.3.0	$\geq$2.3.0 $\wedge$ <2.4.0
Caret ($^\wedge$)	Only update patches and minor releases	$^\wedge$2.3.0	$\geq$2.3.0 $\wedge$ <3.0.0
or / and / ...	Combine multiple logical constraints	2.5.3 || >=2.8.1	2.5.3 $\vee$ 2.8.1 $\vee$ >2.8.1

3   Measuring Technical Lag

The technical lag of a package release can designate anything that makes the release out of date to its upstream versions [10]. For example, bugs or security vulnerabilities could have been fixed, or new functionalities may have been integrated into newer versions of the package. In the remainder of this section, we introduce the necessary terminology to formally define technical lag, and accompany it with illustrative examples.

Definition 1. *Let* **P** *be the set of all* ***packages*** *belonging to the ecosystem, and R the set of all corresponding package* ***releases***. *We define:*

- ***releases*** $: \mathbf{P} \rightarrow 2^R$ *returns the set of releases of a given package. As a shortcut, for a package $p \in \mathbf{P}$ we denote $R_p = releases(p)$*
- ***version*** $: R_p \rightarrow \mathbb{N} \times \mathbb{N} \times \mathbb{N} : r \rightarrow (Major, Minor, Patch)$ *associates a semantic version number to a release.*
- ***major*** $: R_p \rightarrow \mathbb{N}$, ***minor*** $: R_p \rightarrow \mathbb{N}$ *and* ***patch*** $: R_p \rightarrow \mathbb{N}$ *obtain the first, second and third component of a version number, i.e., $version(r) = (major(r), minor(r), patch(r))$*
- ***time*** $: R_p \rightarrow Date$ *returns the release date of a package release.*
- ***latest*** $: \mathbf{P} \rightarrow R : p \rightarrow r$ *such that $r \in R_p$ and $time(r) = max_{q \in R_p}(time(q))$ returns the latest available package release of p.*
- *A* ***dependency*** $d \in \mathbf{D}$ *is a pair (q, c) where $q \in \mathbf{P}$ is a* ***required package***, *and $c : R_q \rightarrow Boolean$ is a* ***version constraint*** *expressing the range of allowed releases of q.*
- ***deps*** $: R_p \rightarrow 2^{\mathbf{D}}$ *returns the set of dependencies of a package release.*
- *Given a dependency $d = (q, c) \in deps(r_p)$ we define* ***lastAllowed***$(d) = r_q \in R_q$ *such that $time(r_q) = max_{\{r \in R_q | c(r) = true\}}(time(r))$*

We use the technical lag of a package release to expresses the inability of that release to benefit from the most recent version of a required package, because the dependency constraint provides an upper bound on the allowed version of the required package. Lag can be expressed as a time difference (referred to as **time lag**), by measuring the elapsed time between the date of the used version of a dependency and the date of the latest available version of this dependency.

Lag can also be expressed as a difference in version numbers (referred to as **version lag**), indicating how many major, minor or patch versions the release of a required dependency is behind. More specifically:

Definition 2 [Technical Lag]. *Let r be a package release, and $d = (q, c) \in deps(r)$ a dependency of r on a package q satisfying the dependency constraint c. Assume that d is an outdated dependency, i.e., $lastAllowed(d) < latest(q)$. We define the* **time lag** *of d (at the release date of r) as:*

$$\mathbf{tLag}(d) = time(latest(q)) - time(lastAllowed(d))$$

If $tLag(d) = 0$, the dependency is up to date with the most recent available version. If $tLag(d) > 0$, the dependency is outdated, since a more recent version of the required package exists. We define the **version lag** *of d (at the release date of r) as:*

$$\mathbf{vLag}(d) = (\varDelta Major, \varDelta Minor, \varDelta Patch), \text{where}$$

$\varDelta Major = major(latest(q)) - major(lastAllowed(d))$
$\varDelta Minor$ *is the amount of successive version numbers between $lastAllowed(d)$ and $latest(q)$ that changed their minor number without changing the major number. $\varDelta Patch$ is the amount of successive version numbers between $lastAllowed(d)$ and $latest(q)$ that changed their patch number without changing the minor and major numbers.*

For example, suppose that required package q of dependency d has the following series of version numbers (1.0.0, 1.0.1, 1.0.2, 1.1.0. 1.1.1, 2.0.0). The major number changed once (1.1.1 → 2.0.0), the minor number changed once without changing the major number (1.0.2 → 1.1.0), and the patch number changed three times without changing the minor and major numbers (1.0.0 → 1.0.1, 1.0.1 → 1.0.2 and 1.1.0 → 1.1.1). This results in a version lag of $vLag(d) = (1, 1, 3)$.

Table 2 illustrates the evolution of the different releases of npm package jasmine over time, in terms of its dependency on the glob package. jasmine version 2.0.1 released in *2014-08-22* contains a dependency $d = $ (glob, ^3.2.11). This dependency implies that all versions of glob ranging between >= 3.2.11 and < 4.0.0 are allowed. At the release date of jasmine 2.0.1, the most recent version of glob in that allowed range was 3.2.11 (released in *2014-05-20*), but the latest available version of glob at that date was 4.0.5, which was released in *2014-07-28*. Since this version does not satisfy the dependency constraint, jasmine 2.0.1 had a technical lag $tLag(d) = 69$ days, for this dependency d at the time of its release. Its version lag was $vLag(d) = (1, 0, 5)$ since, between release 3.2.11 and 4.0.5 of glob, one major version and 5 patch versions were released.

Version 2.5.1 was released in *2016-09-07* and contains a dependency $d = $ (glob, ^7.0.6). The latter constraint implies that all versions of glob ranging between >= 7.0.6 and < 8.0.0 are allowed. At the release date of jasmine 2.5.1, the last available version of glob was 7.1.2 (released in *2017-05-19*). Since this version satisfies the dependency constraint, jasmine 2.5.1 did not suffer from technical lag w.r.t. this specific dependency at the time of its release.

Table 2. Evolution of jasmine's dependency on the glob package.

Release date	jasmine version	glob dep. constraint	lastAllowed(glob) version : date	latest(glob) version : date	tLag	vLag
2014-08-22	2.0.1	^3.2.11	3.2.11 : 2014-05-20	4.0.5 : 2014-07-28	69	(1,0,5)
2014-11-14	2.1.0	^3.2.11	3.2.11 : 2014-05-20	4.0.6 : 2014-09-17	120	(1,0,6)
2014-12-01	2.1.1	^3.2.11	3.2.11 : 2014-05-20	4.3.1 : 2014-12-01	195	(1,3,16)
...	...	...	...	...	...	...
2015-12-03	2.4.1	^3.2.11	3.2.11 : 2014-05-20	6.0.1 : 2015-11-11	540	(3,5,39)
2016-08-31	2.5.0	^3.2.11	3.2.11 : 2014-05-20	7.0.6 : 2016-08-24	827	(4,5,47)
2016-09-07	2.5.1	^7.0.6	7.0.6 : 2016-08-24	7.0.6 : 2016-08-24	0	(0,0,0)

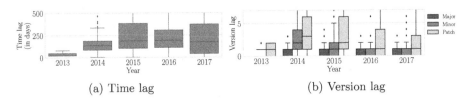

(a) Time lag   (b) Version lag

Fig. 1. Time and version lag distribution, per year, for all outdated dependencies of eslint.

The technical lag of a package release can be computed in terms of the technical lag of all its outdated dependencies. Figure 1 shows the evolution of the time and version lag for all outdated dependencies of the eslint package. Figure 1a shows that the time lag seems to have increased considerably since 2015. Figure 1b seems to reveal a decrease over time in the distribution of the patch, minor and major version lag. This is explained by the fact that at first, eslint was using tilde for its dependency constraints, but after 2015, it started using caret instead. The time lag increased in 2017 because eslint did not update its dependencies karma-babel-preprocessor and cheerio, while these packages did not release new versions after 2015 until mid 2017.

4   Results

RQ_0: How do packages manage their dependencies?

In order to gain insight in how npm package dependencies are managed, we investigate which types of dependency constraints are used, and how packages add, remove or update their dependencies throughout the package release history.

Figure 2 illustrates the proportion of the types of package dependency constraints used. We observe that caret (^) is most frequently used, covering 68.2% (30.6M) of all constraints. This suggests that most package maintainers want to avoid backward incompatible changes, but keep benefiting from bug fixes (patch updates) and new functionalities (minor updates). 15.7% (7M) of all dependencies were specified with an exact version, which is remarkable since this means that they prefer a compatible but possibly older version of a dependency, rather

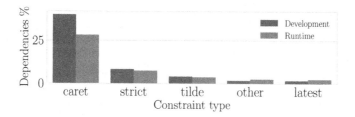

Fig. 2. Proportion of the types of dependency constraints used in npm.

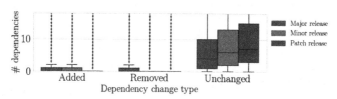

Fig. 3. Number of removed, unchanged and added dependencies between subsequent package releases

than benefiting from updates. 7.8% (3.4M) of all dependencies used a tilde ($\sim$) constraint; and 4.1% (1.8M) of the dependencies use the "latest" version (i.e., *, x, latest, *.*.*, x.x.x*). Other dependency constraints, such as external URLs to Git repositories, local files and explicit boolean comparators, were used by 4.2% (1.9M) of all dependencies. The above findings indicate that developers are mainly concerned with backward compatibility, and that there is a potential of too strict dependency constraints leading to technical lag.

Next, we investigate how npm developers change their dependencies. Figure 3 shows the distribution of added, removed and unchanged dependencies for each type of release during package evolution. Most packages do not appear to change their dependencies over time. If they do, changes in dependencies mainly happen in major releases (both additions and removals). New dependencies are mainly added in major and minor releases, and only very occasionally in patch releases. Dependencies are removed almost exclusively in major releases.

To investigate how packages update their dependencies, for each major, minor or patch release, we identified the type of dependency updates that can occur. Figure 4 shows that only in major releases, packages update their dependencies to a newer available *major* version. Also, packages tend to update to minor releases of their dependencies in both major and minor releases, but not in patches. On the contrary, npm packages update their dependencies at the patch level regardless of their new release type (major, minor and patch). Moreover, we found that 1.2M (i.e., 97.5%) of all dependency version changes were updated to more recent versions, while 29K (i.e., 2.5% of all changes) were downgraded to an older dependency version. 14K (i.e., 49%) of the dependency downgrades were made while the package had major version 0 (i.e., 0.*.*).

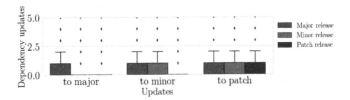

Fig. 4. Number of updated dependencies between package releases, classified by release type of the update.

Findings: npm packages are updated frequently. Dependencies are added or removed rarely, and mostly in major releases. Technical lag is induced because dependency constraints prevent package dependencies from being updated in presence of backward incompatible changes.

RQ_1: How often do packages release new versions?

Technical lag is not only induced by dependency constraints, but also by the rate at which packages produce new releases when they serve as dependencies of other packages. More concretely, packages that release often can cause technical lag in packages using them if these packages cannot keep up with the updating process. We thus analyze how often packages release new versions by only considering required packages, i.e., packages used as dependencies by other packages.

Figure 5 shows the number of releases of required npm packages per year and release type. It shows that the number of releases of required packages increases every year, which is not surprising because of the growing number of npm packages over time. If we consider the entire dataset from 2010 to 2017, the majority of all package releases (80.1%) are patches, while only 15.9% are minor releases, and 4.0% are major releases. This seems to imply that dependent packages in npm mainly benefit from patch releases. It also implies that technical version lag is mainly occurring at the patch level.

Figure 6 shows the time it takes to update the release of a package to a new patch, minor or major version. We found that npm packages take more time to release a major version than a minor or patch version. This is expected since

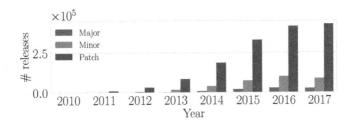

Fig. 5. Number of releases of required packages in npm, per year and per release type.

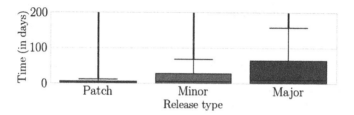

Fig. 6. Time needed to update a package to a patch, minor or major release.

simple bug fixes are very frequent and easier to make, as compared to adding new functionalities. The same is true for backward incompatible changes, i.e., they require more effort to implement, and thus take more time to release. We also found that the average time to release a patch, minor and major versions corresponds to 13 days, 1 month and 2 months respectively. Thus, package maintainers must *monitor and update their dependencies often*. Otherwise, technical lag can pile up throughout time from different outdated dependencies.

Findings: Required packages release new versions frequently, increasing the likelihood of dependent packages suffering from an increased technical lag.

RQ_2: What is the technical lag induced by outdated dependencies?

To identify outdated package dependencies, we use all package releases in our dataset, i.e., 4.2M releases for 610K packages, and all 44.9M dependencies between them. We use the npm-semver constraint definitions to calculate the range of versions that satisfy each constraint. We filter out 2% (743k) of the dependencies for which we don't have any information about the dependency version (i.e., local files, git URLs). In the following step, we use the date of each package release to find the time lag induced by its dependencies. This is achieved by identifying the range of versions that satisfy each dependency constraint, and by comparing the time difference between the latest version that satisfies the constraint and the latest available version of the dependency. We found 27% (i.e., 11.9M) of the 44.1M dependencies to be outdated. These outdated dependencies were used by 60% of all considered packages.

Figure 7 shows the proportion of the types of constraints used for outdated dependencies only. We observe that most of the outdated dependencies used the caret constraint (57%), which is expected since 68.2% of all dependencies use this type of constraint. Constraints using a fixed version can also induce technical lag. Indeed, we found that 28% of all outdated dependencies used an exact version constraint. Contrary to our expectations, only 12% of the outdated dependencies occur due to the tilde constraint. The remaining 3% used yet another constraint type (e.g., 1.2.x). Overall, developers often use caret because it ensures compatibility, but it should only be used when they *closely monitor their dependencies*. Given the fact that most of the outdated dependencies use caret, developers either misuse this constraint or neglect to upgrade their dependencies.

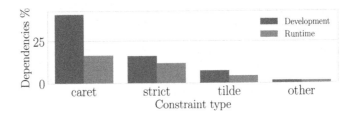

Fig. 7. Proportion of the types of constraints used for outdated dependencies.

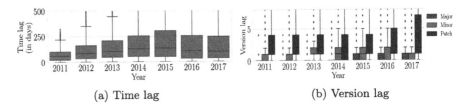

(a) Time lag   (b) Version lag

Fig. 8. Distribution of technical lag, per year, in outdated dependencies.

Figure 8a illustrates the yearly distribution of time lag from 2011 until 2017. From 2011 to 2015, we notice an increase in time lag. This is likely to be a statistical artifact because the time lag is likely to increase as more releases become available. However, from 2015 to 2017, we observe that the time lag started to decrease, although there still is a very high median of 100 days in 2017. This decrease may suggest that developers started to care more about their dependency updates, or simply that a lot of package versions were released after 2015 and they were used as outdated dependencies, but did not have sufficient time yet to be able to accumulate an important time lag.

Figure 8b illustrates the yearly evolution of the version lag distribution. We observe that version lag increases for all release types from 2011 to 2016. In 2017, we notice that the patch version lag is increased compared to the other release types. This means that packages serving as dependencies release much more patch versions in 2017, complying with our earlier observation that time lag decreases in the same year. To statistically verify this, we carried out the non-parametric *Mann-Whitney U* test that does not assume normality of the data. The null hypothesis assumes that the patch distributions of two yearly populations are identical. We rejected H_0 with statistical significance $p < .001$ when comparing the patch distribution of any previous year with the year 2017. We only found a small effect size at $|d| <= 0.2$ using Cliff's Delta, a non-parametric measure quantifying the difference between two groups of observations. However, when we compute the median time lag and version lag over the entire npm lifetime, we find: $tLag = 106$ days and $vLag = (0, 1, 2)$.

Findings: Outdated dependencies induce a median of time lag of three months and a half, and median version lag of one minor and two patch versions.

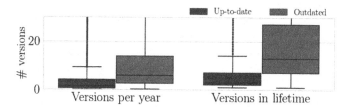

Fig. 9. Number of available versions of packages used by outdated and up-to-date dependencies.

RQ_3: How often do dependencies inducing technical lag release new versions?

This research question investigates if required packages that release often are more likely to lead to technical lag in dependent packages. To this extent, we calculate the number of available versions and the number of versions created each year for such packages. Figure 9 shows the number of available versions of the used outdated and up-to-date dependencies. Packages that are required as dependencies and are outdated have more frequent releases than other required packages. Hence, the package release frequency is a source of technical lag. To statically confirm our observations, we carried out a two-sided *Mann-Whitney U* test between both distributions and we found a statistically significant difference ($p < .001$) for both the available versions per year and throughout their lifetime. Using *Cliff's Delta*, we found a strong effect size at $|d| = 0.54$ and $|d| = 0.65$, implying that the observed difference between the two groups is big.

Findings: Packages that are required as dependencies and are outdated have more frequent releases than other required packages.

RQ_4: What is the appropriate moment to update dependencies?

If a required package has updated to a new (minor or major) release, dependent packages may wish to delay upgrading to this new release, as it may still be unstable or contain bugs. We thus analyze how long it takes before a patch, minor or major release of a package is updated to new patch versions. Answering this question will help package maintainers to choose the suitable moment to update their dependencies.

Figure 10 shows the distributions of the time require to update a package release to a more recent patch. We observe that it takes slightly less time to release a patch version after a minor release (*mean* = 17 *days*) than after a major release (*mean* = 21 *days*). It takes even less time to update a patch release with another patch (*mean* = 13 *days*). We also notice that the time required to make a patch to the first package release is very short (*mean* = 14 *days, median* = 0 *days*). A possible explanation could be that first releases tend to be unstable and immature, since most of them have major release number 0. Studying the different behaviour of releases with major version 0 is part of future work.

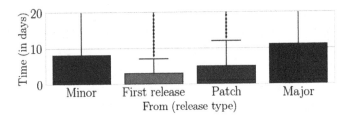

Fig. 10. Time required to update a package release to a more recent patch.

New major releases seem to be more stable. To verify if there is a statistically significant difference between the distributions of Fig. 10, we used the *Wilcoxon rank-sum* non-parametric test. We indeed found statistically significant differences in the mean ranks of each release type with $p < .001$.

Findings: New major releases take longer to receive a patch update.

This suggests that developers should not start using newly available packages immediately because they may still contain bugs that need new patches.

5 Discussion

Ideally, deployed packages would depend on the most recent available version of their dependencies, thus benefiting from the latest functionality and bug fixes. In practice, however, packages have a certain technical lag because many developers choose not to upgrade certain dependencies ("if it ain't broke, don't fix it"). Moreover, in many cases developers choose not to update because new major releases may include new functionality that is not needed. Dietrich et al. [8] found that 75% of all version upgrades in 109 Java programs are not backward compatible, but only few are actually affected by the incompatible changes. In npm, where there is a strong presence of micropackages for trivial functions, developers are concerned with the risk of breakages such packages introduce [1]. In a similar spirit, our findings show concrete evidence of technical lag and the need to monitor dependencies.

Our findings suggest that npm packages could benefit of better procedures for updating. However, it is essential to mention that one should always balance between being up-to-date and the increasing effort, cost and risk of updating. Therefore, further analysis is required to investigate how much functionality is added, how many bugs were fixed and which other changes occurred to the package when updating.

There are many ways to quantify technical lag of package releases w.r.t. outdated dependencies. In this paper we focused only on two definitions, time lag and version lag. We computed these metrics at the package dependency level, but it is also possible to compute them at the package release level by aggregating the lag of all outdated dependencies, e.g.,

$$\mathbf{vLag}(r) = \Big(\sum_{d \in lag(r)} major(vLag(d)), \sum_{d \in lag(r)} minor(vLag(d)), \sum_{d \in lag(r)} patch(vLag(d)) \Big)$$

As an example, the aggregated lag of jasmine 2.0.1 is caused by 4 outdated dependencies (commander, grunt-contrib-jshint, glob and shelljs), which cause an aggregated lag of 1 major, 5 minor and 7 patch releases in total. Since different lag definitions may produce different results; we intend to ask feedback from package maintainers about how informative each definition and way of measurement is when inspecting technical lag.

The concept of technical lag is related to, but different from, the metaphor of technical debt [5,9]. Technical debt refers to the qualitative difference between code "as it should be" and code "as it is". Technical lag refers to the increasing lag between the latest available upstream versions of packages used by a software system and those actually used in the deployed system. As real-world software systems increasingly rely on reusable libraries, techniques for managing their deployment are compulsory. In this work, we studied technical lag as a useful way to assess reuse in large open source deployments. By analyzing npm package dependencies, we found that a large number of package releases suffer from technical lag. This finding opens the door for comparative research with other package repositories of reusable libraries (e.g., Maven for Java, RubyGems for Ruby) and other ways of assessing technical lag.

During our npm analysis, we observed some specific use of version numbers that seems to go against the semantic versioning policy. For example, many packages remain in major version zero (0.*.*) for a long time. If packages are in the initial development phase for long, then a (0.*.*) version should be used. On the contrary, if packages have progressed beyond this phase, then they should upgrade to a (1.*.*) version.

We noticed that many package releases append pre-release tags (e.g., -alpha.1, -beta.3, -rc.0) to their version number or dependency constraints. The semantics of these pre-release constraints is different from normal version constraints according to npm semantic versioning. For example, constraint $^{\wedge}$1.2.3-alpha accepts releases in the range $\geq$1.2.3-alpha.3 and $<$2.0.0, but pre-releases in other patch or minor versions are not allowed (e.g., 1.2.3-alpha.4 would be allowed, but 1.2.4-alpha.5 would not). In this paper we ignored such pre-release tags. Taking them into account when computing technical lag is part of future work.

6   Related Work

In order to help developers to decide when to use which version of a library, Mileva et al. [13] mined hundreds of open-source projects for their library dependencies, and determined global and important emerging trends in library usage. Decan *et al.* [6,7] analyzed the evolution of multiple package dependency networks (including npm, CRAN and RubyGems). They studied the presence and impact of package updates on (transitively) dependent packages, and provided an initial exploration of the presence of semantic versioning and dependency constraints. They observed that, for npm and RubyGems, both the proportion of packages and dependencies that declare a minimal dependency constraint is relatively stable through time, but the proportion of packages or dependencies that declare maximal constraints increases over time. The latter suggests that an increasing number of packages relies on maximal constraints to prevent, limit or control dependency updates. They also observed a high proportion of strict dependency constraints for npm and RubyGems. In September 2016, this accounted for around 15% of all the dependencies in npm. Our work additionally measures the technical lag induced by the use of such dependency constraints in npm.

Kula et al. [11] analyzed 6,374 systems in *Maven* to investigate the latency when adopting the latest library release. They found that maintainers are less likely to adopt the latest releases at the beginning of project; and *Maven* libraries are becoming more inclined to adopt the latest releases when introducing new libraries. In a more recent work [12], they empirically studied library migration that covers over 4,600 GitHub projects and 2,700 library dependencies, and found that 81.5% of the studied systems still keep their outdated dependencies. Surveying the developers, they found that 69% of the interviewees claim that they were unaware of their vulnerable dependencies. In contrast to these works, we analyze the npm ecosystem, where the use of micropackages is prevalent. We do not only measure the number of packages with outdated dependencies, but we quantify the technical lag incurred by outdated dependencies, suggesting the need to monitor such dependencies.

Gonzalez-Barahona et al. [10] proposed for the first time the theoretical model of "technical lag", for measuring how software systems are outdated. In their work, they explored many ways in which technical lag can be implemented and could be used when deciding about upgrading in production. They also presented some specific cases in which the evolution of technical lag is computed. Extending [10], we define technical lag in terms of time lag and version lag and empirically investigate how technical lag is induced by the dependency constraints used by packages at the ecosystem level.

7   Threats to Validity

We relied on the libraries.io dataset for our analysis. If the dataset is incomplete (e.g., due to missing package releases), then there is a risk of underestimating technical lag. To mitigate this threat, we manual inspected a sample of the dataset, and did not find any major information missing.

We ignored dependencies that use constraints formed by a reference to a URL or a local file. This does not bias our findings, since the proportion of such dependencies is only 2% of all the dependencies in our dataset.

While package dependencies are a major source of software reuse, our empirical study did not differentiate between dependency types (runtime, development and optional), package age or size when studying version or time lag. This means that packages created one year ago or packages with 100 lines of code (LOC) are compared on equal terms with packages created many years ago or containing thousands LOC. If the amount of reused functionality were to be considered, then the dependency type, package size and age should also be taken into account to provide further insight into the factors influencing technical lag.

When choosing the allowed versions for each dependency constraint, we rely on npm semver specifications. This may bias our results, since we found that in the past, npm semver had faced issues such as considering pre-releases when using the * constraint[4]. However, we are still confident about our analysis since these issues were bugs and not changes in the npm semver specifications.

A final threat to validity concerns the definitions of technical lag that may influence our findings. For example, the time lag is an over-approximation of the actual one because we include the period of time from the latest allowed version until the next release. However, installing the package during that period of time, will fetch the latest allowed release based on the dependency constraint.

8   Conclusion

This paper presented an empirical analysis of package dependency updates in the npm ecosystem, in order to assess technical lag between the deployed version and the latest available version of package dependencies. We found that a large number of packages suffer from technical lag, where their outdated dependencies are several months behind the latest release. We analyzed when patch versions are released and our results suggested that package maintainers should wait a few days before updating to the new available dependency release. These findings can be turned into actionable guidelines about npm dependency updates, and may open the door for more research about technical lag measurements in package libraries.

In future work, we aim to extend our analysis of technical lag by taking into account other issues such as vulnerabilities and bugs. We also aim to carry out similar analyses for other package managers, while considering transitive dependencies, and carry out cross-ecosystem comparisons.

Acknowledgements. This work was partially supported by EU Research Framework Programme H2020-MSCA-ITN-2014-642954 Seneca, bilateral FRQ-FNRS research program 30440672 SECOHealth, research project TIN2014-59400-R SobreVision funded by the Spanish Government, and Excellence of Science project 30446992 SECO-Assist financed by FWO - Vlaanderen and F.R.S.-FNRS.

---

[4] https://github.com/npm/node-semver/issues/123.

References

1. Abdalkareem, R., Nourry, O., Wehaibi, S., Mujahid, S., Shihab, E.: Why do developers use trivial packages? An empirical case study on npm. In: International Symposium Foundations of Software Engineering, pp. 385–395. ACM (2017)
2. Bogart, C., Kästner, C., Herbsleb, J., Thung, F.: How to break an API: cost negotiation and community values in three software ecosystems. In: International Symposium on Foundations of Software Engineering, pp. 109–120. ACM (2016)
3. Borges, H., Valente, M.T., Hora, A., Coelho, J.: On the popularity of GitHub applications: a preliminary note. arXiv preprint arXiv:1507.00604 (2015)
4. Constantinou, E., Mens, T.: An empirical comparison of developer retention in the RubyGems and npm software ecosystems. Innov. Syst. Softw. Eng. **13**(2–3), 101–115 (2017)
5. Cunningham, W.: The WyCash portfolio management system. ACM SIGPLAN OOPS Messenger **4**(2), 29–30 (1993)
6. Decan, A., Mens, T., Claes, M.: An empirical comparison of dependency issues in OSS packaging ecosystems. In: SANER, pp. 2–12. IEEE (2017)
7. Decan, A., Mens, T., Grosjean, P.: An empirical comparison of dependency network evolution in seven software packaging ecosystems. Empirical Softw. Eng., 1–36 (2018). https://doi.org/10.1007/s10664-017-9589-y
8. Dietrich, J., Jezek, K., Brada, P.: Broken promises: an empirical study into evolution problems in Java programs caused by library upgrades. In: CSMR-WCRE, pp. 64–73 (2014). https://doi.org/10.1109/CSMR-WCRE.2014.6747226
9. Digkas, G., Lungu, M., Chatzigeorgiou, A., Avgeriou, P.: The evolution of technical debt in the Apache ecosystem. In: Lopes, A., de Lemos, R. (eds.) ECSA 2017. LNCS, vol. 10475, pp. 51–66. Springer, Cham (2017). https://doi.org/10.1007/978-3-319-65831-5_4
10. Gonzalez-Barahona, J.M., Sherwood, P., Robles, G., Izquierdo, D.: Technical lag in software compilations: measuring how outdated a software deployment is. In: Balaguer, F., Di Cosmo, R., Garrido, A., Kon, F., Robles, G., Zacchiroli, S. (eds.) OSS 2017. IAICT, vol. 496, pp. 182–192. Springer, Cham (2017). https://doi.org/10.1007/978-3-319-57735-7_17
11. Kula, R.G., German, D.M., Ishio, T., Inoue, K.: Trusting a library: a study of the latency to adopt the latest Maven release. In: International Conference on Software Analysis, Evolution, and Reengineering, pp. 520–524 (2015). https://doi.org/10.1109/SANER.2015.7081869
12. Kula, R.G., German, D.M., Ouni, A., Ishio, T., Inoue, K.: Do developers update their library dependencies? Empirical Softw. Eng. **23**(1), 384–417 (2017). https://doi.org/10.1007/s10664-017-9521-5
13. Mileva, Y.M., Dallmeier, V., Burger, M., Zeller, A.: Mining trends of library usage. In: Proceedings of (IWPSE) and (Evol) Workshops, pp. 57–62. ACM (2009)
14. Nesbitt, A., Nickolls, B.: Libraries.io open source repository and dependency metadata (2017). https://doi.org/10.5281/zenodo.808273
15. Raemaekers, S., van Deursen, A., Visser, J.: Semantic versioning versus breaking changes: a study of the Maven repository. In: SCAM, pp. 215–224 (2014). https://doi.org/10.1109/SCAM.2014.30

On-Demand Automated Traceability Maintenance and Evolution

Muhammad Atif Javed[1,2], Faiz UL Muram[1,2(✉)], and Uwe Zdun[2]

[1] School of Innovation, Design and Engineering, Mälardalen University,
Västerås, Sweden
{muhammad.atif.javed,faiz.ul.muram}@mdh.se,
{muhammad.atif.javed,faiz.ulmuram}@univie.ac.at
[2] Faculty of Computer Science, Software Architecture Research Group,
University of Vienna, Vienna, Austria
uwe.zdun@univie.ac.at

Abstract. After the painstaking process of traceability construction, a substantial evolution of a software system, such as a new major version leads to the decay of traceability links. To date, however, none of the published studies have considered the on-demand update of traceability links. This paper presents an on-demand automated approach for case-based maintenance and evolution of traceability links in the context of different versions of a software project. The approach focuses on the component-to-component features for identification and prioritization of previous traceability cases, which are then used to perform reuse and adaptation of traceability links based on the matches and mismatches, respectively. The adapted (i.e., newly constructed) traceability links can then be verified by a human analyst and stored in a case base. The approach has been validated using an open-source framework for mobile games, named Soomla Android store.

1 Introduction

The constructed traceability links need to be maintained continuously or on-demand as a project evolves so that up-to-date traceability links are available when needed. The need for continuous traceability maintenance is triggered by changes to any of the software artefacts (like any architecture component) that, in turn, can be triggered by changes to artefacts within a traceability chain (e.g., underlying requirements and the code classes that implement the component). The semi-automatic support for such maintenance is achieved in some existing approaches [2,6,10]. However, continuous traceability maintenance might not be a feasible solution in case of a substantial evolution of a software system, such as a new major version in large real-world project in which hundreds of developers are involved, maybe even at different distributed locations. For such new major versions, traceability links are subject to and undergo reconstruction in general.

The proposed on-demand traceability maintenance and evolution approach consists of four phases: First, the pre-existing traceability links need to be organized as cases. Second, the extracted features of a new component are used to

© Springer International Publishing AG, part of Springer Nature 2018
R. Capilla et al. (Eds.): ICSR 2018, LNCS 10826, pp. 111–120, 2018.
https://doi.org/10.1007/978-3-319-90421-4_7

identify and prioritize the stored traceability cases. Third, the new requirements and code classes are matched with the requirements and code classes in previously implemented components. The links concerning the matched requirements and code classes are reused; however, adaptation is performed for mismatches between the requirements, architectural components and code classes. Finally, the adapted (i.e., newly constructed) links can be verified by a human analyst and stored in the dedicated case base for future use. The feasibility of the proposed approach is demonstrated by maintaining and evolving the traceability links of the Soomla Android store[1] Version 2.0 to the Version 3.6.17.

The rest of this paper is organized as follows: Sect. 2 discusses the related work. Section 3 describes the on-demand maintenance and evolution of traceability links. Section 4 presents a case study. Section 5 compares the results of the proposed approach to an information retrieval methods based tool. Section 6 concludes the paper and discusses future work.

2   Related Work

Hammad et al. [6] developed a tool, called SrcTracer that supports traceability from the source code to the design to maintain consistency with the design during code evolution. The approach examines the source code changes based on a lightweight analysis and syntactic differentiation to evaluate whether a particular change alters the design or not. The changes in the source code that lead to design changes include adding or removing of classes, methods and their relationships. Cleland-Huang et al. introduce a concept for the identification of change types that are applied to requirements in their event-based traceability approach [3]. The authors capture seven types of change activities to requirements, in particularly create, inactivate, modify, merge, refine, decompose and replace. However, the approach concentrates more on the manual construction of traceability links instead of maintaining them.

Mäder et al. [10] introduce a semi-automatic strategy, called traceMaintainer to determine changes in UML models to update pre-existing traceability relations. The approach records all changes to model elements and uses this information to find a match within a set of predefined patterns of recurring development activities. Buchgeher and Weinreich [2] introduce the LISA approach that captures traceability relations through observing the developer as she/he is working on the architecture design and implementation. These approaches, however, focus on the continuous maintenance of traceability links that might not be feasible when a large real-world project substantially evolve (i.e., a new major version). The research in Borg et al. [1] focus on the extraction of traceability information that has been specified as a by-product of completing impact analyses reports by using history mining and storage of extracted traceability information in a semantic network. They have not considered the use of extracted traceability as a way to either update or validate the traceability record.

---

[1] http://soom.la/.

3 Building a Case-Based Reasoner for Traceability Maintenance and Evolution

An overview of the proposed on-demand traceability maintenance and evolution approach is shown in Fig. 1. It describes the procedure used for case-based representation of software traceability (Sect. 3.1), similarity assessment and retrieval of stored traceability cases (Sect. 3.2), reuse and adaptation of traceability links at the architectural level (Sect. 3.3), and revision and retention of traceability links (Sect. 3.4).

3.1 Case Representation of Software Traceability

In case-based reasoning paradigm, a problem situation is organized as a case which consists of two parts, as shown in Listing 1.1: problem description and solution. The former describes the components as software architecture elements and their interconnections, while the later contains the traceability links to artefacts produced in the other activities of the development process, such as requirements and implementation.

The idea with the problem description part is the selection of substitutable component(s) among a variety of candidate components that might solve a given problem. The information about an architectural component might be enclosed inside particular XML tags and attributes. The component identification number distinguishes a component from others components, the name represents a name of the component and the description specifies functionalities offered by a component. A port describes an interaction point; it would have provided or required interfaces that provide specific information about the services offered or

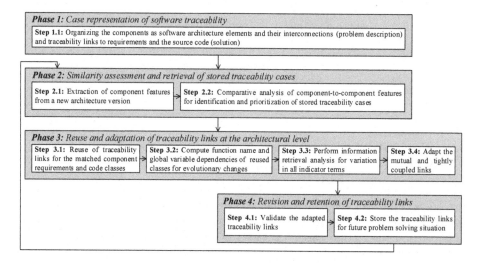

Fig. 1. The steps of the on-demand traceability maintenance and evolution approach

required by a component. A connector defines a pathway of interaction between components and have source and target ends.

The solution part of a case comprises of traceability links to the underlying requirements that can be distinguished by an identification number and the code classes that implement the particular requirement within the component. For efficient reuse and adaptation, it was decided to separate each requirement and its corresponding implementation classes so that unaffected traceability links shall be avoided from adaptation.

Listing 1.1. Features and traceability links of the StoreAssets component in the Soomla Android store Version 2.0

```
<Case ID = "C53">
   <Problem Part>
      <Feature List>
         <Component ID="SC1" Name="StoreAssets" Description="The StoreAssets component implements
            the virtual currencies, virtual goods, as well as their classification and price models."
            />
         <Port Name="Assets" Kind="Prov" Interfaces="" />
         <Port Name="AssetsInfo" Kind="Prov" Interfaces="" />
         <Connector Source="Assets" Target="ControlAssets" TargetComponent="StoreController" />
         <Connector Source="AssetsInfo" Target="InfoStorage" TargetComponent="DatabaseServices"
            />
      </Feature List>
   </Problem Part>
   <Solution Part>
      <Trace Links>
         <Requirement ID="1.2.0" Description="The SOOMLA Android store supports consumable items.
            The user is expected to consume virtual goods and repurchase them. Tokens, coins and gems
            are some examples of virtual currencies. To purchase the virtual goods, the static and
            balance driven price models should be implemented. After some time, when the virtual
            currency is insufficient, the user would have to purchase a virtual currency pack, such as
            10 coins pack or 20 coins pack. The pack holds the virtual currency and its corresponding
            price, i.e., the cost of the pack." />
         <Code Classes="VirtualCurrency.java, VirtualCurrencyPack.java, VirtualItemNotFoundException.
            java, AbstractPriceModel.java, StaticPriceModel.java, BalanceDrivenPriceModel.java,
            JSONConsts.java" />
      </Trace Links>
      <Trace Links>
         <Requirement ID="2.2.0" Description="SOOMLA also supports non-consumable items that are
            expected to last forever. This type of goods will be used to implement additional
            levels, a remove ads feature, or upgrading to a premium version of the game." />
         <Code Classes="NonConsumeableItem.java, VirtualGood.java, VirtualCategory.java,
            GoogleMarketItem.java, AbstractVirtualItem.java" />
      </Trace Links>
   </Solution Part>
</Case>
```

3.2 Similarity Assessment and Retrieval of Stored Traceability Cases

The assessment of component-to-component features for case retrieval includes two steps. First, all the components together with their features are extracted from the given software architecture. Second, the stored cases are traversed in order to find the similar cases, i.e., a set of candidate components whose characteristics/features match with the new architectural component.

Let $Sim1$ and $Sim2$ be the similarity values of two previous cases $Cpr1$ and $Cpr2$, respectively. Of course, for a new case problem Cpn, a case $Cpr1$ is more preferable if $Sim1$ is higher than $Sim2$, because $Cpr1$ is more similar to the new case problem. The global similarity $GSIM$ (Eq. 1) concerns the overall features while the local similarity $LSIM$ (Eq. 2) focuses on matching f_i (*ith* feature) of a new component with the f'_j (*jth* feature) of a previous component incorporated in a traceability case. It was decided to assign the similarity weights (W_i) ranging from 1.0–3.0. In particular, the highest weight is assigned to component interfaces or otherwise its description; whereas the component name, port name and port kind are weighted 2.0, 1.5 and 1.0, respectively. Algorithm 1 illustrates the case retrieval mechanism.

$$GSIM([f_1, f_2, ..., f_n][f'_1, f'_2, ..., f'_m]) = \sum_{i=1}^{n} \sum_{j=1}^{m} W_i . LSIM(f_i, f'_j) \qquad (1)$$

$$LSIM(f, f') = \begin{cases} 1, & \text{if } f = \text{f'} \\ 0, & \text{otherwise} \end{cases} \qquad (2)$$

Algorithm 1. Algorithm for retrieval of traceability cases

1: **Input:** A new case problem Cpn would have a set of features $f = \{f_1, f_2, ..., f_n\}$, where n
2: refers to the number of new component features
3: **Output:** The degree of similarity between the versions of an architectural component
4: **Local variables:** The component features $f' = \{f'_1, f'_2, ..., f'_m\}$ within in the problem part of
5: a previous case Cpr, where m concerns the number of features
6: The weight factor W is assigned to the components' features so that $w = \{w_1, w_2, ..., w_n\}$
7: **Begin**
8:     start from $i = 1$ -> select one case Cpn_i $(0 \leq j \leq m)$
9:     **Begin**
10:         for each f'_j of Cpr do $(0 \leq j \leq n)$
11:         **Begin**
12:             compare individual features f and f':
13:             do Eq. 2
14:         **End**
15:     calculate the similarity of overall features using Eq. 1
16:     **End**
17: **End**

3.3 Reuse and Adaptation of Traceability Links at the Architectural Level

The artefacts produced in the other activities of the development process, such as requirements and source code are matched with the solution part of retrieved traceability case(s) that underlies requirements and code classes implemented in a previous component. If component requirements and code classes are matched, the relevant traceability links are reused. However, adaptation is performed for mismatches between the requirements, architectural components and the code classes.

Based on our experiences and observations from various empirical investigations and open source software systems, we have noticed that a main driver for trusted and cost-effective traceability construction is the achievement of highest precision for the initial traceability links [7,9]. It is therefore decided to use the unchanged traceability links, if available, as an active countermeasure to arbitrarily making traceability decisions and to maintain and preserve the trust in further traceability construction [8]. The reuse and adaptation is performed in four steps: (i) the links for matched parts are reused, (ii) the function name and global variable dependencies of reused classes are computed, (iii) the information retrieval analysis based on the indicator terms for variation in architectural components, requirements and undetected classes is performed, and (iv) the mutual and tightly coupled classes are linked with the corresponding development artefacts. The availability of reused links demonstrated better results for on-demand traceability maintenance and evolution.

3.4   Revision and Retention of Traceability Links

The validation by a human analyst is strongly required in automated traceability tools. Nevertheless, the problems in automated traceability might not be completely eliminated when extensive set of traceability links are candidates for validation [5]. The focus on reuse and adaptation of traceability links would reduce the burden on a human analyst, in particularly the already verified traceability links from the past (i.e., reused links) in both matched and partially matched cases might be omitted from validation. However, only adapted traceability links for evolutionary changes would be made available to human analyst for validation. The revised solution part is combined with the problem description part in order to be stored as a new case so that the new traceability case becomes available for future problem solving situation.

4   Case Study

The Soomla Android store allows mobile game developers to easier implement virtual currencies (e.g., tokens, coins, gems), virtual goods and in-app purchases. Due to the added support for virtual goods, rewards, store events and payment mechanisms, the migration from older to later versions ($\geq 3.6.X$) of the Soomla Android store is recommended. The complete maintenance and evolution of traceability links cannot be discussed due to space limitations and similar technical details. Therefore, the rest of this section describes one of the affected component, named as StoreAssets.

Listing 1.2. Upgradation of previously constructed traceability links of the StoreAssets component to the Version 3.6.17

```
<Case ID="75">
  <Problem Part>
    <Feature List>
      <Component ID="SC1" Name="StoreAssets" Description="The StoreAssets component implements
        the virtual currencies, virtual goods, rewards as well as their classification." />
      <Port Name="Assets" Kind="Prov" Interfaces="" />
      <Port Name="AssetsInfo" Kind="Prov" Interfaces="" />
      <Connector Source="Assets" Target="ControlAssets" TargetComponent="StoreController" />
      <Connector Source="AssetsInfo" Target="InfoStorage" TargetComponent="DatabaseServices"
        />
    </Feature List>
  </Problem Part>
  <Solution Part>
    <Trace Links>
      <Requirement ID="1.3.6.17" Description="The SOOMLA Android store supports consumable items.
        The user is expected to consume virtual goods and repurchase them. Tokens, coins and gems
        are some examples of virtual currencies. After some time, when the virtual currency is
        insufficient, the user would have to purchase a virtual currency pack, such as 10 coins
        pack or 20 coins pack. The pack holds the virtual currency and its corresponding price,
        i.e., the cost of the pack. In addition, the user should be able to earn a specific
        reward after achieving certain criteria in game progress." />
      <Code Classes="VirtualCurrency.java, VirtualCurrencyPack.java, VirtualItemNotFoundException.
        java, BadgeReward.java, RandomReward.java, Reward.java, SequenceReward.java,
        VirtualItemReward.java, Schedule.java, SoomlaEntity.java,
        JSONConsts.java, JSONFactory.java" />
    </Trace Links>
    <Trace Links>
      <Requirement ID="2.3.6.17" Description="SOOMLA also supports non-consumable items that
        are expected to last forever. This type of goods will be used to implement additional
        levels, a remove ads feature, or upgrading to a premium version of the game."
        />
      <Code Classes="VirtualGood.java, VirtualItem.java, VirtualCategory.java, EquippableVG.java,
        LifetimeVG.java, SingleUseVG.java, SingleUsePackVG.java, UpgradeVG.java, MarketItem.java,
        PurchasableVirtualItem.java" />
    </Trace Links>
  </Solution Part>
</Case>
```

The adaptation of traceability links is performed in three steps. First, the function name and global variable dependencies of reused classes are computed. This led to the identification of eleven classes for the first underlying requirement. In case of second requirement, five classes are identified out of which four classes are strongly linked as means of «extends» relationship. Second, the information retrieval analysis based on the indicator terms is performed, which leads to the identification of nine and twelve classes for the requirements, respectively. The variation in first requirement text covers the variation in component description. Besides that, the undetected classes are not used for adaptation as the indicator terms in excluded requirement text are matched with the deleted classes. The mutual terms, if available, would be used for the recovery. Finally, the mutual and tightly coupled classes are linked with the requirements in Version 3.6.17, as shown in Listing 1.2. The adaptation process correctly identified all the classes realizing the particular requirements within a StoreAssets component.

5   Experimental Evaluation

In circumstances of a new major version, the information retrieval techniques are commonly used to reconstruct the traceability links. As means of comparison, the traceability links for Soomla Android store Version 3.6.17 are reconstructed using an information retrieval based tool, called Traceclipse[2]. Particularly, the latent semantic indexing is used for traceability construction.

Table 1 summarizes the achieved results for the Soomla Android store. For statistical analysis of the retrieved results, the Cliff's δ [4] – a robust non-parametric test – is used to evaluate the significance of the found results. The results from the Cliff's δ test are shown in Table 2. It is noticeable to see that significant differences emerged for all comparisons except with the recall of all traceability links. The main reason behind particular result is the rather higher number of generated links by the Traceclipse tool. The results for the Soomla Android store Version 3.6.17 provide strong evidence that our on-demand maintenance and evolution approach improved the precision and f-measure of traceability links for the new version of a software project, compared to an IR-based tool called Traceclipse.

Table 1. Summary of achieved results for the Soomla Android store Version 3.6.17

Factors	On-Demand Maintenance and Evolution (OME)				Traceclipse Tool Weight >= 0.1 (TWF)			Traceclipse Tool All Links (TAL)		
	Reused	Adapted	Irrelevant	Missed	Generated	Irrelevant	Missed	Generated	Irrelevant	Missed
StoreAssets	6	16	0	0	84	67	5	170	149	1
StoreController	11	43	8	1	24	13	36	85	38	0
DatabaseServices	4	3	0	0	40	37	4	85	78	0
Billing	0	43	36	0	32	27	2	83	76	0
CryptDecrypt	3	1	0	0	8	7	3	84	83	3

Table 2. Cliff's δ test for the Soomla Android store Version 3.6.17

	Recall		Precision		F-measure	
	OME vs. TWF	OME vs. TAL	OME vs. TWF	OME vs. TAL	OME vs. TWF	OME vs. TAL
Cliff's delta	−0.5158	−0.1548	−0.5995	−0.6319	−0.6019	−0.5859
Cohen's delta	−2.8780	−0.6614	−2.1561	−2.1100	−2.6114	−2.0095
Standard deviation of delta	0.1792	0.2340	0.2780	0.2994	0.2304	0.2915
z/t score of delta	−4.5505	−1.0458	−3.4091	−3.3362	−4.1290	−3.1774
Confidence interval low	−0.8301	−0.5656	−1.0435	−1.0863	−0.9867	−1.0131
Confidence interval high	−0.2014	0.2559	−0.1555	−0.1774	−0.2170	−0.1587
Degrees of freedom	4.0112	4.0066	5.3214	6.5339	4.5955	7.7932
p-value	**0.0103**	0.3545	**0.0172**	**0.0138**	**0.0108**	**0.0134**

---

[2] http://www.cs.wm.edu/semeru/traceclipse/.

6   Conclusions and Future Work

This paper has proposed an on-demand traceability maintenance and evolution approach in which the component-to-component features are used for identification and prioritization of stored traceability cases, which are then used to perform reuse and adaptation of traceability links based on the matches and mismatches, respectively. The previous traceability links for the exactly matched parts are not only reused, but also not considered for validation by a human analyst. However, the adapted solution (i.e., newly constructed traceability links) can be verified by a human analyst and stored in the case base for future problem solving situations. The proposed approach demonstrated reliable results than the information retrieval based tool, called Traceclipse. In the future, our plan is to build a catalogue of guidelines as best practices for traceability reuse and adaptation across projects, organizations, domains, product lines and supporting tools.

References

1. Borg, M., Gotel, O.C.Z., Wnuk, K.: Enabling traceability reuse for impact analyses: a feasibility study in a safety context. In: 7th International Workshop on Traceability in Emerging Forms of Software Engineering, TEFSE 2013, pp. 72–78 (2013)
2. Buchgeher, G., Weinreich, R.: Automatic tracing of decisions to architecture and implementation. In: 9th Working IEEE/IFIP Conference on Software Architecture, WICSA 2011, pp. 46–55 (2011)
3. Cleland-Huang, J., Chang, C.K., Ge, Y.: Supporting event based traceability through high-level recognition of change events. In: 26th International Computer Software and Applications Conference on Prolonging Software Life: Development and Redevelopment, COMPSAC 2002, pp. 595–600 (2002)
4. Cliff, N.: Dominance statistics: ordinal analyses to answer ordinal questions. Psychol. Bull. **114**, 494–509 (1993)
5. Dekhtyar, A., Dekhtyar, O., Holden, J., Hayes, J., Cuddeback, D., Kong, W.-K.: On human analyst performance in assisted requirements tracing: statistical analysis. In: 19th IEEE International Requirements Engineering Conference, RE 2011, pp. 111–120 (2011)
6. Hammad, M., Collard, M.L., Maletic, J.I.: Automatically identifying changes that impact code-to-design traceability during evolution. Softw. Quality Control **19**(1), 35–64 (2011)
7. Javed, M.A., Stevanetic, S., Zdun, U.: Cost-effective traceability links for architecture-level software understanding: a controlled experiment. In: 24th Australasian Software Engineering Conference, ASWEC 2015, vol. 2, pp. 69–73 (2015)
8. Javed, M.A., Stevanetic, S., Zdun, U.: Towards a pattern language for construction and maintenance of software architecture traceability links. In: 21st European Conference on Pattern Languages of Programs, EuroPlop 2016, pp. 24:1–24:20 (2016)

9. Javed, M.A., Zdun, U.: On the effects of traceability links in differently sized software systems. In: 19th International Conference on Evaluation and Assessment in Software Engineering, EASE 2015, pp. 11:1–11:10 (2015)
10. Mäder, P., Gotel, O.: Towards automated traceability maintenance. J. Syst. Softw. **85**(10), 2205–2227 (2012)

Assuring Virtual PLC in the Context of SysML Models

Mounifah Alenazi, Deepak Reddy, and Nan Niu[✉]

Department of Electrical Engineering and Computer Science,
University of Cincinnati, Cincinnati, OH 45221, USA
alenazmh@mail.uc.edu, kasuvy@mail.uc.edu, nan.niu@uc.edu

Abstract. In complex industrial projects, textual information has been recognized as an important factor for automatically recovering trace links in software development. The goal of this paper is to empirically investigate if the trace links in the simulation result can assist in validating a virtual Programmable Logic Controller (PLC) in the context of System Modeling Language (SysML). We integrate the concept of obstacle analysis to recover situations in which a safety requirement will not be satisfied. Therefore, we use fault tree analysis to validate the safety requirements, and further use the elements of the fault tree to evaluate the quality of the automatically recovered trace links. We showed that the identified impacts of assuring virtual PLC (V-PLC) elements using traceability information can be reused to ensure a number of other PLCs or requirements in the systems models. This paper presents our experience of applying our approach using an automatic transmission systems built in SysML models.

Keywords: Systems Modeling Language (SysML)
Programmable Logic Controller (PLC) · Trace links
Natural Language Processing (NLP) similarity measures
Fault Tree Analysis

1 Introduction

Model-Based Systems Engineering (MBSE), outlined in the International Council on Systems Engineering (INCOSE) Vision 2020, is a methodology of modeling to support systems requirements, design, analysis, and verification and validation activities starting from the conceptual design phase and continuing through development and later lifecycle phase [9]. The overall objective of the vision is to replace a document-centric approach through a model-centric one, i.e., shifting the records of authority from documents to digital models such as UML and SysML, which enables engineering from multiple domains to easily capture requirements, understand design change impacts, define traceability paths, and analyze system design before it is built [16].

The Systems Modeling Language (SysML) is now commonly used in many industry sectors and has become a *de facto* standard for systems engineering [30].

© Springer International Publishing AG, part of Springer Nature 2018
R. Capilla et al. (Eds.): ICSR 2018, LNCS 10826, pp. 121–136, 2018.
https://doi.org/10.1007/978-3-319-90421-4_8

SysML, proposed by the Object Modeling Group (OMG) and INCOSE, is a graphical modeling language intended to unify the universe of modeling languages used by systems engineers [16]. SysML is used for specifying, analyzing, designing, and verifying complex systems among various participants. In other words, SysML allows engineers to simulate the physical world of a system (e.g., an autonomous car) to fulfill stakeholder requirements. This is very important especially for safety critical systems.

Programmable logic controllers (PLCs) are often used to implement safety critical systems [25]. PLCs based on IEC 61131 represent the state of art in industrial automation systems. However, these PLCs have limited capabilities for describing heterogeneous disciplines [6]. To integrate the specific knowledge of each discipline, MBSE was introduced [16]. Brecher *et al.* [6] proposed an approach of integrating a PLC into a model-based development system. The aim of the proposed approach is to validate a virtual PLC (V-PLC) before connecting it to the real system by using executable SysML models. The challenge is that the simulation model of any system is only an approximation of the actual system, no matter the amount of time spent on building the model [20]. However, in requirements engineering, a technique such as obstacle analysis is used to recover situations in which a safety requirement will not be satisfied. Dealing with obstacles is very important for safety critical system [34].

In safety critical systems, safety analysis is performed using safety analysis techniques such as Fault Tree Analysis (FTA) and Failure Modes and Effects Analysis (FMEA) [28]. System validation is performed in a model-based paradigm using simulation. In our paper, we integrate the simulation details of the V-PLC with the safety assessment technique FTA. FTA is one of the most prominent techniques in safety analysis and is used by a wide range of industries [28]. It was developed extensively by the nuclear and aerospace industries and can be viewed as a systematic technique for acquiring information about a system [3]. A fault tree is a graphical method that models how failures propagate through the system. In other words, it models how component failures lead to the undesired event of system failures [28].

We showed that the identified impacts of assuring V-PLC elements using traceability information can be reused to assure a number of other PLCs or requirements in the system models. The availability of traceability has proven vital to several engineering activities such as verification and validation (V&V) and software reuse [1,24,32]. Traceability refers to the ability to interrelate any uniquely identifiable artifact to any other [8]. Several authors have applied information retrieval (IR) techniques to recover trace links between different components. The reason is that most of the models and diagrams contain textual information. Therefore, artifacts having high textual similarity probably share several concepts, so they are likely good candidates to be traced from one another [19]. Nejati *et al.* [23] proposed an approach to automatically identify the impact of requirements changes on system design when the requirements and design elements are expressed in SysML models. Based on model slicing, this approach uses natural language processing (NLP) methods to rank the resulted elements from slicing. Although significant efforts have been devoted to retrieving traceability links, little is known about how the retrieved links are used to assure a V-PLC when integrated with safety analysis techniques.

The main goal of this paper is to answer the following research question: To what extent can the trace links of textual information assist engineers in validating a virtual PLC in the context of SysML models? In other words, how much confidence engineers can claim about the V-PLC when relying only on the textual information?

This paper presents our experience of applying our approach using an automatic transmission system[1], built in SysML. The rest of this paper is structured as follows: Sect. 2 reviews background and related work and Sect. 3 describes our experimental setup. Results and analysis are presented in Sect. 4. Section 5 discusses the main findings of the paper. Section 6 concludes the paper and outlines future work.

2 Background and Related Work

This section provides some preliminaries on PLC, SysML and FTA in the context of safety analysis, reviews some prior research on the integration of SysML and safety analysis, and presents some related work on the use of textual information for automatically recovering trace links.

2.1 Virtual PLC

A PLC is a specialized computer widely used in automation production systems. PLCs can read all the inputs provided by sensors and write all the output variables to operate the actuators based on a custom program. These operations continually take place in a repeating loop. In many real applications, a PLC is a part of a large system that contains several PLCs and computers coupled and working together [29]. SysML diagrams can be used to model such systems. The PLC and the system are both "virtual," i.e., no physical PLC exists. The behavior of the real PLC can be learned by introducing necessary characteristics to the virtual PLC. The conceptual tool that is offered by SysML to simulate processing done by a PLC is a state diagram, or a model that describes the states an object can have and how events (input signals) affect those states over time [29]. The state diagram of the V-PLC is then executed to observe its behavior.

2.2 SysML-Safety Analysis Integration

The specification of SysML is classified into three basic types of diagrams: Requirements diagrams, behavior diagrams, and structure diagrams. According to [5], the information contained in a SysML model can support the elicitation and representation of safety information. This information is useful in the

---

[1] http://www.cvel.clemson.edu/auto/systems/transmission_control.html.

analysis and design of safety-critical systems. For instance, interfaces between system components can be a cause of a system failure. SysML internal block diagrams and sequence diagrams that define how system components interact can be analyzed to identify the specific cause of the failure [5].

Fault trees have been broadly used for safety assessment and reliability of systems for over 40 years [21]. FTA is a graphical representation of the relationship between certain events. The FTA begins with a stated top-level undesired event and is broken down into events until an event is no longer desired to be decomposed for further analysis. The relationship between multiple events are modeled as boolean logic gates.

Several approaches exist to integrate SysML and safety analysis techniques. These approaches are based on either a heavy-weight intermediate stage with model transformation, or a light weight solution based on system modeling with safety information [21]. Mhenni *et al.* [21] present an extension to SysML models that is dedicated for safety analysis. The proposed approach generates fault trees automatically from structural diagrams (e.g., SysML internal block diagram). The fault tree is generated automatically by transforming the internal block diagrams into a directed graph using a graph traversal algorithm. However, it is component-oriented only and thus requires knowledge, which might not be available in early stages [22]. Biggs *et al.* [5] describe a SysML profile designed for modeling safety information of a safety critical system. The profile is expressed based on the important concepts found in safety standards and safety analysis techniques integrated with system design information. This profile can be used to present information to engineers involved in system development.

2.3   NLP and IR-Based Traceability

Various research approaches use IR-based or NLP-based methods to automatically recover trace links between different types of artifacts within software boundary [17,19,35]. Beyond the software boundary, the use of textual information has also been examined. Nejati *et al.* [23] proposed an approach to automatically identifying the impact of requirements changes on system design, when the requirements and design elements are expressed in SysML models. Two main steps are involved in their approach: extracting a set of impacted elements by computing reachability over intra-block control, inter-block data flow, and data flow dependencies, and ranking the resulting set using NLP techniques. NLP support was also used by Arunthavanathan *et al.* [2] in their traceability tool *SATAnalyzer* to extract information from different artifacts. The author claimed that the addition of NLP methods helps to improve the performance measure of the tool. However, the design models are expressed in UML models. Delgoshaei *et al.* [10] proposed an approach to requirements traceability using semantic platforms in MBSE development for cyber-physical systems (CPSs). The proposed approach is based on the use of domain ontologies and rule-based reasoning to enable validation of requirements. Briand *et al.* [7] devised a mechanism to establish traceability between textual requirements and design models. The proposed methodology is based on extracting design slices (model fragments) containing information relevant to each requirement. Although significant effort has been devoted to retrieving traceability links, little is known about how the retrieved links are used to assure a virtual PLC when integrating with safety analysis techniques.

3   Experimental Setup

Our objective is to validate a virtual PLC when it is integrated into a model-based development process. The virtual PLC with its behavior is modeled as a part of the overall system (e.g., SysML models). In our approach, we use the simulation model that represents the behavior of the virtual PLC (e.g., a safety requirement). In most cases, SysML models are exported in the XML format. However, in our case, we use the simulation results of the executed model. In particular, the simulation model consists of a static user interface (UI) and a dynamic simulation log file. The static UI contains elements that we utilize as a trace query. The simulation log file records all the details of the engineers' actions during model execution. The capability of recording all the details is a key advantage of using simulations to perform safety analysis. The steps of our approach are as follows:

1. Manually generating FTA for a safety requirement in the V-PLC.
2. Representing the behavior of the V-PLC in the system models (e.g., SysML).
3. In addition to V-PLC representation, a query set of elements (i.e., textual content) based on the targeted requirement is required from the engineers. This query is based on the textual information presented in the user interface of the V-PLC.
4. Applying NLP similarity measures on the simulation file to identify the set of elements that impact the targeted safety requirement of the V-PLC.
5. Assessing the retrieved results by comparing it to the answer set derived from FTA.

The main purpose of our approach is to assess how much assurance we can claim about the tracing results of the virtual PLC when engineers rely only on the textual information. Our work can further inform how these tracing results can be reused to assure other V-PLCs or requirements in the system model.

3.1   Subject System

The case study we conducted in this paper is the Transmission Control Module (TCM) described in [33] (Fig. 1). TCM consists of not only mechanical parts but also electronics. It controls gearbox and switch between gears based on input from several sensors as well as data provided by engine control module (ECM). It then processes this input to calculate how and when to shift gears in the transmission and generates the signals that drive actuators to complete this shifting. Electronic sensors monitor the selection of gear position, vehicle

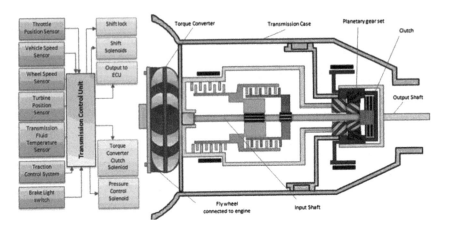

Fig. 1. Transmission Control Module (TCM) [33].

speed, throttle position, and many other attributes. This information helps the control module to adjust the current supplied to solenoids in the transmission that control the position of various valves and gears. For example, the gear position selector switch communicates to the TCM which gear has been selected by the operator. The crankshaft position sensor provides information to the TCM to determine the current rotational speed of the engine. This information is used by the TCM to determine when to change gears. The brake pedal position sensor helps to assure that the driver has applied the brake before shifting into park or reverse. To describe transmission controller and demonstrate how gears in the gearbox are changed, SysML models are used, i.e., structure diagrams, behavior diagrams, and parametric diagrams. A user interface (UI) is then added to simulate the model.

Our goal is to assure a safety requirement of the TCM. The safety requirement we have considered is: $R = Revolution\ Per\ Minute\ (RPM)\ value\ shall\ not\ exceed\ 3900$. An obstacle to this goal is $O = RPM\ value\ exceed\ 3900$ (the top undesired event shown in Fig. 2). This obstacle is called a "hazard" obstacle since it obstructs the satisfaction of a safety goal [34]. Obstacles recover situations in which a goal or a requirement is violated. The obstacle O is refined using AND/OR structure (directed acyclic graph) which shows how the occurrence of other events and which combination of them can lead to the top event. To help identify obstacles to the high-level requirement R, we selected FTA because it enables the analysis of individual risks. Moreover, according to Lee *et al.* [18], as systems become more complex and the consequences of accidents become catastrophic, a safety technique such as FTA should be applied. Figure 2 shows the FTA of obstacle O which corresponds to our case study (Fig. 1). Our construction of the FTA was manual and inspired by the autonomous car described in [4].

As mentioned above, a UI is created to execute the SysML models. Figure 3 shows the UI of the Transmission System. From this UI, engineers can use the

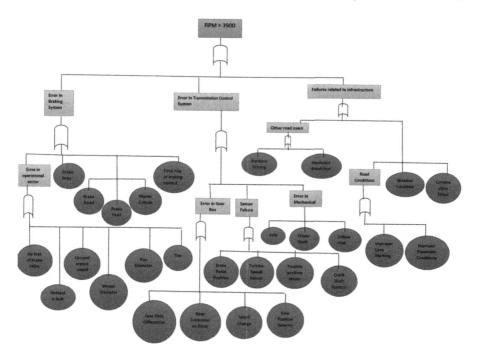

Fig. 2. Fault Tree Analysis

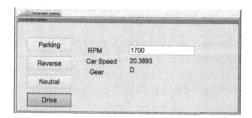

Fig. 3. User interface of the V-PLC [33]

textual elements as trace queries. We represent the trace queries as follows:
$TQ = \{parking, reverse, neutral, drive, RPM, carSpeed, gear\}$. The next step
after executing the model is to represent the behavior of this V-PLC as an
XML or a text file. We use Cameo simulation toolkit plugin by MagicDraw[2].
It provides a simulation log file that records all the simulation details during
execution.

A preprocessing technique for the simulation file is needed. The main objective of preprocessing is to obtain the key-terms from the simulation which can
be used for NLP similarity measures. Several methods are used for preprocessing

---

[2] https://www.nomagic.com/products/cameo-systems-modeler.

such as tokenization, stemming, and stop word removal. We denote the retrieved results as *TraceSet*.

We use the Rapid-Miner tool for data preprocessing[3]. RapidMiner is a data science software platform that provides an integrated environment for data preprocessing, machine learning, text mining, and predictive analysis [11]. RapidMiner is used for both research and real-world data mining tasks. The data mining process can be made up of various nestable operators, described in XML files and created in RapiddMiner's graphical user interface. It provides more than 500 operators for all main machine learning procedures. It integrates learning schemes of Weka machine learning environment and also statistical schemes of R project [11]. After preprocessing the data, we apply NLP-similarity measures using *TQ* and *TraceSet* obtained from the UI and the Simulation file, respectively.

We use the concept of query expansion and run multiple iterations to assess if the retrieved results are improved. Query expansion is defined as *"a method for improving retrieval performance by supplementing an original query with additional terms"* [12]. The main purpose of query expansion is to improve the overall recall of the related elements. Once the first candidate trace links are obtained, different query expansion techniques can be applied. We added to the *TQ* additional links that were retrieved after computing the similarity measures, i.e., the top links previously retrieved. This process is known as *relevance feedback*. Next, a brief description of NLP-similarity measures (syntactic and semantic) of the textual information used in our study is reviewed.

3.2   Natural Language Processing (NLP)

Since engineers have the textual information presented in the user interface of the V-PLC, our approach explicitly includes syntactic and semantic information integration. The simulation file of the virtual PLC with the textual information displayed on the UI enables us to use NLP-similarity measures since the file contains rich textual information that can be used for retrieving more traces other than the ones displayed in the UI, e.g., *TQ*. NLP-similarity measures can be syntactic or semantic. Syntactic measures are based on their syntactical representation (their string format), whereas semantic measures use general-purpose dictionaries such as WordNet. WordNet[4] started in 1990 as a language project by Miller and Christian at the Cognitive Science Laboratory, Princeton University [26]. It is defined as a large lexical database of English language. Nouns, verbs, adjectives, and adverbs are grouped into sets of cognitive synonyms (synsets), each expressing a distinct concept. These sets are linked by a different type of relations (i.e., 'is-a' relationship). As a result, WordNet produces a combination of a thesaurus and dictionary which can be used for many applications such as text analysis. The recent online version of WordNet is v.3.1, announced in June 2011, containing around 117,659 synsets and 206,941 word-sense pairs [31].

---

[3] https://rapidminer.com/.

[4] https://wordnet.princeton.edu/.

For the choice of similarity measures, we follow the same strategy in [23], i.e., three syntactic measures (SoftTFIDF, Levenshtein, and Monge-Elkan) and four semantic measures (Resnik, JCN, Path, and Lin). While the goal in [23] was to rank already computed impacted elements of SysML with a change of requirements statement, our goal is to identify the impacted elements of the V-PLC modeled in SysML diagrams relying only on the textual information displayed on the UI. Next is a brief description of the similarity measures used in this study.

- **Resnik:** RES similarity measure depends on the amount of information two concepts (synsets) have in common. That is the information content of their most specific common subsumer. If there is no common concept, then the similarity between two concepts will be 0 [13].
- **Jian and Conrath:** While RES depends only on the information content shared by two concepts, JCN is based on a combination of edge counts in the WordNet 'is-a' hierarchy and the amount of information shared by two concepts. In other words, this measure uses the sum of individual distances between the nodes in the shortest path and the information content as a decision factor [13].
- **PATH measure:** This method computes similarity between two concepts by counting the number of nodes along the shortest path in 'is-a' hierarchy in WordNet taxonomy.
- **Lin:** Lin extended RES measure of the information content by considering the information required to describe what the concepts are. Lin is like JCN method but with a small modification, i.e., the similarity between two concepts is stated as the ratio of the amount of information two concepts have in common and the information required to describe these concepts [13].
- **Soft-TFID** is a variation of TFIDF. It combines two measures the TF-IDF and Jaro-Winkler. Soft-TFID first applies Jaro-Winkler to all pairs of tokens between the two concepts and then uses the TF-IDF measure to tokens that have a similarity score above the threshold [15].
- **Levenshtein** defines the distance between two strings by counting the minimum number of operations needed to transform one string into the other. Operations include insertion, deletion, or substitution of a single character, or a transposition of two adjacent characters [15].
- **Monge-Elkan** measure is a hybrid similarity measure that combines internal character-based (e.g., edit distance) and token-based (i.e., word level) methods. Monge-Elkan takes the average score of the best matching tokens from the secondary measure such as Levenshtein, Jaro, and Smith-Waterman [15].

3.3 Evaluation Metrics

In this study, the retrieved links are evaluated using recall, precision, and F2 metrics. In the field of IR, recall and precision are the standard measures often used to assess the quality of the retrieved trace links. Recall can be defined as the relevant links that are successfully retrieved, while precision measures the accuracy of the retrieved links. More specifically, recall and precision can be calculated as follows:

$$Recall = \frac{TP}{TP + FN} \tag{1}$$

$$Precision = \frac{TP}{TP + FP} \tag{2}$$

where TP is the true positive, FP is the false positive, and FN is the false negative. For example, suppose that 70 links were extracted out of 100 words in an answer set and among those 70, 30 links were correct, then the recall is $30/(70 + 30) = 0.30$, while precision $30/(30 + 40) = 0.43$.

To minimize noise, as in line with common practice [23], a threshold score is established such that all links above or at the threshold are retrieved, and all links below the threshold are rejected.

Because it is not feasible to achieve identical recall values across every trace set, it can be challenging to compare recall and precision results across experiments [17]. Therefore, we use another metric known as the F-Measure, which computes the harmonic mean of recall and precision. In this paper, we used a variant of the F-measure, known as the F2-Measure, which weights recall values more highly than precision (by placing more emphasis on false negatives). This weighting is appropriate in the traceability domain where it is essential to recall as many of the correct links as possible [27]. F2 can be calculated as follows:

$$F2 = \frac{5.Precision.Recall}{(4.Precision) + Recall} \tag{3}$$

4   Results and Analysis

4.1   Results

We assess the usefulness of the similarity measures by comparing the retrieved links with the answer set derived from our FTA. Table 1 shows our results of applying similarity measures. After applying similarity measures, a postprocessing step for the retrieved results is done, i.e., we removed all the duplicates since two trace queries may retrieve the same set of traces. For example, *parking* using RES measure retrieves {*parking, reverse, suspension, RPM, speed, Driving*} and *reverse* using the same measure retrieves {*reverse, suspension, RPM, speed, parking, light, tire*}. Our results show that Levenshtein and Monge-Elkan result in 70% recall of set-based coverage with 29% precision (54% F2), while softTFIDF results in high precision 50% with low recall 25% (27% F2). The reason is that Levenshtein and Monge-Elkan assume all tokens have equal weight and assign a similarity score between every two key-terms (high recall), while softTFIDF considers only similarity between tokens that are above the threshold, so it assigns 0 for non-closely matching terms (high precision). For example, the retrieved trace set using the term *Drive* as a query set are: *Drive, Driver, drivershaft* because SoftTFIDF allows partial matching of words instead of only

Table 1. NLP similarity measures results before query expansion

	TFIDF	Levenshtein	MongeElkan	softTFIDF	RES	JCN	PATH	Lin
Recall	0.15	**0.70**	**0.70**	0.25	0.40	0.25	0.25	0.30
Precision	0.43	0.29	0.29	**0.50**	0.25	0.19	0.13	0.15
F2 measure	0.17	**0.54**	**0.54**	0.27	0.35	0.22	0.21	0.25

Table 2. NLP similarity measures results after query expansion

	TFIDF	Levenshtein	MongeElkan	softTFIDF	RES	JCN	PATH	Lin
Recall	0.15	**0.75**	**0.75**	0.25	0.40	0.25	0.25	0.30
Precision	0.43	**0.32**	**0.32**	0.50	0.25	0.19	0.13	0.15
F2 measure	0.17	**0.59**	**0.59**	0.27	0.35	0.22	0.21	0.25

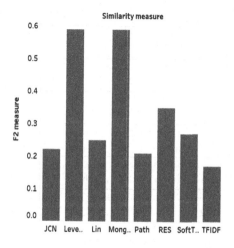

Fig. 4. F2 metric for similarity measures

allowing exact matching such as in TFIDF; this is why we received the lowest recall in TFIDF of only 15%.

Table 2 shows our results after applying query expansion. The results show that Levenshtein and Monge-Elkan perform better with the additional terms yielding a recall of 75% with 32% precision. However, the rest of the methods perform the same even after query expansion, especially the semantic measures (considering that we removed the duplicate traces). Semantic measures such as RES and JCN retrieved most of the trace queries using only a subset of the TQ. However, the overall performance is still low even with query expansion. The reason for that is the small dataset of the V-PLC used plus WordNet does not include much domain-specific terminology. From this result, we can see that textual information only gives 59% assurance using set-based measure. Due to the space constraint, only the F2 statistics are summarized in Fig. 4.

4.2 Threats to Validity

Several factors can affect the validity of our study. Construct validity is the degree to which the variables accurately measure the concepts they claim to measure [36]. To mitigate the threats, we adopt standard IR metrics (recall and precision), which are used extensively in requirements traceability research.

Threats to internal validity are influences that can affect the independent variable with respect to causality [36]. A potential threat to our study's internal validity is our manual construction of the FTA, (i.e., error prone and time-consuming).

Threats to external validity [36] impacts the generalizability of results. A threat to the external validity could be the answer set of the constructed fault tree. In particular, the elements of the fault tree we used to evaluate the similarity measures. However, these elements were chosen according to the component of the V-PLC in the transmission system. Another external validity is that our chosen tool provides a simulation details for any executed model. However, this may not apply to other SysML tools.

5 Discussion

Studies show that the performance of the similarity measures is affected by characteristics such as text length, spelling accuracy, and presence of abbreviations [14]. Another common observation is that measures that demonstrate good performance and robustness for one data set can perform poorly on another [14]. In our study, we used the simulation details of the V-PLC built in SysML models as our data set. We assessed the usefulness of the textual information displayed in the UI and the simulation results by applying NLP-similarity measures and compared the automatically recovered trace links by the elements of the fault tree. Our results show that textual information gives only 59% assurance.

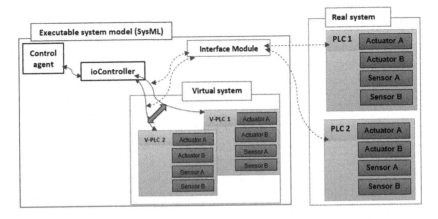

Fig. 5. Integrating a virtual PLC in SysML models adapted from [6].

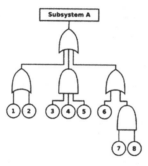

Fig. 6. Fault Tree Analysis example

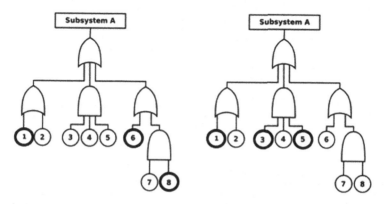

Fig. 7. Tree-based coverage for similarity measure *S1*(*left*) and *S2*(*right*)

As we mentioned earlier, our requirement R may need multiple PLCs to check its fulfillment, and the same V-PLC can be used to verify more than one requirement. In our approach, we considered the safety requirement to be that *RPM value should not exceed 3900* and analyzed how different components of a V-PLC are responsible for the success or failure of the above-stated requirement. The recovered trace links using the set-based measures on the FTA help us identify the components of TCM that can be reused to verify other V-PLCs (Fig. 5). For example, when we consider the braking system, some of the retrieved results of the braking system are overlapped with impacted elements of the TCM.

Set-based evaluation versus tree-based evaluation is an important comparison because it could explain which similarity measure is more effective. To explain this, let us randomly consider any of the two similarity methods Syntactic or Semantic (*S1* and *S2*). As mentioned earlier in our approach, we use these two methods to retrieve trace links from the simulation file, based on our query requirement. Suppose we found that these two methods have returned the same "Recall" and "Precision" values, i.e., number of relevant and retrieved trace links are the same for both *S1* and *S2*. Now consider the example Fault Tree in Fig. 6.

Let the results obtained from both similarity measures *S1* and *S2* be 1, 6, 8 and 1, 3, 5 respectively, and the relevant nodes for this Fault Tree are 1, 2, 3, 5, 6, 8. We observe that both *S1* and *S2* have the same recall and precision values. But when we try to analyze the coverage of these results on a Fault Tree, it is very different. Let us observe Fig. 7 for the tree-based coverage of results obtained from similarity methods 'S1' (*left*) and 'S2' (*right*) respectively. Assessing which similarity measures could be more effective using tree-based or set-based may reveal new insights.

6   Conclusion

In this paper, we investigate how trace links assist engineers in validating a virtual PLC in the context of SysML models relying only on the textual information of the user interface. We integrate FTA to validate the safety requirements, and further use the elements of the fault tree to evaluate the quality of the automatically recovered trace links. Our results show that Monge-Elkan and Levenshtein methods give only 59% confidence in assuring the executed V-PLC. We illustrated that the identified impacts of assuring the V-PLC can be reused to verify other V-PLCs and also additional requirements.

Our future work includes applying our approach on different datasets, and comparing set-based evaluation versus tree-based evaluation. Analyzing the coverage of tree-based results and explaining which similarity method can be more effective could be a potential way to describe the effectiveness of a similarity measure when used in the context of identifying the system failures, rather than just depending on the set-based evaluation measures.

Acknowledgments. This research is partially supported by the U.S. National Science Foundation (Award CCF-1350487).

References

1. Alenazi, M., Niu, N., Wang, W., Gupta, A.: Traceability for automated production systems: a position paper. In: 2017 IEEE 25th International Requirements Engineering Conference Workshops (REW), pp. 51–55. IEEE (2017)
2. Arunthavanathan, A., Shanmugathasan, S., Ratnavel, S., Thiyagarajah, V., Perera, I., Meedeniya, D., Balasubramaniam, D.: Support for traceability management of software artefacts using natural language processing. In: Moratuwa Engineering Research Conference (MERCon 2016), pp. 18–23. IEEE (2016)
3. Balakrishnan, N.: An overview of system safety assessment. In: Dependability in Medicine and Neurology, pp. 33–81. Springer, Cham (2015). https://doi.org/10.1007/978-3-319-14968-4_2
4. Bhavsar, P., Das, P., Paugh, M., Dey, K., Chowdhury, M.: Risk analysis of autonomous vehicles in mixed traffic streams. Transp. Res. Rec. J. Transp. Res. Board **2625**, 51–61 (2017)
5. Biggs, G., Sakamoto, T., Kotoku, T.: A profile and tool for modelling safety information with design information in SysML. Softw. Syst. Model. **15**(1), 147–178 (2016)

6. Brecher, C., Nittinger, J.A., Karlberger, A.: Model-based control of a handling system with SysML. Procedia Comput. Sci. **16**, 197–205 (2013)
7. Briand, L., Falessi, D., Nejati, S., Sabetzadeh, M., Yue, T.: Traceability and SysML design slices to support safety inspections: a controlled experiment. ACM Trans. Softw. Eng. Methodol. (TOSEM) **23**(1), 9 (2014)
8. Cleland-Huang, J., Gotel, O.C., Huffman Hayes, J., Mäder, P., Zisman, A.: Software traceability: trends and future directions. In: Proceedings of the on Future of Software Engineering, pp. 55–69. ACM (2014)
9. Crisp, H.: INCOSE systems engineering vision 2020. Technical report, INCOSE-TP-2004-004-02, September 2007
10. Delgoshaei, P., Austin, M.A., Veronica, D.A.: A semantic platform infrastructure for requirements traceability and system assessment. In: The Ninth International Conference on Systems (ICONS 2014), pp. 215–219 (2014)
11. Dong, Z., Zhang, P.: Emerging Techniques in Power System Analysis. Springer, Berlin (2010). https://doi.org/10.1007/978-3-642-04282-9
12. Efthimiadis, E.N.: Query expansion. Ann. Rev. Inf. Sci. Technol. (ARIST) **31**, 121–187 (1996)
13. Elavarasi, S.A., Akilandeswari, J., Menaga, K.: A survey on semantic similarity measure. Int. J. Res. Advent Technol. **2**(3), 389–398 (2014)
14. Gali, N., Mariescu-Istodor, R., Fränti, P.: Similarity measures for title matching. In: 2016 23rd International Conference on Pattern Recognition (ICPR), pp. 1548–1553. IEEE (2016)
15. Gomaa, W.H., Fahmy, A.A.: A survey of text similarity approaches. Int. J. Comput. Appl. **68**(13), 13–18 (2013)
16. Hart, L.E.: Introduction to model-based system engineering (MBSE) and SysML. In: Delaware Valley INCOSE Chapter Meeting, Ramblewood Country Club, Mount Laurel, New Jersey (2015)
17. Hayes, J.H., Dekhtyar, A., Osborne, J.: Improving requirements tracing via information retrieval. In: Proceedings of the 11th IEEE International Requirements Engineering Conference, pp. 138–147. IEEE (2003)
18. Lee, W.S., Grosh, D.L., Tillman, F.A., Lie, C.H.: Fault tree analysis, methods, and applications a review. IEEE Trans. Reliab. **34**(3), 194–203 (1985)
19. Mahmoud, A., Niu, N.: On the role of semantics in automated requirements tracing. Requirements Eng. **20**(3), 281–300 (2015)
20. Martis, M.S.: Validation of simulation based models: a theoretical outlook. Electron. J. Bus. Res. Methods **4**(1), 39–46 (2006)
21. Mhenni, F., Choley, J.Y., Nguyen, N.: SysML extensions for safety-critical mechatronic systems design. In: 2015 IEEE International Symposium on Systems Engineering (ISSE), pp. 242–247. IEEE (2015)
22. Müller, M., Roth, M., Lindemann, U.: The hazard analysis profile: linking safety analysis and SysML. In: 2016 Annual IEEE Systems Conference (SysCon), pp. 1–7. IEEE (2016)
23. Nejati, S., Sabetzadeh, M., Arora, C., Briand, L.C., Mandoux, F.: Automated change impact analysis between SysML models of requirements and design. In: Proceedings of the 2016 24th ACM SIGSOFT International Symposium on Foundations of Software Engineering, pp. 242–253. ACM (2016)
24. Niu, N., Wang, W., Gupta, A.: Gray links in the use of requirements traceability. In: Proceedings of the 2016 24th ACM SIGSOFT International Symposium on Foundations of Software Engineering, pp. 384–395. ACM (2016)
25. Oh, Y., Yoo, J., Cha, S., Son, H.S.: Software safety analysis of function block diagrams using fault trees. Reliab. Eng. Syst. Saf. **88**(3), 215–228 (2005)

26. Pedersen, T., Patwardhan, S., Michelizzi, J.: WordNet::Similarity: measuring the relatedness of concepts. In: Demonstration Papers at HLT-NAACL 2004, pp. 38–41. Association for Computational Linguistics (2004)

27. Powers, D.M.: What the f-measure doesn't measure. Technical report, Beijing University of Technology, China & Flinders University, Australia (2014)

28. Ruijters, E., Stoelinga, M.: Fault tree analysis: a survey of the state-of-the-art in modeling, analysis and tools. Comput. Sci. Rev. **15**, 29–62 (2015)

29. Sacha, K.: Automatic code generation for PLC controllers. In: Winther, R., Gran, B.A., Dahll, G. (eds.) SAFECOMP 2005. LNCS, vol. 3688, pp. 303–316. Springer, Heidelberg (2005). https://doi.org/10.1007/11563228_23

30. Schafer, W., Wehrheim, H.: The challenges of building advanced mechatronic systems. In: Future of Software Engineering, FOSE 2007, pp. 72–84. IEEE (2007)

31. Slimani, T.: Description and evaluation of semantic similarity measures approaches. arXiv preprint arXiv:1310.8059 (2013)

32. Spanoudakis, G., Zisman, A.: Software traceability: a roadmap. Handb. Softw. Eng. Knowl. Eng. **3**, 395–428 (2005)

33. Strolia, Z., Pavalkis, S.: Building executable SysML model - automatic transmission system (part 1) (2017). https://blog.nomagic.com/building-executable-sysml-model-automatic-transmission-system-part-1/

34. Van Lamsweerde, A., Letier, E.: Handling obstacles in goal-oriented requirements engineering. IEEE Trans. Software Eng. **26**(10), 978–1005 (2000)

35. Wang, W., Gupta, A., Niu, N., Xu, L., Cheng, J.R.C., Niu, Z.: Automatically tracing dependability requirements via term-based relevance feedback. IEEE Trans. Industr. Inf. **14**(1), 342–349 (2018)

36. Wohlin, C., Runeson, P., Höst, M., Ohlsson, M.C., Regnell, B., Wesslén, A.: Experimentation in Software Engineering. Springer, Berlin (2012). https://doi.org/10.1007/978-3-642-29044-2

Software Product Lines, Features and Reuse of Code Rewriters

Guiding Clone-and-Own When Creating Unplanned Products from a Software Product Line

Eddy Ghabach[1,2(✉)] ⓘ, Mireille Blay-Fornarino[1], Franjieh El Khoury[2,3],
and Badih Baz[2]

[1] Université Côte d'Azur, I3S, CNRS UMR 7271, Sophia Antipolis, France
{ghabach,blay}@i3s.unice.fr
[2] Université Saint-Esprit de Kaslik, Kaslik, Lebanon
badih.baz@usek.edu.lb
[3] Université de Lyon, Université Lyon 1, ERIC EA 3083, Lyon, France
franjieh.elkhoury@eric.univ-lyon2.fr

Abstract. Clone-and-own is a simple and intuitive practice adopted to construct new product variants based on existing ones. However, when the developed family of products becomes rich, maintaining shared assets and managing variability between the clones become tedious tasks. Therefore, migrating the family of products into a software product line becomes essential. Despite that, software engineers remain interested in constructing new product variants that are not provided by the software product line. In this short paper, we briefly present our approach to guide software engineers in deriving new products from a software product line based on clone-and-own. This approach consists of proposing the possible configuration scenarios by means of operations to perform at asset level, in order to derive a new product variant.

Keywords: Software product line · Clone-and-own
Product derivation

1 Introduction

A software product line (SPL) is a set of software products that belong to the same domain and have some characteristics in common [1]. These characteristics are known as features [2]. A feature model (FM) is one of the abstract representations of SPL products variability [3]. A configuration is a selection of features that respects the constraints imposed by the FM and generally reflects a product of the SPL [4]. SPLs permit a systematic reuse of software artifacts, which reduces development cost and increases time to market and software quality [5]. SPLs are considered as an expensive up-front investment, since artifacts must be initially defined in a domain engineering phase, before deriving new products through an application engineering phase [5]. Therefore, organizations that are not able to deal with such an up-front investment, tend to develop a family of software products using simple and intuitive practices such as clone-and-own.

© Springer International Publishing AG, part of Springer Nature 2018
R. Capilla et al. (Eds.): ICSR 2018, LNCS 10826, pp. 139–147, 2018.
https://doi.org/10.1007/978-3-319-90421-4_9

Clone-and-own (C&O) is an approach that consists in cloning an existing product variant (PV) then modifying it to add and/or remove some functionalities in order to obtain a new PV [6,7]. This approach is practically adopted by several organizations as "favorable and natural" solution to develop a family of related software systems, due to its simplicity, availability and rapidity [8]. However, when the number of variants increases, it becomes difficult to manage them efficiently [8]. Thus, it becomes essential to migrate the developed PVs into an SPL [9], in order to manage their variability and benefit from a systematic reuse. This process is known as extractive [10] or bottom-up [11] adoption, or re-engineering [9,12] of SPLs. In our approach, we are interested in organizations that adopt C&O to develop a family of software products, and desire to develop new PVs after integrating the existing products into an SPL. Such organizations are in need of a guidance in reusing the existing products artifacts to derive the new "desired product". Hence, our approach consists of proposing the possible configuration scenarios by means of operations to perform, in order to derive a new PV from the SPL based on C&O. In addition, our approach allows the integration of the newly developed products into the SPL, in order to benefit from its reuse in future derivations.

2   Approach Overview

We illustrate our approach on a running example, representing an excerpt of three PVs for managing soccer matches[1]. The features, assets and FM of the running example are illustrated in Tables 1, 2, and Fig. 1 respectively.

2.1 $\mathcal{SPL}$ Definition and Correlations

We define $\mathcal{SPL}$ as a software product line, where $\mathcal{P} = \{p_1, ..., p_x\}$ is the set of products that can be derived through the valid configurations of the $\mathcal{SPL}$ feature model, $\mathcal{F} = \{f_1, ..., f_y\}$ is the set of features *implemented* by its products and $\mathcal{A} = \{a_1, ..., a_z\}$ is the set of assets *employed* by the products to implement the features. We note $F(p_j)$ the set of features implemented by a product p_j. A product p_j *employs* a set of assets $A(p_j)$ and for each employed asset $a_k \in A(p_j)$, p_j *exploits* one of its instances a_k^i to fulfill the implementation, where $a_k^i \in AI(a_k)$ the set of instances of a_k. The set of asset instances *exploited* by p_j are noted as $AI(p_j)$. We call *assets* the identified files and *asset instances* their corresponding versions. For example, referring to Table 2, we can identify 1 instance for asset *match.jsp* and 3 instances for asset *style.css*.

We designate *correlations* as the mappings between features and assets, and between features and asset instances. Instead of mapping a feature or set of features (features interaction) to an implementation block, which can be composed of fragments of several assets, we map each feature to the set of assets that supposedly contribute in its implementation. Hence, a feature might be correlated

---

[1] The implementation files of the PVs of the running example are available on: https://github.com/eddyghabachi3s/SoccerManager.

Table 1. Product variants with their corresponding features

Product	Feature			
	ManageMatches	AddMatches	ModifyMatches	DeleteMatches
p_1	✓	✓	✓	
p_2	✓	✓	✓	✓
p_3	✓	✓		

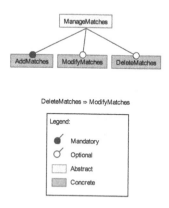

DeleteMatches ⇒ ModifyMatches

Legend:
- ● Mandatory
- ○ Optional
- ▢ Abstract
- ▤ Concrete

Fig. 1. Running example SPL FM

Table 2. Product variants with an excerpt of their corresponding assets

Product	Asset^{version}
p_1	match.jsp^1
	SaveMatch.java^1
	style.css^1
p_2	match.jsp^1
	SaveMatch.java^1
	style.css^2
	DeleteMatch.java^1
p_3	match.jsp^1
	SaveMatch.java^2
	style.css^3

to several assets, and an asset might be correlated to several features as well. We consider that a correlation has to be identified between a feature and an asset instance, if we find at least a product implementing the feature and exploiting the asset instance, with a constraint that no other product exploits the same asset instance without implementing the feature, or implements the feature without exploiting any instance of the asset. Thus, given an instance a^i of an asset a, a correlation between a feature f and a^i noted as $c(f, a^i)$ holds if $\exists p_j, f \in F(p_j), a^i \in AI(p_j) \land \nexists p_k, (a^i \in AI(p_k), f \notin F(p_k) \lor f \in F(p_k), a \notin A(p_k))$. For example, the correlation $c(ModifyMatches, match.jsp^1)$ does not hold, because the same instance $match.jsp^1$ exploited by p_1 and p_2 which implement $ModifyMatches$, is also exploited by p_3 that does not implement $ModifyMatches$. Moreover, the correlation $c(AddMatches, DeleteMatch.java^1)$ does not hold, because except p_2, the products p_1 and p_3 implement the feature $AddMatches$ without exploiting any instance of the asset $DeleteMatch.java$. A correlation between a feature and an asset is identified if there exists at least one of the instances of the asset in correlation with the feature. Thus, given a feature f and an asset a, a correlation $c(f, a)$ holds if $\exists a^i \in AI(a) \land c(f, a^i)$.

We consider an $\mathcal{SPL}$ *complete* if each of its features, assets and asset instances has at least one correlation. To guarantee the *completeness* of an $\mathcal{SPL}$, we impose the following rules: given two products $(p_j, p_k) \in \mathcal{P}$, ① there has to be at least a feature in common between them which is the root feature, ② no two products have exactly the same implementation (same set of asset instances), thus, if $A(p_j) = A(p_k) \Rightarrow AI(p_j) \neq AI(p_k)$, ③ if p_k implements all the features implemented by p_j and more, p_k has to employ all the assets employed by p_j and – not necessarily but most likely – more, thus, if $F(p_j) \subset F(p_k) \Rightarrow A(p_j) \subseteq A(p_k)$.

2.2 Product Configuration and Derivation

A *restrictive FM* allows an automated derivation of the exact set of products $\mathcal{P}$ provided by the $\mathcal{SPL}$. However, a software engineer might be interested in creating a product that is not provided by the $\mathcal{SPL}$, such as p_4 that implements the features *ManageMatches*, *AddMatches* and *DeleteMatches*. Thus, we define a *free FM*, a constraint-free version of the *restrictive FM* where all features except the root are optional. Hence, a *free FM* allows a software engineer to select the features required for a *desired* product, in addition to extension points allowing to add new features that are not provided yet by the $\mathcal{SPL}$.

We define a configuration cf consisting of two sets of features: $EF(cf)$ the features required for the desired product and offered by the $\mathcal{SPL}$, and $NF(cf)$ the features required and not offered by the $\mathcal{SPL}$. For instance, the configuration cf_4 relative to the derivation of p_4 has $EF(cf_4) = \{ManageMatches, AddMatches, DeleteMatches\}$ and $NF(cf_4) = \{\phi\}$. When $NF \neq \{\phi\}$, software engineers are asked to determine the assets to be added and/or modified to introduce the new features. Inspired from [13], we categorize the potential products to achieve a certain configuration into three categories: given a product p and a configuration cf, ① p *realizes* cf if $EF(cf) = F(p)$, ② p *covers* cf if $EF(cf) \subset F(p)$, ③ p *contributes in* cf if $EF(cf) \not\subset F(p) \wedge \exists f \mid f \in EF(cf) \wedge f \in F(p)$. If no product *realizes* a certain configuration, several scenarios might be possible to achieve the configuration. Hence, we identify for each configuration cf a set of *configuration scenarios* $\{cs_1(cf), ..., cs_n(cf)\}$. A configuration scenario $cs_i(cf)$ is defined as a pair $\langle \{\langle p_k, \{f_q, ..., f_s\}\rangle\}, \{f_x, ..., f_z\}\rangle$, where $\{\langle p_k, \{f_q, ..., f_s\}\rangle\}$ is a combination of products where each p_k *covers* or *contributes in* cf, while $\{f_q, ..., f_s\}$ refers to the *unrequired features* of p_k and $\{f_x, ..., f_z\}$ is $NF(cf)$, if any. Table 3 shows the possible configuration scenarios for cf_4.

A configuration scenario is a way to identify the suitable assets and operations to perform over their instances to achieve the configuration. An asset a is required

Table 3. Possible configuration scenarios for configuration cf_4

cs_1	$\langle\{\langle p_2, \{ModifyMatches\}\rangle\}, \{\phi\}$
cs_2	$\langle\{\langle p_1, \{ModifyMatches\}\rangle, \langle p_2, \{ModifyMatches\}\rangle\}, \{\phi\}$
cs_3	$\langle\{\langle p_2, \{ModifyMatches\}\rangle, \langle p_3, \{\phi\}\rangle\}, \{\phi\}$
cs_4	$\langle\{\langle p_1, \{ModifyMatches\}\rangle, \langle p_2, \{ModifyMatches\}\rangle, \langle p_3, \{\phi\}\rangle\}, \{\phi\}$

for a configuration cf if $F(a) \cap EF(cf) \neq \{\phi\}$ where $F(a) = \{f_j \mid c(f_j, a)\}$. We define three types of actions that can be performed on an asset instance:

1. Clone and Retain (CRT): consists of cloning a required asset instance and retaining it as it is, without modifying its implementation.
2. Clone and Remove (CRM): consists of cloning a required asset instance, and removing from it the implementation fragments corresponding to the features that it is in correlation with but are not required by the configuration.
3. Extract and Add (ETA): consists of extracting from an asset instance the implementation fragments of some features required by the configuration, and adding them to a cloned asset instance under construction. An ETA action is used only as a subsequent to a CRT or CRM action.

We define an *action* ac as a triple $\langle type, a^i, \{f_j, ..., f_n\}\rangle$, where $type$ is one of the action types defined earlier $\{CRT, CRM, ETA\}$. For CRT and CRM, a^i is the asset instance to clone, while for ETA, a^i is the asset instance to extract from. $\{f_j, ..., f_n\}$ is the set of features to be removed or extracted from a^i, if $type$ is CRM or ETA respectively. Hence, we define an *operation* op as a triple $\langle a, \{ac_1, ..., ac_n\}, a^i\rangle$ where a is the operation asset, $\{ac_1, ..., ac_n\}$ noted as $AC(op)$ is the set of actions to be made to obtain the suitable asset instance a^i. For instance, the operation $\langle style.css, \{\langle CRM, style.css^1, \{ModifyMatches\}\rangle, \langle ETA, style.css^2, \{DeleteMatches\}\rangle\}, style.css^4\rangle$ consists of cloning the asset instance $style.css^1$ and removing from it the feature $ModifyMatches$, then extracting the feature $DeleteMatches$ from $style.css^2$ and adding the extraction to the clone, which produces a new instance $style.css^4$. Several operations might be identified for a required asset, where only one of them has to be chosen.

A software engineer might be interested in choosing the configuration scenario dealing with the products that she is most familiar with, or that involves the least number of products (i.e. cs_1 involves only p_2), or the one having the least number of operations that require a modification of assets (i.e. cs_3 requires less modifications than cs_1). For these purposes, we auto-generate an FM (see Fig. 2) based on the identified configuration scenarios and operations. The generated FM uses a classic FM formalism, but serves only in supporting the selection of the operations. If one of the operations has a CRT action, it is chosen by default since it does not involve any modification to the asset instance in concern. The generated FM can be configured from several dimensions. A software engineer can make her choice of operations within or outside a configuration scenario, and she can deselect the products or asset instances that she is not familiar with as well, in order to reduce the possible choices.

It is essential to permit the reuse of the newly derived products. Therefore, to enable an incremental evolution of the $\mathcal{SPL}$, we enrich the $\mathcal{SPL}$ with the derived products. We perform a *FAMILIAR merge* operation [14] on the *restrictive FM* and the newly derived product FM to obtain an updated *restrictive FM*. As well, we re-generate the *free FM* and we update the correlations.

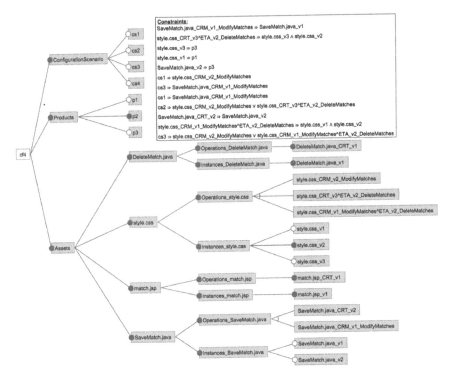

Fig. 2. Generated FM upon configuration of cf_4

3   Experiments and Limitations

We demonstrate the feasibility of our approach on a case study of 8 PVs, by performing an incremental derivation and integration of 5 PVs into an SPL composed initially of 3 PVs. The SPL comprises when it has its 8 PVs a total of 93 features, 271 assets and 296 asset instances with an average of 66 features, 214 assets and 4.7KLOCs per PV. Table 4 illustrates some significant metrics that we collected from the configurations. Metrics show that the number of configuration scenarios per configuration increases as long as the SPL becomes rich. Further, despite that the number of required assets can be large, the number of operations to perform might be few. The interest in our approach is that it can identify the assets to be modified and the ones to retain without modification. Further, the deselection of some undesired products or asset instances from the generated FM considerably reduces the choice of a configuration scenario. Moreover, metrics show that, if selection is made by operations regardless the configuration scenarios that they belong to, the number of operations to perform is less, compared to a selection made by configuration scenario. Thus, a software engineer who is familiar with the SPL can rely on this dimension.

A limitation of our approach is that it is dependent on the architecture of the developed SPL. A change in structure or naming of the SPL artifacts affects

Table 4. Metrics of 5 sequential configurations to derive new PVs

Configuration	cf_4	cf_5	cf_6	cf_7	cf_8
NB of CSs	7	10	16	48	56
AVG NB of Products per CS	1.714	2.5	3	3.3	4.214
NB of required Assets	185	221	211	211	244
NB of Assets to modify if selection made by OPs	4	3	2	2	2
AVG NB of Assets to modify if selection made by CSs	7.143	3.5	4.5	3.167	2.286
NB of features added by the configuration	0	0	25	0	0
NB of Assets added after derivation	0	0	8	0	24
NB of Asset instances added after derivation	3	1	11	1	25

NB: number – AVG: average – CS: configuration scenario – OP: operation

the identified correlations. However, adhering to the proposed operations during product derivation avoids such inconsistencies. Another limitation is that correlations are identified at file level, while several related works when performing feature location, map features to implementation blocks of several files. Such techniques can be complementary to our approach, since we consider that guidance is the most meaningful when provided at file level.

4 Related Work

Fischer et al. developed the *ECCO* approach [7] that allows an automated derivation of existing PVs and supports the derivation of new PVs by an automated extraction of the required artifacts, and a guidance during the manual completion of the PV. Further, it allows an incremental enrichment of the new PVs. In our approach, we focus on guiding developers in manual derivation, since we consider automated derivation can degrade ownership level and trust of developers in the newly derived products. Martinez et al. proposed a bottom-up extractive approach that migrates PVs from several artifact types into an SPL [11]. The approach performs feature identification when features are not provided, and feature location when features are known. Moreover, it provides word cloud visualization, which helps software engineers to name the identified features. This proposed approach allows an automated derivation of existing and new PVs as well, however, contrarely to our approach the new PVs cannot be incrementally integrated in the SPL. Rubin and Chechik proposed a framework to manage PVs developed using C&O approach [15]. They consider features as the main unit of reuse and they define a set of useful operators to manage PVs and derive new ones. Narwane et al. define operators to investigate traceability between features and assets [13]. Although the functionality of some operators from [13,15] are provided by our approach, we consider that integrating these operators in our approach can be an added value.

5   Conclusion and Future Work

In this paper, we presented our approach in guiding software engineers to derive new PVs based on C&O and incrementally integrating them into an SPL. Our experiments showed that the configuration scenarios and operations to perform that we propose upon a new configuration can guide software engineers to construct new PVs, so they can maintain their ownership and trust on the developed PVs since they built it by themselves. As future work, we plan to enhance the provided guidance by a cost estimation for the identified operations, so software engineers can rely on it as an additional parameter during derivation. Further, we aim to compare our approach to related works, and measure its effectiveness in terms of efforts and time saving when compared to the classic C&O approach.

References

1. Clements, P., Northrop, L.: Software Product Lines: Practices and Patterns. Addison-Wesley, Boston (2001)
2. Berger, T., Lettner, D., Rubin, J., Grünbacher, P., Silva, A., Becker, M., Chechik, M., Czarnecki, K.: What is a feature? A qualitative study of features in industrial software product lines. In: Proceedings of the 19th International Software Product Line Conference, pp. 16–25 (2015)
3. Kang, K.C., Cohen, S.G., Hess, J.A., Novak, W.E., Peterson, A.S.: Feature-Oriented Domain Analysis (FODA) Feasibility Study. Carnegie-Mellon Univ Pittsburgh Pa Software Engineering Inst. (1990)
4. Bagheri, E., Ensan, F., Gasevic, D., Boskovic, M.: Modular feature models: representation and configuration. J. Res. Pract. Inf. Technol. **43**(2), 109 (2011)
5. Pohl, K., Böckle, G., van der Linden, F.J.: Software Product Line Engineering: Foundations, Principles and Techniques. Springer, Heidelberg (2005). https://doi.org/10.1007/3-540-28901-1
6. Lapeña, R., Ballarin, M., Cetina, C.: Towards clone-and-own support: locating relevant methods in legacy products. In: Proceedings of the 20th International Systems and Software Product Line Conference, Beijing, China, pp. 194–203 (2016)
7. Fischer, S., Linsbauer L., Lopez-Herrejon, R.E., Egyed, A.: Enhancing clone-and-own with systematic reuse for developing software variants. In: Proceedings of IEEE International Conference on Software Maintenance and Evolution, pp. 391–400 (2014)
8. Dubinsky, Y., Rubin, J., Berger, T., Duszynski, S., Becker, M., Czarnecki, K.: An exploratory study of cloning in industrial software product lines. In: 17th European Conference on Software Maintenance and Reengineering (CSMR), pp. 25–34 (2013)
9. Ziadi, T., Henard, C., Papadakis, M., Ziane, M., Le Traon, Y.: Towards a language-independent approach for reverse-engineering of software product lines. In: Proceedings of the 29th Annual ACM Symposium on Applied Computing, pp. 1064–1071 (2014)
10. Krueger, C.W.: Easing the transition to software mass customization. In: van der Linden, F. (ed.) PFE 2001. LNCS, vol. 2290, pp. 282–293. Springer, Heidelberg (2002). https://doi.org/10.1007/3-540-47833-7_25
11. Martinez, J., Ziadi, T., Bissyandé, T.F., Klein, J., Le Traon, Y.: Bottom-up adoption of software product lines: a generic and extensible approach. In: Proceedings of the 19th International Software Product Line Conference, pp. 101–110 (2015)

12. Assunção, W.K.G., Lopez-Herrejon, R.E., Linsbauer, L., Vergilio, S.R., Egyed, A.: Reengineering legacy applications into software product lines: a systematic mapping. Empirical Softw. Eng. **22**(6), 2972–3016 (2017)
13. Narwane, G.K., Duarte, J.G., Krishna, S.N., Benavides, D., Millo, J., Ramesh, S.: Traceability analyses between features and assets in software product lines. Entropy MDPI **18**(8), 269 (2016)
14. Acher, M., Collet, P., Lahire, P., France, R.B.: FAMILIAR: a domain-specific language for large scale management of feature models. Sci. Comput. Program. **78**, 657–681 (2013)
15. Rubin, J., Czarnecki, K., Chechik, M.: Managing cloned variants: a framework and experience. In: Proceedings of the 17th International Software Product Line Conference, pp. 101–110 (2013)

Supporting Product Line Adoption by Combining Syntactic and Textual Feature Extraction

András Kicsi[1]([✉]), László Vidács[1,2], Viktor Csuvik[1], Ferenc Horváth[1],
Árpád Beszédes[1], and Ferenc Kocsis[3]

[1] Department of Software Engineering, University of Szeged, Szeged, Hungary
{akicsi,lac,csuvikv,hferenc,beszedes}@inf.u-szeged.hu
[2] MTA-SZTE Research Group on Artificial Intelligence, University of Szeged,
Szeged, Hungary
[3] SZEGED Software Ltd., Szeged, Hungary
kocsis.ferenc@szegedsw.hu

Abstract. Software product line (SPL) architecture facilitates systematic reuse to serve specific feature requests of new customers. Our work deals with the adoption of SPL architecture in an existing legacy system. In this case, the extractive approach of SPL adoption turned out to be the most viable method, where the system is redesigned keeping variants within the same code base. The analysis of the feature structure is a crucial point in this process as it involves both domain experts working at a higher level of abstraction and developers working directly on the program code. In this work, we propose an automatic method to extract feature-to-program connections starting from a very high level set of features provided by domain experts and existing program code. The extraction is performed by combining and further processing call graph information on the code with textual similarity between code and high level features. The context of our work is an industrial SPL adoption project of a large scale logistical information system written in an 4G language, Magic. We demonstrate the benefits of the combined method and its use by different stakeholders in this project.

Keywords: Product lines · SPL · Feature extraction
Variability mining · Magic · 4GL · Information retrieval · Call graphs

1 Introduction

Maintaining parallel versions of a software satisfying various customer needs is challenging. Many times the clone-and-own solution [1] is chosen because of short term time and effort constraints. As the number of product variants increases, a more viable solution is needed through systematic code level reuse. A natural step towards more effective development is the adoption of product line architecture [2]. The extractive approach analyzes existing products to obtain feature models and build the product line architecture [3]. An advantage of the

© Springer International Publishing AG, part of Springer Nature 2018
R. Capilla et al. (Eds.): ICSR 2018, LNCS 10826, pp. 148–163, 2018.
https://doi.org/10.1007/978-3-319-90421-4_10

extractive approach in general is that several reverse engineering methods exist to support feature extraction and analysis [4–6].

Product line adoption is usually approached from three directions: the proactive approach starts with domain analysis and applies variability management from scratch. The reactive approach incrementally replies to the new customer needs when they arise. When there are already a number of systems in production, the extractive approach seems to be the most feasible choice. During the extractive approach the adoption process benefits from systematic reuse of existing design and architectural knowledge.

In this paper, we report on an ongoing product line adoption project in which the extractive approach is being used. Our subject is a legacy high market value, wholesaler logistics system, which was adapted to various domains in the past using clone-and-own method. It is developed using a fourth generation language (4GL) technology, Magic [7], and in this project the product line architecture is to be built based on an existing set of products developed in the Magic XPA language. Although there is reverse engineering support for usual maintenance activities [8,9], the special structure of Magic programs makes it necessary to experiment with targeted solutions for coping with features. Furthermore, approaches used in mainstream languages like Java or C++ need to be re-considered in the case of systems developed in 4GLs. For instance, in the traditional sense there is no source code, rather the developer sets up user interface and data processing units in a development environment and the flow of the program follows a well-defined structure.

In this work, we concentrate on the feature identification and analysis phase of the project and describe an efficient method for this purpose. This is a well studied topic in the literature for mainstream languages [5], but the same for 4GL is less explored. The method starts from a very high level set of features provided by domain experts, and uses information extracted from the existing program code. The extraction is performed by combining and further processing call graph information on the code with textual similarity between code and high level features, essentially working simultaneously with structural (syntactic) and conceptual (text based) information. Similar approaches have been previously proposed for traditional object oriented systems, e.g. by Al-msie'deen et al. [10].

In previous work [11], we presented our information retrieval approach to feature extraction similar to our textual analysis, but that information alone proved to be very noisy and incomplete. We not only combine conceptual information with structural one, but present an efficient method for filtering the data as well. This results in a set of information that is more suitable for performing the SPL adoption by various stakeholders of the project including domain experts, architects and programmers. In summary, the contributions of this paper are the following:

1. A method for feature extraction by combining syntactic and textual information.
2. Details for applying the approach in an 4GL technology, and the associated experimental results.

3. Details on the use of the approach in an ongoing SPL adoption industrial project from various stakeholder perspectives.

The paper is organized as follows. We present the background of our project with the peculiarities of the underlying technology and the overview of our method in Sect. 2. The details of our method for combining structural and conceptual feature extraction for Magic systems and the associated experimental results are presented in Sect. 3. Section 4 deals with the benefits of the approach and how it is used in other phases of the SPL adoption project. Related work is briefly introduced in Sect. 5, before concluding the paper Sect. 6.

2   Feature Extraction and Abstraction of Magic Applications

2.1   Product Line Adoption in a Clone-and-Own Environment

The decision of migrating to a new product line architecture is hard to make. Usually there is a high number of derived specific products and the adoption process poses several risks and may take months [12–14]. The subject system of our analysis is a leading pharmaceutical wholesaler logistics system started more than 30 years ago. Meanwhile more than 20 derived variants of the system were introduced at various complexity and maturity levels with independent life cycles and isolated maintenance. Our industrial partner is the developer of market leading solutions in the region, which are implemented in the Magic XPA 4GL language.

This work is part of an industrial project aiming to create a well-designed product line architecture over the isolated variants. The existing set of products provide appropriate environment for an extractive SPL adoption approach. Characterizing features is usually a manual or semi-automated task, where domain experts, product owners and developers co-operate. Our aim is to help this process by automatic analysis of the relation of higher level features and map program level entities to features.

The 4GL environment used to implement the systems requires different approaches and analysis tools than today's mainstream languages like Java [8,15]. For example there is no source code in its traditional sense. The developers work in a fully fledged development environment by customizing several properties of programs. Magic program analysis tool support is not comparable to mainstream languages, hence this is a research-intensive project. In our current work we used our previously available tools for static analysis of Magic applications and IR-based feature extraction [11].

The feature extraction process is challenged, since product variants themselves are written in 4 different language versions as shown in Fig. 1. In case of the oldest Magic V5 systems, there is a high demand on the migration to a newer version. UniPaaS 1.9 introduced huge changes in the language by using the .NET engine for applications. Most systems are implemented in that version. The newest Magic XPA 3.x line of the language lies close to the uniPaaS v1.9

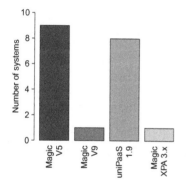

Fig. 1. The magic language versions of the 19 currently active product variants

Table 1. Overview of the common program base of application variants

Variants	Largest application size		
	Programs	Models	Tables
19	4 251	822	1 065

systems. The overall size of the common codebase of product variants is shown in Table 1. The first column states that there are 19 currently active variants of the application, while the remaining columns contain the main specifications of the largest variant. Magic is a data-intensive language, which clearly reflects on these values as well, containing a large amount of data tables.

2.2 Feature Extraction Approach

During product line adoption's feature extraction phase various artifacts are obtained to identify features in an application [16]. This phase is also related to feature location. The analysis phase targets common and variable properties of features and prepares the reengineering phase. This last phase migrates the subject system to the product line architecture.

In this phase of the research project we address the feature extraction phase. Our inputs are the high level features of the system and the program code. We apply a semi-automated process as in [4]. High level features are collected by domain experts from the developer company. The actual task is to establish a link between features and main components of the Magic applications. Although there exists a common analysis infrastructure for reverse engineering 4GL languages [8,9,17], the actual program models differ.

Figure 2 illustrates our current approach to feature extraction. We assign a number of elements for each high level feature, this information helping the work of developers and domain experts working on the new product line architecture. During the assignment we mainly rely on structural information attained on call dependency by constructing a call graph of the variant in question. This results in high number of located elements, crucial for the development of product line architecture, but the large amount of data can be hard to grasp in its entirety.

We combine this method with information retrieval, which can also make it easier to cope with a 4GL language by utilizing conceptual connections, and is successfully applied in software development tasks, such as in traceability

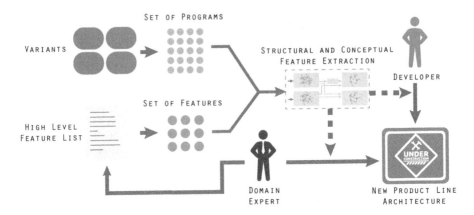

Fig. 2. An illustration of feature extraction as a part of product line adoption

scenarios for object oriented languages [18]. A comprehensive overview of Natural Language Processing (NLP) techniques – including Latent Semantic Indexing, the technique we chose – is provided by Falessi et al. [19]. In our previous work [11] we already presented our LSI-based approach to feature extraction. LSI is already known to be capable of producing quality results combined with structural information [10].

2.3   The Structure of a Magic Application

Being a fourth generation language, Magic does not completely follow the structure of a traditional programming language. Figure 3 represents the most important components of the Magic language from our current point of view.

Each software written in Magic is called an application. These can be built up from one or more projects. In turn, each project can have any number of programs which contain the actual logic of the software. The tasks branching

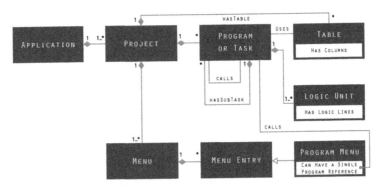

Fig. 3. Illustration on the elements of a magic application

directly from a project are called programs. These can have their own subtasks and be called anywhere in the project like methods in a traditional programming environment, however their subtasks can only be called by the (sub)task containing them. Any task or subtask can access data through tables.

It is also possible for a program to be called through menus, which are controls designed to provide user intervention and usually start a process by calling programs. Having sufficient information on menus, we used these as a base for the call graph in structural feature extraction, deriving calls from menus.

3 Feature Extraction Experiments

In this section we present the feature extraction methods used based on call dependency and textual similarity, as well as the combination and possible filtering options. Figure 4 illustrates the processes described in this section. Our static analysis is specific to the Magic language. One of the variants of our subject system was selected by domain experts to be used as a starting point for the product line adoption. It is a specific variant involving 4251 programs, 822 models and 1065 data tables. Our experiments presented in this paper were done on this specific variant. We have been provided with a feature list structured in a tree format consisting of three levels which have 10, 42 and 118 unique elements respectively. From these we chose the upper level to display our results, the features of this level are listed in Fig. 5. The numbers shown here are in accordance with the numbers we present on our later graph examples.

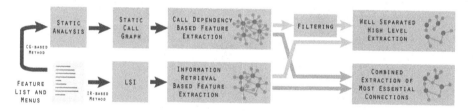

Fig. 4. A more detailed view on the feature extraction process

1 – Manufacturing	6 – Administrator interventions
2 – Interface	7 – Supplier order management
3 – Access management	8 – Invoicing
4 – Quality control	9 – Master file maintenance
5 – Stock control	10 – Customer order reception

Fig. 5. The higher level features of the system

3.1 Feature Extraction Using (task) Call Dependency

This approach relies mostly on the program structure, but especially on the call dependencies between programs and task. To construct a call graph from these dependencies we use the process that can be seen in Fig. 6. For the sake of simplicity, this figure represents only a minimalistic example of a Magic application. We emphasis tasks and programs with squares, while other program elements like projects, logic units, logic lines, etc. are shown as circles.

We have the abstract semantic graph (ASG) as the base, which is provided by our static source code analyzer tool. As the next step we add the call edges to the graph by examining Magic components that operate as calls between tasks and programs. Finally, in the last two step of the process we eliminate some nodes and edges from the graph, keeping only the necessary ones *i.e.,* call edges, tasks and programs. From the CG we obtain the features by running a customized breadth-first search algorithm from specific staring points determined by menu entries. In Fig. 7 a graph representation of the CG based results can be seen.

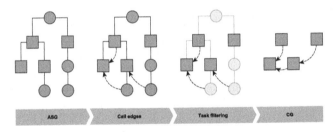

Fig. 6. The process of calculating the call graph

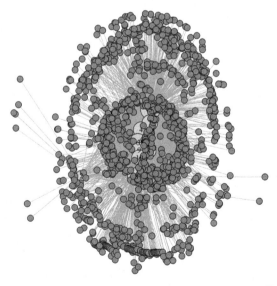

Fig. 7. Graph visualization of the set of results obtained by the call graph technique

3.2   Textual Similarity

Information retrieval (IR) techniques focus on the information content of data, dealing with natural language at a semantic level. This results in a more versatile approach concerning the form of the data, like the language used. In our specific case this can be a huge boon, since the systems processed use different versions of the Magic language, and this would cause serious problems for a technique dealing with the specific syntax of the language. With IR techniques on the other hand, we can process the natural language parts of code, freeing us from the burden of having to solve differences of language versions and syntax of Magic. Latent Semantic Indexing (LSI) [20] is an IR technique capable of measuring semantic similarity between textual data. It is widely used throughout software engineering, mainly in cases involving natural language.

A more complete summary of our feature extraction work with LSI is presented in our previous work. Our current experiments differ from these in some respects, the main differences being that these experiments work on a completely different base variant of the system, and consider the top level of features of an updated, more precise feature list obtained from domain experts.

In Fig. 8 we can see a graph representation of the results of the top features paired with the programs of a system. Though the structural information obtained from call graph is more thorough, it is more suitable for the developers rather than domain experts. With purely structural information it is hard to separate along the features, having many programs laying the groundwork for any single feature it is hard to grasp the overall aim. Conceptual analysis

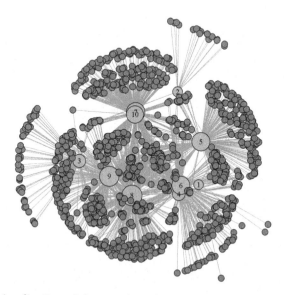

Fig. 8. Graph visualization of the set of results obtained by the information retrieval technique

separates more agreeably along the semantics of the feature, hence it can be more valuable for domain experts.

3.3   Combined Technique

As already introduced, the two methods we used for program assignment to features use fundamentally different methods for achieving their results. Consequently, the results themselves also show a significant difference, overlapping only partially. The set of programs for the techniques presented are shown on the left side of Fig. 9. Each slice of the diagram represents a top level feature and its colors indicate the number of programs detected by each technique. IR represents the result set of the information retrieval technique, CG represents the pairs attained by call graph, while ESS represents the set of programs considered most essential, detected by both techniques. The left side of Fig. 11 shows the number of programs assigned in each set, the abbreviations match the ones explained for the previous figure.

The call graph dependency technique produces vast amounts of matches for each feature. These matches build on the real calls inside the code, hence they

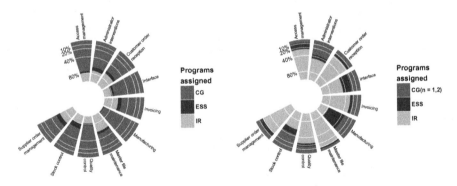

Fig. 9. The size of our result sets for each feature. Results shown on the left, results with filtering on the right (Color figure online)

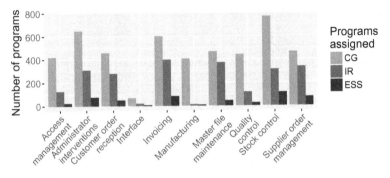

Fig. 10. Number of programs found most essential for each feature

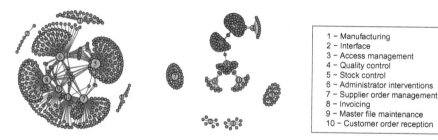

Fig. 11. Graph visualization of the set of programs deemed most essential. Results shown on the left, results with filtering on the right

are considered a reliable source of information. It is important to note that this is only static and not dynamic call information, thus at runtime it is not necessary for every call to occur. The abundance of programs found by this technique can undoubtedly be useful for developers, but it also presents a problem of coping with the large amount of data not distinguishable in any manner.

The conceptual method produces fewer programs for each feature, but further examination of random cases revealed that even considering this, a significant amount of noise presents itself. Textual similarity works with very little information in these cases, hence it is likely for similar wording or more general words like "list" to produce misleading matches, occurring in the text of many features.

Looking at only the intersection of the connections found by these two techniques we find that this set of connections takes into account both the structural and conceptual information, producing only connections which are indeed present on both levels. This results in a clearer, more straightforward set of connections, which contains the most essential findings of the two techniques (Fig. 10).

As we could see before, the structural information produces a rather large amount of matches for each feature, and we observed that there is a considerable overlap between features. We decided to attempt to clear these matches too with a filtering technique applied on the structural information output, which filters out less specific programs. The filtering technique works with a number n, which denotes the maximal number of features a program can connect before it is considered less specific and is filtered out from the program set of features. This removes the programs with less information value and results in even more straightforward groups of programs for each feature. On the right side of Figs. 9 and 11 we can see the results of the common structural and conceptual connections of this filtered approach, featuring only programs with maximum two connections. It is apparent from the graph that features are much better separated, providing a suitable high level glance at the background of features without much technical details, ideal for top level understanding.

Examining the graphs we can come to many interesting conclusions. For example feature number 7 is behaving like any other feature considering the purely conceptual or purely structural viewpoint, its common graph provides a clearer picture, apparently connecting through a group of more general features to large number of other features. In the filtered case however, it is nicely separated with a group of unique programs specific to the feature itself.

4   Discussion

Figure 12 highlights how various feature extraction techniques can be used to help in building the new product line architecture.

- Structural Extraction - Provides a detailed, widespread analysis. It is good for developers, since they are required to have knowledge of all of the programs called by a feature, too much for domain experts.
- Conceptual Extraction - For domain experts on the other hand, all called programs can be too much. This approach however introduces conceptual dependencies, although with too much noise for smooth work.
- Combination (ESS) - Grasps the essence of features, more fit for domain experts. While constructing the new architecture, the domain experts need to judge properly which parts of the variants should be adopted. In this decision making process the results of this extraction highly decreases complexity, additionally in the future it can facilitate test planning.

Besides these, we would like to mention some other possible ways to use the results. Firstly, connections are not necessarily observable through the calls of the system, programs can for instance connect by accessing to the same data objects. This means that not every connection will present itself on the call graph. These however can be found via conceptual feature extraction, since it is likely that programs using the same data are conceptually connected to the same feature. This is why the programs detected by the conceptual extraction

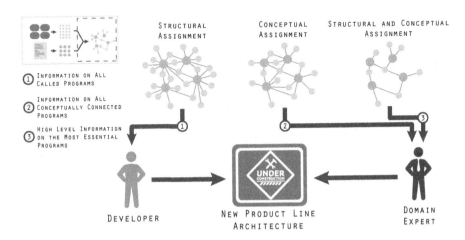

Fig. 12. The possible ways of usage of the results of various feature extraction techniques in helping product line adoption

and not discovered via structural information can still be valuable. This data is rather noisy, but still represents a ready source of the semantically connected programs to each feature, hence it can be a reliable starting point with manual evaluation for domain experts looking for connected programs.

Additionally, the structural information produced can be tailored according to our intent, filtering out the more general programs, which provides the possibility to form even better separated sets of programs, making it easier to attain a high level knowledge about the procedures and the basic structure of a system.

We provided our results to our industrial partner, who has already commenced on constructing the new SPL architecture. The work is proceeding well, product line adoption seems to go according the plans and the results of our experiments are utilized in the process.

5   Related Work

The literature of reverse engineering 4GL languages is not extensive. By the time the 4GL paradigm arisen, most papers coped with the role of those languages in software development, including discussions demonstrating their viability. The paradigm is still successful, although only a few works are published about the automatic analysis and modeling 4GL or specifically Magic applications. The maintenance of Magic applications is supported by cost estimation and quality analysis methods [17,21,22]. Architectural analysis, reverse engineering and optimization are visible topics in the Magic community [8,9,15,23], and after some years of Magic development migration to object-oriented languages [24] as well.

SPL has a widespread literature, and over the last 8–10 years it has gained even more popularity. All three phases of feature analysis (identification, analysis, and transformation) are tackled by researchers. A recommended mapping study on recent works on feature location can be read in [5].

Software product line extraction is a time-consuming task. To speed up this activity, many semi-automatic approaches has been proposed [25–27]. Reverse engineering is a popular approach which has recently received an increased attention from the research community. With this technique missing parts can be recovered, feature models can be extracted a set of features, etc. [25,28]. Applying these approaches companies can migrate their system into a software product line. However, changing to a new development process is risky and may have unnecessary costs. The work of Krüger et al. [29] supports cost estimations for the extractive approaches and provides a basis for further research.

Feature models are considered first class artifacts in variability modeling. Haslinger et al. [27] present an algorithm that reverse engineers a FM for a given SPL from feature sets which describe the characteristics each product variant provides. She et al. [30] analyze Linux kernel (which is a standard subject in variability analysis) configurations to obtain feature models. LSI is applied for recovering traceability links between various software artifacts. The work of Marcus and Maletic [18] is an early paper on applying LSI for this purpose. Eyal-Salman et al. [6] use LSI for recovering traceability link between features and source code with about 80% success rate, but experiments are done only for a small set of features of a simple java program. IR-based solution for feature extraction is combined with structural information in the work of Al-msie'deen et al. [10]. Further research deals with constraints in a semi-automatic way [31] both for functional and even nonfunctional [32] feature requirements.

A possible future goal could be to make the system dynamically configurable, which is a problem known as Dynamic SPL [33–39]. Today, many application domains demand runtime reconfiguration, for which the two main limitations are handling structural changes dynamically and checking the consistency of the evolved structural variability model during runtime [36]. However, as reported in [40], the current research on runtime variability is still heavily based on the decisions made during design time. Coping with uncertainty of dynamic changes also needs to be addressed [41].

Several existing approaches can be adapted to 4GL environment, although none of the above cited papers cope with 4GL product lines directly.

6   Conclusions

An ongoing industrial project was presented, which undergoes a software product line adoption process. In this work, we concentrated on the feature extraction and analysis aspects of the project, which are fundamental parts of the effort because further architecture redesign and implementation are and will be based on this information. For feature extraction we used two fundamental approaches: one based on computing structural information form the code in for of call-graphs, and the other in which conceptual information was automatically extracted from the textual representation of high level feature models and the code. However, the combination of the two pieces of information had to be performed and processed in such a way that the resulting models are most useful for project participants.

Experimental results show that the final models are significantly more com-prehensible, and hence directly usable (though in various forms) by domain experts, architects, developers and other stakeholders of the project. The extracted information and the associated toolset is currently in use by our indus-trial partner in this ongoing effort, however in later phases further refinements of the approach are to be expected. For instance, (semi-)automatic classification of the feature sets will probably be needed.

Although the approach was implemented in Magic, a 4GL technology, we believe that the fundamental method could be suitable for other more traditional paradigms as well after the necessary adaptations.

Acknowledgment. Ferenc Kocsis was supported in part by the Hungarian national grant GINOP-2.1.1-15-2015-00370. András Kicsi, László Vidács, Viktor Csuvik, Ferenc Horváth and Árpád Beszédes were supported in part by the European Union, co-financed by the European Social Fund (EFOP-3.6.3-VEKOP-16-2017-00002).

References

1. Fischer, S., Linsbauer, L., Lopez-Herrejon, R.E., Egyed, A.: Enhancing clone-and-own with systematic reuse for developing software variants. In: 2014 IEEE International Conference on Software Maintenance and Evolution, pp. 391–400. IEEE, September 2014
2. Clements, P., Northrop, L.: Software Product Lines: Practices and Patterns. Addison-Wesley Professional, Reading (2001)
3. Krueger, C.W.: Easing the transition to software mass customization. In: van der Linden, F. (ed.) PFE 2001. LNCS, vol. 2290, pp. 282–293. Springer, Heidelberg (2002). https://doi.org/10.1007/3-540-47833-7_25
4. Kästner, C., Dreiling, A., Ostermann, K.: Variability mining: consistent semi-automatic detection of product-line features. IEEE Trans. Softw. Eng. 40(1), 67–82 (2014)
5. Assunção, W.K.G., Vergilio, S.R.: Feature location for software product line migration. In: Proceedings of the 18th International Software Product Line Conference on Companion Volume for Workshops, Demonstrations and Tools - SPLC 2014, pp. 52–59. ACM Press, New York (2014)
6. Eyal-Salman, H., Seriai, A.D., Dony, C., Al-msie'deen, R.: Recovering traceability links between feature models and source code of product variants. In: Proceedings of the VARiability for You Workshop on Variability Modeling Made Useful for Everyone - VARY 2012, pp. 21–25. ACM Press, New York (2012)
7. Magic Software Enterprises Ltd.: Magic Software Enterprises. http://www.magicsoftware.com. Last visited May 2017
8. Nagy, C., Vidács, L., Ferenc, R., Gyimóthy, T., Kocsis, F., Kovács, I.: MAGISTER: quality assurance of magic applications for software developers and end users. In: 26th IEEE International Conference on Software Maintenance, pp. 1–6. IEEE Computer Society, September 2010
9. Nagy, C., Vidács, L., Ferenc, R., Gyimóthy, T., Kocsis, F., Kovács, I.: Solutions for reverse engineering 4GL applications, recovering the design of a logistical wholesale system. In: Proceedings of CSMR 2011 (15th European Conference on Software Maintenance and Reengineering), 343–346. IEEE Computer Society, March 2011
10. Al-msie'deen, R., Seriai, A.D., Huchard, M., Urtado, C., Vauttier, S.: Mining features from the object-oriented source code of software variants by combining lexical and structural similarity. In: 2013 IEEE 14th International Conference on Information Reuse & Integration (IRI), pp. 586–593. IEEE, August 2013
11. Kicsi, A., Vidács, L., Beszédes, A., Kocsis, F., Kovács, I.: Information retrieval based feature analysis for product line adoption in 4GL systems. In: Proceedings of the 17th International Conference on Computational Science and its Applications - ICCSA 2017, pp. 1–6. IEEE (2017)
12. Clements, P.C., Jones, L.G., McGregor, J.D., Northrop, L.M.: Getting there from here: a roadmap for software product line adoption. Commun. ACM 49(12), 33 (2006)
13. Clements, P., Krueger, C.: Eliminating the adoption barrier. IEEE Softw. 19(4), 29–31 (2002)
14. Catal, C.: Cagatay: barriers to the adoption of software product line engineering. ACM SIGSOFT Softw. Eng. Notes 34(6), 1 (2009)
15. Harrison, J.V., Lim, W.M.: Automated reverse engineering of legacy 4GL information system applications using the ITOC workbench. In: Pernici, B., Thanos, C. (eds.) CAiSE 1998. LNCS, vol. 1413, pp. 41–57. Springer, Heidelberg (1998). https://doi.org/10.1007/BFb0054218

16. Ballarin, M., Lapeña, R., Cetina, C.: Leveraging feature location to extract the clone-and-own relationships of a family of software products. In: Kapitsaki, G.M., Santana de Almeida, E. (eds.) ICSR 2016. LNCS, vol. 9679, pp. 215–230. Springer, Cham (2016). https://doi.org/10.1007/978-3-319-35122-3_15

17. Nagy, C., Vidács, L., Ferenc, R., Gyimóthy, T., Kocsis, F., Kovács, I.: Complexity measures in 4GL environment. In: Murgante, B., Gervasi, O., Iglesias, A., Taniar, D., Apduhan, B.O. (eds.) ICCSA 2011. LNCS, vol. 6786, pp. 293–309. Springer, Heidelberg (2011). https://doi.org/10.1007/978-3-642-21934-4_25

18. Marcus, A., Maletic, J.: Recovering documentation-to-source-code traceability links using latent semantic indexing. In: 2003 Proceedings of the 25th International Conference on Software Engineering, pp. 125–135. IEEE (2003)

19. Falessi, D., Cantone, G., Canfora, G.: A comprehensive characterization of NLP techniques for identifying equivalent requirements. In: Proceedings of the 2010 ACM-IEEE International Symposium on Empirical Software Engineering and Measurement - ESEM 2010, p. 1. ACM Press, New York (2010)

20. Deerwester, S.C., Dumais, S.T., Landauer, T.K., Furnas, G.W., Harshman, R.A.: Indexing by latent semantic analysis. J. Am. Soc. Inf. Sci. **41**(6), 391–407 (1990)

21. Verner, J., Tate, G.: Estimating size and effort in fourth-generation development. IEEE Softw. **5**, 15–22 (1988)

22. Witting, G., Finnie, G.: Using artificial neural networks and function points to estimate 4GL software development effort. Australas. J. Inf. Syst. **1**(2), 87–94 (1994)

23. Ocean Software Solutions: Homepage of Magic Optimizer. http://www.magic-optimizer.com. Last visited May 2017

24. M2J Software LLC: Homepage of M2J. http://www.magic2java.com. Last visited May 2017

25. Valente, M.T., Borges, V., Passos, L.: A semi-automatic approach for extracting software product lines. IEEE Trans. Softw. Eng. **38**(4), 737–754 (2012)

26. Assunção, W.K.G., Lopez-Herrejon, R.E., Linsbauer, L., Vergilio, S.R., Egyed, A.: Multi-objective reverse engineering of variability-safe feature models based on code dependencies of system variants. Empirical Softw. Eng. **22**(4), 1763–1794 (2017)

27. Haslinger, E.N., Lopez-Herrejon, R.E., Egyed, A.: Reverse engineering feature models from programs' feature sets. In: 18th Working Conference on Reverse Engineering, pp. 308–312. IEEE, October 2011

28. Lima, C., Chavez, C., de Almeida, E.S.: Investigating the recovery of product line architectures: an approach proposal. In: Botterweck, G., Werner, C. (eds.) ICSR 2017. LNCS, vol. 10221, pp. 201–207. Springer, Cham (2017). https://doi.org/10.1007/978-3-319-56856-0_15

29. Krüger, J., Fenske, W., Meinicke, J., Leich, T., Saake, G.: Extracting software product lines: a cost estimation perspective. In: Proceedings of the 20th International Systems and Software Product Line Conference on - SPLC 2016, pp. 354–361. ACM Press, New York (2016)

30. She, S., Lotufo, R., Berger, T., Wąsowski, A., Czarnecki, K.: Reverse engineering feature models. In: Proceeding of the 33rd International Conference on Software Engineering - ICSE 2011, p. 461. ACM Press, New York (2011)

31. Bagheri, E., Ensan, F., Gasevic, D.: Decision support for the software product line domain engineering lifecycle. Autom. Softw. Eng. **19**(3), 335–377 (2012)

32. Siegmund, N., Rosenmüller, M., Kuhlemann, M., Kästner, C., Apel, S., Saake, G.: SPL conqueror: toward optimization of non-functional properties in software product lines. Softw. Qual. J. **20**(3–4), 487–517 (2012)

33. Lee, K., Kang, K.C., Lee, J.: Concepts and guidelines of feature modeling for product line software engineering. In: Gacek, C. (ed.) ICSR 2002. LNCS, vol. 2319, pp. 62–77. Springer, Heidelberg (2002). https://doi.org/10.1007/3-540-46020-9_5

34. Baresi, L., Quinton, C.: Dynamically evolving the structural variability of dynamic software product lines. In: 10th International Symposium on Software Engineering for Adaptive and Self-Managing Systems (2015)

35. Bashari, M., Bagheri, E., Du, W.: Dynamic software product line engineering: a reference framework. Int. J. Softw. Eng. Knowl. Eng. **27**(02), 191–234 (2017)

36. Capilla, R., Bosch, J., Trinidad, P., Ruiz-Cortés, A., Hinchey, M.: An overview of dynamic software product line architectures and techniques: observations from research and industry. J. Syst. Softw. **91**(1), 3–23 (2014)

37. Uchôa, A.G., Bezerra, C.I.M., Machado, I.C., Monteiro, J.M., Andrade, R.M.C.: ReMINDER: an approach to modeling non-functional properties in dynamic software product lines. In: Botterweck, G., Werner, C. (eds.) ICSR 2017. LNCS, vol. 10221, pp. 65–73. Springer, Cham (2017). https://doi.org/10.1007/978-3-319-56856-0_5

38. Hinchey, M., Park, S., Schmid, K.: Building dynamic software product lines. IEEE Comput. Soc. **45**(10), 22–26 (2012)

39. Lee, J.: A feature-oriented approach to developing dynamically reconfigurable products in product line engineering. In: 10th International Software Product Line Conference, pp. 131–140 (2006)

40. Bencomo, N., Lee, J., Hallsteinsen, S.: How dynamic is your Dynamic Software Product Line? DiVA project (EU FP7 STREP), pp. 61–67 (2010)

41. Classen, A., Hubaux, A., Sanen, F., Truyen, E., Vallejos, J., Costanza, P., De Meuter, W., Heymans, P., Joosen, W.: Modelling variability in self-adaptive systems: towards a research agenda. In: Proceedings of International Workshop on Modularization, Composition and Generative Techniques for Product-Line Engineering, vol. 1(2), pp. 19–26 (2008)

A Delta-Oriented Approach to Support the Safe Reuse of Black-Box Code Rewriters

Benjamin Benni[1]([✉]) [iD], Sébastien Mosser[1], Naouel Moha[2], and Michel Riveill[1]

[1] Université Côte d'Azur, CNRS, I3S, Sophia Antipolis, France
{benni,mosser,riveill}@i3s.unice.fr
[2] Université du Québec à Montréal, Montreal, Canada
moha.naouel@uqam.ca

Abstract. The tedious process of corrective and perfective maintenance is often automated thanks to rewriting rules using tools such as `Spoon` or `Coccinelle`. These tools consider rules as black-boxes, and compose multiple rules by giving the output of a given rewriting as input to the next one. It is up to the developer to identify the right order (if it exists) among all the different rules. In this paper, we define a formal model compatible with the black-box assumption that reifies the modifications (Δs) made by each rule. Leveraging these Δs, we propose a way to safely compose multiple rules when applied to the same program by *(i)* ensuring the isolated application of the different rules and *(ii)* yield unexpected behaviors that were silently ignored before. We assess this approach by applying rewriting rules used to fix anti-patterns existing in Android applications to external pieces of software available on GitHub.

1 Introduction

It is a commonplace to state that "software evolves", and it is part of software developers' duty to support and operate such an evolution. On the one hand, the adaptive and perfective evolution [8] of a piece of software to address new requirements is taken into account by software development methodologies and project management methods [20]. On the other hand, this evolution [8] is not correlated to the addition of immediate business value in the program. It covers time-consuming and error prone activities, including software migration (*e.g.*, moving from `Python 2.x` to `Python 3.x`); framework upgrade (*e.g.*, supporting upcoming versions of `Android` for a mobile application); implementation of best practices that change along time (*e.g.*, following vendor guidelines to rewrite `Docker` deployment descriptors); code refactoring (*e.g.*, to introduce design patterns) or bugs/anti-patterns correction.

The second form of evolution is usually automated as much as possible, using tools working directly on the source code. For example, migrating from `Python 2.x` to `3.x` is automated using the `2to3` shell command [15]. In a broader way, any up-to-date `IDE` provides automated refactoring options to ease the work of software developers. In 2006, Muller *et al.* coined the term of *collateral*

R. Capilla et al. (Eds.): ICSR 2018, LNCS 10826, pp. 164–180, 2018.
https://doi.org/10.1007/978-3-319-90421-4_11

evolution to address the issues that appear when developing linux drivers: the kernel libraries continuously evolve, and device-specific drivers must be ported to support the new APIs. To tame this challenge, they develop the `Coccinelle` tool [13], used to rewrite C code and generate patches automatically applied to the `Linux` kernel to correct bugs or adapt drivers, in a fully automated way. In the `Java` ecosystem, the `Spoon` tool [14] (also released in 2006) allows one to write processors that adapt `Java` source code in various way, such as code refactoring, automated bug-fixing or anti-patterns fixing [5]. At runtime, both tools consider rewriting rules as black boxes, applied to a program to generate a patched one.

Contrarily to *abstract rewriting machines* that focus on the confluence, fixed point identification and termination of the rewriting process [7] for a given set of rewriting rules, the previously cited tools took an opposite point of view. They do not consider the confluence of rules application, and generalize the classical function composition operator ($\circ$) to compose rules: each rule r_i is a black-box that consumes a program p to produce a new program p'. Rules are sequentially applied to the input program to yield the final one, passing intermediate results to each others.

$$p' = apply(p, [r_1, \ldots, r_n]) = r_1 \circ \cdots \circ r_n(p) = r_1(\ldots(r_n(p)))$$

The main issue with this assumption is the impact of overlapping rules on the yielded program. Considering large software systems where separation of concerns matters, each code rewriting function is defined independently. As a consequence, if two rules do not commute ($r_1(r_2(p)) \neq r_2(r_1(p))$), it is up to the developer to *(i)* identify that these rules are conflicting inside the rules sequence, and *(ii)* fix the rules or the application sequence to yield the expected result. Classical term rewriting methods cannot be applied to these tools, as it breaks the underlying black-box assumption: a rewriting function cannot be opened to reason on its intrinsic definition, and only the result of its application on a given program can be analyzed.

In this paper, **we propose an approach to support the safe reuse of code rewriters defined as black-boxes**. The originality of the approach is to reason on the modifications (*i.e.*, the *deltas*) produced by code rewriters, when the application to the program guarantees that each one is successfully applied, or to detect conflicts when relevant. We give in Sect. 2 background information about black-box rewriters, using `Coccinelle` and `Spoon` as examples. Then, Sect. 3 defines a formal model to represent deltas and Sect. 4 describes how conflicts can be identified based on this representation. The approach is implemented in the `Java` ecosystem, and Sect. 5 describes how the contribution is implemented and then applied to identify rewriting conflicts when automatically patching `Android` mobile applications with respect to `Google` guidelines. Finally, Sect. 6 describes related work and Sect. 7 concludes the paper by describing perspectives of this work from both theoretical and empirical point of views.

2   Background and Challenges

In this section, we focus on two tools that exist in the state of practice (Coccinelle and Spoon) to automate code rewriting, so to identify the challenges our contribution addresses.

2.1   Using Coccinelle to Patch the Linux Kernel

As stated in the introduction, the Coccinelle tool is used to automatically fix bugs in the C code that implements the Linux kernel, as well as backporting device-specific drivers [16]. These activities are supported by allowing a software developer to define *semantic patches*. A semantic patch contains *(i)* the declaration of free variables in a header identified by *at* symbols (@@), and *(ii)* the patterns to be matched in the C code coupled to the rewriting rule. Statements to remove from the code are prefixed by a minus symbol (-), statements to be added are prefixed by a plus symbol (+), and placeholders use the . . . wildcard. For example, the rule R_k (Fig. 1a) illustrates how to rewrite legacy code in order to use a new function available in the kernel library instead of the previous API. It describes a semantic patch removing any call to the kernel memory allocation function (kmalloc, *l.5*) that is initialized with 0 values (memset, *l.8*), and replacing it by an atomic call to kzalloc (*l.6*), which do both at the very same time. Wildcards can define guards, for example here the patch cannot be applied if the allocated memory was changed in between (using the **when** keyword). Fig. 1b describes another semantic patch used to fix a very common bug, where the memory initialization is not done properly when using pointers (*l.8*). These two examples are excerpts of the examples available on the tool webpage[1].

Considering these two semantic patches, the intention of applying the first one (R_k) it to use call to kzalloc whenever possible in the source code, and the intention associated to the second one (R_m) is to fix bad memory allocation. In the state of practice, applying the two patches, in any orders, does not produce any error. However, the application order matters. For example, when applied to the sample program p_c described in Fig. 1c:

- $p_{km} = R_k(R_m(p_c))$: The erroneous memset is fixed (Fig. 1c, *l.13*), and as a consequence the kzalloc optimization is also applied to the fixed memset, merging *l.11* and *l.13* into a single memory allocation call. In this order, the two initial intentions are respected in p_{km}: all the erroneous memory allocations are fixed, and the atomic function kzalloc is called whenever possible. This is the expected result depicted in Fig. 1d.
- $p_{mk} = R_m(R_k(p_c))$: In this order, the erroneous memory allocations are fixed after the kzalloc merge. As a consequence, it is possible to forgot some of these kzalloc calls when it implies badly defined memset. Considering p_c, *l.5* and *l.7* are not mergeable until *l.7* pointer is fixed, leading to a program p_{mk} where the intention of R_k is not respected: the kzalloc method is not called whenever it is possible in the final program.

---

[1] http://coccinelle.lip6.fr/impact_linux.php: *(i)* "kzalloc treewide" for R_k and *(ii)* "Fix size given to memset" for R_m.

```
1 @@
2 type T;
3 expression x, E, E1,E2;
4 @@
5 - x = kmalloc(E1,E2);
6 + x = kzalloc(E1,E2);
7 ... when != \( x[...]=E; \| x=E; \)
8 - memset((T) x, 0, E1);
```

```
1 @@
2 type T;
3 T *x;
4 expression E;
5 @@
6
7 - memset(x, E, sizeof(x))
8 + memset(x, E, sizeof(*x))
```

(a) kmalloc∧memset(0) ↦ kzalloc (R_k)

(b) Fix size in memset call (R_m)

```
1 struct Point {
2    double x;
3    double y;
4 };
5 typedef struct Point Point;
6
7 int main()
8 {
9    Point *a;
10   // ....
11   a = kmalloc(sizeof(*a), 0);
12   // not using a
13   memset(a, 0, sizeof(a));
14   // ...
15   return 0;
16 }
```

```
1 struct Point {
2    double x;
3    double y;
4 };
5 typedef struct Point Point;
6
7 int main()
8 {
9    Point *a;
10   // ....
11   a = kzalloc(sizeof(*a), 0);
12   // not using a
13
14   // ...
15   return 0;
16 }
```

(c) Example of a C program (p_c)

(d) Expected program: $R_k(R_m(p_c))$

Fig. 1. Coccinelle: using semantic patches to rewrite C code

2.2 Using Spoon to Fix Anti-patterns in Android Applications

Spoon is a tool defined on top of the Java language, which works at the *Abstract Syntax Tree* (AST) level. It provides the AST of a Java source code and let the developer define her transformations. A Spoon rewriter is modeled as a Processor, which implements an AST to AST transformation. It is a Java class that analyses an AST by filtering portions of it (identified by a method named isToBeProcessed), and applies a process method to each filtered element, modifying this AST. Spoon reifies the AST through a meta-model where all classes are prefixed by Ct: CtClasses contains CtMethods made of CtExpressions.

We consider here two processors defined according to two different intentions. The first one, implemented in a file NPGuard.java (R_{np}), is a rewriter used to protect setters[2] from null pointer assignment by introducing a test that prevents an assignment to the *null* value to an instance variable in a class. The second one (IGSInliner.java, R_{igs}) implements a guideline provided by Google when developing mobile application in Java using the Android framework. Inside a given class, a developer should directly use an instance variable instead of accessing it through its own getter or setter (*Internal Getters Setters* anti-pattern).

---

[2] We use the classical definition of a setter, *i.e.*, "a setter for a private attribute *x* is a method named *setX*, with a single parameter, and doing a single-line and type-compatible assignment from its parameter to *x*".

```
1  public class NPGuard extends AbstractProcessor<CtClass> {
2
3    @Override public boolean isToBeProcessed(CtClass candidate) {
4      List<CtMethod> allMethods = getAllMethods(candidate);
5      settersToModify = keepSetters(allMethods);
6      return !settersToModify.isEmpty();
7    }
8
9    @Override public void process(CtClass ctClass) {
10     List<CtMethod> setters = settersToModify;
11     for (CtExecutable currentSetterMethod : setters) {
12       if (isASetter(currentSetterMethod)) {
13         CtParameter parameter =
14           (CtParameter) currentSetterMethod.getParameters().get(0);
15         CtIf ctIf = getFactory().createIf();
16         ctIf.setThenStatement(currentSetterMethod.getBody().clone());
17         String snippet = parameter.getSimpleName() + " != null";
18         ctIf.setCondition(getFactory()
19           .createCodeSnippetExpression(snippet));
20         currentSetterMethod.setBody(ctIf);
21       }
22     }
23   }
24 }
```

Fig. 2. Spoon: using processors to rewrite Java code (`NPGuard.java`, R_{np})

This is one (among others) way to improve the energy efficiency of the developed application with `Android`[3].

Like in the `Coccinelle` example, these two processors work well when applied to `Java` code, and always yield a result. However, order matters as there is an overlap between the add of the *null* check in R_{np} and the inlining process implemented by R_{igs}. As described in Fig. 3, when composing these two rules, if the guard mechanism is introduced before the setters are inlined, the setters will *not* be inlined as they do not conform to the setter definition with the newly introduced `if` statement. We depict in Fig. 3 how these processor behave on a simple class p_j. Inlining setters yields p_{igs}, where internal calls to the `setData` method are replaced by the contents of the associated method (Fig. 3b, *l.11*). When introducing the *null* guard, the contents of the `setData` method is changed (Fig. 3c, *l.5–8*), which prevents any upcoming inlining: $R_{igs}(R_{np}(p_j)) = R_{np}(p_j)$. It is interesting to remark that, when considering R_{igs} and R_{np} to be applied to the very same program, one actually expects the result described in Fig. 3d: internal setters are inlined with the initial contents of `setData`, and any external call to `setData` is protected by the guard.

2.3   Challenges Associated to Rewriting Rules Reuse

Based on these two examples that come from very different worlds, we identify the following challenges that need to be addressed to properly support the safe reuse of code rewriters. These challenges define the scope of requirements associated to our contribution. As rewriting tools are part of the state of practice in

---

[3] http://stackoverflow.com/a/4930538.

```
 1 public class C {
 2
 3   private String data;
 4
 5   public String setData(String s) {
 6     this.data = s;
 7   }
 8
 9   public void doSomething() {
10     // ...
11     setData(newValue)        /* <<<< */
12     // ...
13   }
14 }
```

(a) Example of a Java class (C.java, p_j)

```
 1 public class C {
 2
 3   private String data;
 4
 5   public String setData(String s) {
 6     this.data = s;
 7   }
 8
 9   public void doSomething() {
10     // ...
11     this.data = newValue     /* <<<< */
12     // ...
13   }
14 }
```

(b) $p_{igs} = R_{igs}(p_j)$

```
 1 public class C {
 2
 3   private String data;
 4
 5   public String setData(String s) {
 6     if (s != null)
 7       this.data = s;
 8   }
 9
10   public void doSomething() {
11     // ...
12     setData(newValue)        /* <<<< */
13     // ...
14   }
15 }
```

(c) $p_{np} = p_{igsonp} = R_{igs}(R_{np}(p_j))$

```
 1 public class C {
 2
 3   private String data;
 4
 5   public String setData(String s) {
 6     if (s != null)
 7       this.data = s;
 8   }
 9
10   public void doSomething() {
11     // ...
12     this.data = newValue     /* <<<< */
13     // ...
14   }
15 }
```

(d) $p_{npoigs} = R_{np}(R_{igs}(p_j))$

Fig. 3. Spoon: applying processors to Java code

software engineering (*e.g.*, for scalability purpose when patching the whole Linux kernel), an approach supporting the reuse of rewriting rules must be aligned with the assumptions made by these tools, *i.e.*, consider their internal decisions as black boxes.

C_1 *Rules isolation.* When rules overlaps, it is not possible to apply the two rules in isolation, as the result of a rule is used to feed the other one. It is important to support isolation when necessary.

C_2 *Conflict detection.* As each rewriter is associated to an *intention*, it is important to provide a way to assess if the initial intention is still valid in the composed result.

3   Using Deltas to Isolate Rule Applications (C_1)

In this section, we focus on the definition of a formal model that supports the safe reuse of code rewriters, *w.r.t.* the challenges identified in the previous section. This model directly addresses the first challenge of *rule isolation* (C_1). It also provides elementary bricks to support the *conflict detection* one (Sect. 4).

We model a code rewriter $\rho \in P$ as a pair of two elements: *(i)* a function $\varphi \in \Phi$ used to rewrite the AST, coupled to *(ii)* a checker function $\chi \in X$ used to validate a postcondition associated to the rewriting[4]. The postcondition validation is modeled as a boolean function taking as input the initial AST and the resulting one, returning *true* when the postcondition is valid, and false elsewhere. For a given $p \in AST$, applying φ to it yields an AST p' where $\chi(p, p')$ holds. This model supports the formalization of the rewriting rules exemplified in the previous section, and also automates the validation of the developer's intention on the yielded program.

$$\text{Let } \rho = (\varphi, \chi) \in (\Phi \times X) = P, \quad (\varphi : AST \to AST) \in \Phi$$
$$\chi : AST \times AST \to \mathbb{B} \in X, \quad \forall p \in AST, \ \chi(p, \varphi(p)) \tag{1}$$

Working with functions that operate at the AST level does not provide any support to compose these functions excepting the classical composition operator $\circ$. When combined with the postcondition validation introduced in the model, it supports the *apply* operator that classically exists in the rewriting tools. The rules $[\rho_1, \ldots, \rho_n]$ to be applied are consumed in sequence, leading to a situation where only the last postcondition (χ_1) can be ensured in the resulting program, by construction.

$$apply : AST \times P_<^n \to AST$$
$$p, [\rho_1, \ldots, \rho_n] \mapsto \text{Let } p_{2.n} = (\underset{i=2}{\overset{n}{\circ}} \varphi_i)(p), \ p' = \varphi_1(p_{2.n}), \quad \chi_1(p_{2.n}, p') \tag{2}$$

Using this operator leads to scheduling issues, as it implies strong assumptions on the functions to be commutative. We build here our contribution on top of two research results: PRAXIS [2] and a parallel composition operator [12]. These two approaches share in common the fact that instead of working on a model (here an AST), they rely on the sequence of elementary actions used to build it. PRAXIS demonstrated that for any model m, there exists an ordered sequence of elementary actions $[\alpha_1, \ldots, \alpha_n] \in A_<^*$ yielding m when applied to the empty model. The four kinds of actions available in A are *(i)* the creation of a model element, *(ii)* the deletion of a model element, *(iii)* setting a property to a given value in a model element and *(iv)* setting a reference that binds together two model elements. For example, to build the Java program p_j described in Fig. 3a, one can use a sequence of actions S_{p_j} that creates a class, names it C, creates an instance variable, names it data, sets its type to String, adds it to C, ...

$$S_{p_j} = [create(e_1, Class), setProperty(e_1, name, \{\text{``C''}\}), \ldots] \in A_<^*$$

Considering a rewriting rule as an action producer introduces the notion of *deltas* in the formalism. We consider the rewriting not through its resulting AST but through the elementary modifications made on the AST (*i.e.*, a Δ)

---

[4] We do not formalize preconditions, as the tools silently return the given AST when they are not applicable.

by the rule to produce the new one. This is compatible with the "rules are black boxes" assumption for two reasons. On the one hand, rewriting tools use a similar mechanism in their rewriting engine, for example by relying on patches for `Coccinelle` (*i.e.*, Δs containing elements to add or remove) or on an action model for `Spoon` (*e.g.*, *l.15* in Fig. 2 creates an `if` statement, and *l.20* binds the contents of the setter to this new conditional statement). We model here the application of a sequence of actions to a given AST to modify it, as a generic operator denoted by $\oplus$ (where executing a given action on the AST is a language-specific operation). On the other hand, it is possible for certain languages to define a differentiation tool working at the AST level. For example, the `GumTree` tool [4] exposes the differences between two `Java` ASTs as the minimal sequence of actions necessary to go from the right one to the left one. We denote such a *diff* operation using the $\ominus$ symbol (language-specific).

$$\oplus : AST \times A_<^* \to AST$$

$$(p, S) \mapsto \begin{cases} S = \emptyset & \Rightarrow p \\ S = \alpha | S' & \Rightarrow exec(\alpha, p) \oplus S' \end{cases} \tag{3}$$

$$\ominus : AST \times AST \to A_<^*$$

$$(p', p) \mapsto \Delta, \text{ where } p' = p \oplus \Delta$$

This representation is compatible with the previously defined semantics for the *apply* composition operator.

$$\text{Let } p \in AST, \ \rho_1 = (\varphi_1, \chi_1) \in P, \rho_2 = (\varphi_2, \chi_2) \in P$$

$$p_1 = \varphi_1(p) = p \oplus (p_1 \ominus p) = p \oplus \Delta_1, \qquad\qquad \chi_1(p, p_1)$$

$$p_2 = \varphi_2(p) = p \oplus (p_2 \ominus p) = p \oplus \Delta_2, \qquad\qquad \chi_2(p, p_2)$$

$$p_{12} = apply(p, [\rho_1, \rho_2]) = \varphi_1 \circ \varphi_2(p) = \varphi_1(\varphi_2(p)) \tag{4}$$

$$= \varphi_1(p \oplus \Delta_2) = (p \oplus \Delta_2) \oplus \Delta_1', \qquad\qquad \chi_1(p_2, p_{12})$$

$$p_{21} = apply(p, [\rho_2, \rho_1]) = \varphi_2 \circ \varphi_1(p) = \varphi_2(\varphi_1(p))$$

$$= \varphi_2(p \oplus \Delta_1) = (p \oplus \Delta_1) \oplus \Delta_2', \qquad\qquad \chi_2(p_1, p_{21})$$

However, the need for the user to decide an order is implied by the way the rewriting tools are implemented. At the semantic level, the user might not want to order the different rewriting (as seen in the `Spoon` example). Using our model, it is possible to leverage the Δs to support an isolated composition of multiple rewriting rules, where the rewriting functions are applied on the very same model in an isolated way (Fig. 4). Using this approach, *(i)* we obtain the two sequences Δ_1 and Δ_2 used to yield p_1 and p_2, *(ii)* concatenate[5] them into a single one Δ, and *(iii)* apply the result to the initial program. As a consequence, according to this composition semantic, both postconditions χ_1 and χ_2 must hold in the resulting program p' for it to be valid.

---

[5] We consider a function denoted as ; that implements action sequence concatenation.

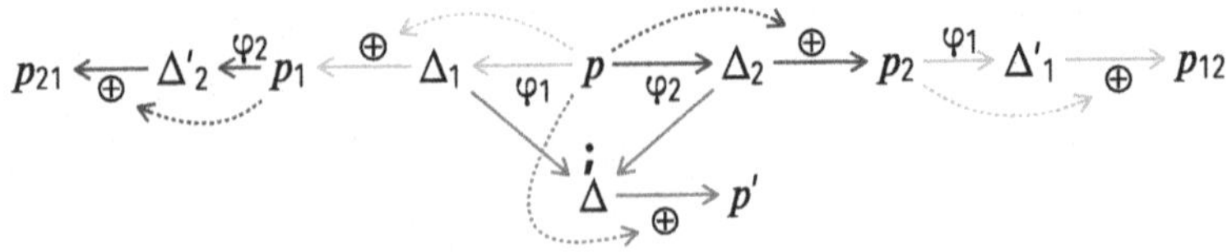

Fig. 4. Sequential $(p \mapsto \{p_{12}, p_{21}\})$ *versus* isolated $(p \mapsto p')$ rewriting

$$p' = p \oplus ((p_1 \ominus p); (p_2 \ominus p)) = p \oplus (\Delta_1; \Delta_2), \quad \chi_1(p, p') \wedge \chi_2(p, p') \qquad (5)$$

An interesting property of the isolated composition is to ensure that all post-conditions are valid when applied to a program. Unfortunately, it is not always possible to apply rules in an isolated way: for example, to yield the expected program in the `Coccinelle` example (Fig. 1d), it is necessary to always execute the error fixing rule before the allocation optimization one. However, we need to detect that one ordering ensures both postconditions, where the other only ensures the last one. As a consequence, we generalize the application of several rewriting rules to a given program according to two new composition operators that complements the legacy *apply* one. Using these operators ensures that all the postconditions hold between the initial program and the final one, no matter what happened in between. The *seq* operator implements the sequential composition of an ordered sequence of rules, and the *iso* operator implements the isolated application of a set of rules.

$$seq : AST \times P_<^n \to AST$$

$$p, [\rho_1, \ldots, \rho_n] \mapsto p_{seq} = (\overset{n}{\underset{i=1}{\circ}} \varphi_i)(p), \qquad \overset{n}{\underset{i=1}{\wedge}} \chi_i(p, p_{seq})$$

$$iso : AST \times P^n \to AST$$

$$p, \{\rho_1, \ldots, \rho_n\} \mapsto p_{iso} = p \oplus (\overset{n}{\underset{i=1}{;}} (\varphi_i(p) \ominus p)), \qquad \overset{n}{\underset{i=1}{\wedge}} \chi_i(p, p_{iso})$$

$$\qquad (6)$$

4   Detecting Syntactic and Semantic Conflicts (C_2)

We discriminate conflicts according to two types: *(i)* syntactic conflicts and *(ii)* semantic conflicts. The latter are related to the violation of postconditions associated to the rewriting rules. The former are a side effect of the *iso* operator, considering that Δs might perform concurrent modifications of the very same tree elements. These two mechanisms address the second challenge of *conflict detection* (C_2, Sect. 2).

4.1   Syntactic Conflicts as Overlapping Deltas

Let p an AST that defines a class C with a *protected* attribute named att. Let ρ_1 and ρ_2 two rewriting rules, applied using the *iso* operator to prevent one to capture the output of the other. On the one hand, applying φ_1 to p creates Δ_1, which makes att *private*, with an associated getter and setter. On the other hand, applying φ_2 to p creates Δ_2, which promotes the very same attribute as a *public* one. As an attribute cannot be *public* and *private* at the very same time, we encounter here a syntactic conflict: applying the two rules ρ_1 and ρ_2 on the same program is not possible as is.

$$\varphi_1(p) \ominus p = \Delta_1 = [\ldots, setProperty(att, visibility, \{\text{``private''}\}), \ldots]$$
$$\varphi_2(p) \ominus p = \Delta_2 = [\ldots, setProperty(att, visibility, \{\text{``public''}\}), \ldots] \quad (7)$$

On the one hand, the *seq* operator cannot encounter a syntactical conflict, as it it assumed to produce a valid AST as output. On the other hand, the *iso* operator can encounter three kinds of conflicts (Eq. 8) at the syntax level[6]: *Concurrent Property Modification* (CPM), *Concurrent Reference Modification* (CRM) and *Dangling reference* (DR). The first and second situation identify a situation where two rules set a property (or a reference) to different values. It is not possible to automatically decide which one is the right one. The last situation is identified when a rule creates a reference to a model element that is deleted by the other one. This leads to a situation where the resulting program will not compile. Thanks to the definition of these conflicting situations, it is possible to check if a pair of Δs is conflicting through the definition of a *conflict?* function. If this function returns *true*, it means that the two rewriting rules cannot be applied independently on the very same program. One can generalize the *conflict?* function to a set of Δs by applying it to the elements that compose the cartesian product of the Δs to be applied on p.

The syntactical conflict detection gives an information to the software developer: among all the rules used to rewrite the program under consideration, there exist a pair of rules that cannot be applied independently. It is still her responsibility to fix this issue, but at least the issue is explicit and scoped instead of being silently ignored.

4.2   Semantic Conflicts as Postcondition Violations

We now consider rewriting rules that are not conflicting at the syntactical level. We focus here on the postconditions defined for each rules, *w.r.t.* the legacy, sequential and isolated composition operators. We summarize in Tables 1 and 2 how the different postconditions hold when applying the *apply*, *iso* and *seq* operators to the examples defined in Sect. 2. When composed using the *apply*

---

[6] See the PRAXIS seminal paper [2] for a more comprehensive description of conflict detection in the general case.

operator $(p' = apply(p, rules))$, the only guarantee is that the last postcondition is true. It is interesting to notice that, in both tables, using the *apply* operator

$$CPM : A_<^* \times A_<^* \to \mathbb{B}$$
$$\Delta, \Delta' \mapsto \exists \alpha \in \Delta, \alpha' \in \Delta', \alpha = setProperty(elem, prop, value)$$
$$\alpha' = setProperty(elem, prop, value'), value \neq value'$$

$$CRM : A_<^* \times A_<^* \to \mathbb{B}$$
$$\Delta, \Delta' \mapsto \exists \alpha \in \Delta, \alpha' \in \Delta', \alpha = setReference(elem, ref, elem')$$
$$\alpha' = setReference(elem, ref, elem''), elem' \neq elem''$$

$$DR : A_<^* \times A_<^* \to \mathbb{B}$$
$$\Delta, \Delta' \mapsto \exists \alpha \in \Delta, \alpha' \in \Delta', \alpha = setReference(elem, ref, elem')$$
$$\alpha' = delete(elem''), elem' = elem''$$

$$conflict? : A_<^* \times A_<^* \to \mathbb{B}$$
$$\Delta, \Delta' \mapsto CPM(\Delta, \Delta') \vee CRM(\Delta, \Delta') \vee DR(\Delta, \Delta') \vee DR(\Delta', \Delta) \tag{8}$$

always yields a result that conforms to the associated postcondition, even if the result is not the expected one.

Table 1. Identifying semantic conflicts on the `Coccinelle` example

$p \in AST$	$p' \in AST$	$\chi_k(p, p')$	$\chi_m(p, p')$	Postcondition
p_c	$\varphi_k(p_c)$	✓		✓
p_c	$\varphi_m(p_c)$		✓	✓
$\varphi_m(p_c)$	$apply(p_c, [\rho_k, \rho_m])$	✓	✓	✓
$\varphi_k(p_c)$	$apply(p_c, [\rho_m, \rho_k])$	✗	✓	✓
p_c	$seq(p_c, [\rho_k, \rho_m])$	✓	✓	✓
p_c	$seq(p_c, [\rho_m, \rho_k])$	✗	✓	✗
p_c	$iso(p_c, \{\rho_k, \rho_m\})$	✗	✓	✗

Table 2. Identifying semantic conflicts on the `Spoon` example

$p \in AST$	$p' \in AST$	$\chi_{igs}(p, p')$	$\chi_{np}(p, p')$	Postcondition
p_j	$\varphi_k(p_c)$	✓		✓
p_j	$\varphi_m(p_c)$		✓	✓
$\varphi_{np}(p_j)$	$apply(p_j, [\rho_{igs}, \rho_{np}])$	✓	✓	✓
$\varphi_{igs}(p_j)$	$apply(p_j, [\rho_{np}, \rho_{igs}])$	✓	✓	✓
p_j	$seq(p_c, [\rho_{igs}, \rho_{np}])$	✗	✓	✗
p_j	$seq(p_c, [\rho_{np}, \rho_{igs}])$	✓	✓	✓
p_j	$iso(p_c, \{\rho_{igs}, \rho_{np}\})$	✓	✓	✓

Let $rules = [\rho_1, \ldots, \rho_n] \in P^n$ a set of rewriting rules. When using the *seq* operator, ordering issues are detected. For example, in the `Coccinelle` example, both $apply(p_c, [\rho_k, \rho_m])$ and $apply(p_c, [\rho_m, \rho_k])$ yield a valid result (*i.e.* that do not violate postconditions). However, in the last case, the fixed calls to `memset` introduced by ρ_m make the postcondition invalid. When using the *seq* operator, only $seq(p_c, [\rho_k, \rho_m])$ is valid *w.r.t.* to the postcondition associated to the operator. This detects the fact that fixing the `memset` size error must be applied before the one that merges the `kmalloc` and `memset` calls to support both intentions. The operator also identifies an issue when, in the `Spoon` example, the *guard* rule is applied before the other one.

When composed using the *iso* operator ($p' = iso(p, rules)$), the resulting program is valid only when all the postcondition hold when the rules are simultaneously applied to the input program. On the one hand, when applied to `Coccinelle` example, this is not the case. The fact that at least one postcondition is violated when using the *iso* operator gives a very important information to the developers: these two rewriting rules cannot be applied independently on this program. On the other hand, considering the `Spoon` example, the two rules can be applied in isolation (yielding the result described in Fig. 3d).

5   Implementation and Validation

The approach described in this paper is implemented[7] on top of the `Spoon` framework, in the `Java` ecosystem. Each rule is defined as a `Processor` working at the AST level, and we also used the same mechanism to implement the associated postcondition, as another `Processor` that identifies violations when relevant.

We consider here as a validation example the development of an Android application. Based on the collaborative catalogue *Android Open Source Apps*[8], we selected the *RunnerUp*[9] application. This application is developed by an external team, is open-source, has a large number of installations (between $10,000$ and $50,000$) and positive reviews in the Android Play Store. From a source code point of view, it has 316 stars on its GitHub repository (December 2017) and have involved 28 contributors since December 2011. It defines 194 classes implemented in $53k$ lines of code. This application is dedicated to smartphones and smartwatches thus its energy efficiency is very important.

From the software rewriting point of view, we reused here four different rules. The first one, named R_λ, is used to migrate plain old iterations to the new λ-based API available since `Java` 8, helping the piece of software to stay up to date. The second one, named R_{np}, is used to introduce guards preventing *null* assignments (Fig. 2) in setters, introducing safety in the application. The two others are dedicated to energy consumption anti-pattern fixing: R_h replaces `HashMaps` in the code by a more efficient data structure (`ArrayMaps` are

---

[7] https://github.com/ttben/ICSR-Implementation-validation.

[8] https://github.com/pcqpcq/open-source-android-apps.

[9] https://github.com/jonasoreland/runnerup.

preferred in the Android context), and R_{igs} inlines internal calls to getter and setters (Sect. 2).

We act here as the maintainer of *RunnerUp*, who wants to reuse these four rules. As there is no evident dependencies between the rules, she decides to use the *iso* operator to automatically improve her current version of *RunnerUp*: $p'_{ru} = iso(p_{ru}, \{R_{np}, R_{igs}, R_h, R_\lambda\})$. It happens that all the postconditions hold when applied to p_{ru} and p'_{ru}, meaning that the *iso* operator can be used in this case. The maintainer do not have to wonder about ordering issues *w.r.t.* this set of rules ($4! = 24$ different orders).

To validate the *seq* operator, we consider a slightly different implementation of the R_{igs} rule, named R'_{igs}. This rule rewrites a setter even if it does not contain a single line assignment, and expects as postcondition that the call to the setter is replaced by the contents of the method in the resulting program. With such a rule, $p'_{ru} = iso(p_{ru}, \{R_{np}, R'_{igs}, R_h, R_\lambda\})$ is not valid with respect to its postcondition, as $\chi'_{igs}(p_{ru}, p'_{ru})$ does not hold. Actually, the yielded program contains call to the initial contents of the setter, where the guarded one is expected according to this postcondition. Considering this situation, the maintainer is aware that *(i)* isolated application is not possible when R'_{igs} is involved for p_{ru} and *(ii)* that the conflicting situation might involve this very rule. She can yield a valid program by calling $iso(p_{ru}, \{R_{np}, R_h, R_\lambda\})$, meaning that these three rules do not interact together on p_{ru}, and thus an order involving R'_{igs} must be defined. The main advantage of the *seq* operator is to fail when a postcondition is violated, indicating an erroneous combination that violates the developers intention. Any call to the *seq* operator that does put R'_{igs} as the last rule will fail, thanks to a postcondition violation. Thus, among 24 different available ordering, the expected one is ensured by calling $p'_{ru} = seq(p_{ru}, [\ldots, R'_{igs}])$.

Threats to Validity. This experiment does not aim to empirically validate the *apply*, *seq* and *iso* operators with a large number of programs and rules. The point here is to validate the expressiveness of the three operators when confronted to a legacy piece of software that was not developed by the authors of the approach. Further experiments are necessary to empirically identify conflicting cases on a large scale code rewriting, measuring the scalability of our approach, but is considered out of the scope of this contribution.

6   Related Work

Model transformation is *"the automatic manipulation of input models to produce output models, that conform to a specification and has a specific intent"* [10]. Tool such as T-core [18] targets the definition and execution of rule-based graph transformations. Such transformation rules are defined as *(i)* a right part that describes the pattern that will trigger the rule and *(ii)* a left part indicating the expected result once the rules has been executed. It does not indicate how to go from the right part to the left, and only express the *expected* result. In this paper, we underlined the fact that our rewriting functions are black-boxes that hide their behaviors and inputs (*i.e.*, the right and left parts are hidden). In addition, some rewriting rules implemented in the Android example are not pattern-based and uses a two-pass algorithm to catch relevant elements before processing it.

Aspect-Oriented Programming (AOP [6]) aims to separate cross-cutting concerns into *aspects* that will be weaved on a software. Aspects can be weaved in sequence on the same software, thus interactions between different aspects can occur. Their interactions has been identified and studied [3,19]. These works focus on their interaction in order to find a possible schedule in their application to *avoid* any interactions. In this paper, we want to avoid such a scheduling by using the *iso* composition operator and detect interactions on a given code base. When conflicts are detected, it is possible to reuse aspect-ordering like mechanisms to schedule the application of the rewriting rules.

Transformations can also be directly operated at the code level. Compilers optimize, reorganize, change or delete portions of code according to known heuristics. Works has been done to formalize these transformations and guarantee their correctness [9]. Such tooling, Alive for example, are focused on the correctness of a given rule, expressed in an intermediate domain specific language. A strong assumption of our work is that these transformations are blackboxes, correct, bug-free, and we focus on the interactions between rules instead of rule-correctness itself, making our work complementary to this one.

Other works focus on concurrent modifications that can occurs during a team development. Concurrent refactorings can occur when multiple developers work on the same code and incompatibility can be detected [11]. Such refactoring can be considered as white-boxes graph transformations. Each refactoring is formalized as a function that captures elements in a graph and updates them. This work focus on refactoring operations only, and need to formalize and specify the captured inputs of the refactoring (*i.e.*, the pattern that needs to be captured), breaking the black-box assumption of the contribution described in this paper.

Work has been done in Software Product Lines (SPL) to safely evolve it by applying step-wise modifications [1,17]. A modification is brought by socalled *delta modules* that specify changes to be operated on a core module of a SPL. A delta module can operate a finite set of changes in the SPL (*e.g.*, add/remove a superclass, add/remove an interface), and is considered as a whitebox function. In addition, conflicting applications of delta modules is solved by explicitly defining an ordering. The sequence of application is explicitly defined by chaining the execution of modules. The white-box paradigm, along the explicit dependency declaration does not match our constraints and initial hypothesis. Finally, the delta-oriented programming of SPL is focused on the safety of a delta module: is a given function safe?, will it bring inconsistencies?, will it perform inconsistent queries? It does not deal with the safe application of multiple delta modules.

7   Conclusions and Perspectives

In this paper, we identified the composition problem that exists when composing multiple rewriting rules using state of practice tools such as `Coccinelle` or `Spoon`. We proposed a formal model to represent rewriting rules in a way compatible with such tools. Through the reification of the deltas introduced by each rule on a given program, we defined two composition operators *seq* and *iso* used to safely compose the given rules. The safety is ensured by the validation of postconditions associated to each rule. This enables to detect badly composed rules that would silently ignore developers' intention if sequentially applied. We implemented the model and operators, and applied them on an external Android application, using four rewriting rules designed to identify and fix anti-patterns, following the latest guidelines from `Google` for Android development.

Contrarily to related work approaches that assume an access to the internal definition of the rewriting rules, we advocate from a reuse point of view the necessity to be fully compatible with state of practice tools that do not expose such information. We intent to extend this work by *(i)* introducing results from the state of the art in the existing tools and *(ii)* applying methods from the test community to the rules. For the former, one can imagine an annotation-based mechanism where a rule would describe in a non-invasive way the elements it selects, as well as the one it produces. Such metadata, when available, will provide a more accurate way to identify conflicts in the general case instead of doing it program by program. For the latter, we believe that property-based testing could help to assess rewriting rules composition safety. By generating input programs under given assumptions, it is possible to explore how the rules interact between each others and perform an empirical evaluation of the conflict rate. This might also lead to the reverse engineering of the rules to automatically extract from such applications the selected and rewritten elements.

Acknowledgments. This work is partially funded by the *M4S* project (CNRS INS2I JCJC grant). The authors want to thanks Erick Gallesio for his help on kernel development; Geoffrey Hecht for his knowledge of Android optmizations; Mehdi Adel Ait Younes for having developed the initial versions of the Spoon processors and Mireille Blay-Fornarino and Philippe Collet for their feedbacks on this paper.

References

1. Bettini, L., Damiani, F., Schaefer, I.: Compositional type checking of delta-oriented software product lines. Acta Informatica **50**(2), 77–122 (2013)
2. Blanc, X., Mounier, I., Mougenot, A., Mens, T.: Detecting model inconsistency through operation-based model construction. In: Proceedings of the 30th International Conference on Software Engineering, ICSE 2008, pp. 511–520. ACM, New York (2008)
3. Douence, R., Fradet, P., Südholt, M.: Detection and resolution of aspect interactions. Research Report RR-4435, INRIA (2002)

4. Falleri, J.-R., Morandat, F., Blanc, X., Martinez, M., Monperrus, M.: Fine-grained and accurate source code differencing. In: ACM/IEEE International Conference on Automated Software Engineering, ASE 2014, Vasteras, Sweden, 15–19 September 2014, pp. 313–324 (2014)
5. Hecht, G., Rouvoy, R., Moha, N., Duchien, L.: Detecting antipatterns in Android apps. In: 2nd ACM International Conference on Mobile Software Engineering and Systems, MOBILESoft 2015, Florence, Italy, 16–17 May 2015, pp. 148–149 (2015)
6. Kiczales, G., Lamping, J., Mendhekar, A., Maeda, C., Lopes, C., Loingtier, J.-M., Irwin, J.: Aspect-oriented programming. In: Akşit, M., Matsuoka, S. (eds.) ECOOP 1997. LNCS, vol. 1241, pp. 220–242. Springer, Heidelberg (1997). https://doi.org/10.1007/BFb0053381
7. Klop, J.W., et al.: Term rewriting systems. In: Abramsky, S., Gabbay, D., Maibaurn, T. (eds.) Handbook of Logic in Computer Science, vol. 2, pp. 1–116. Oxford University Press, New York (1992)
8. Lientz, B.P., Swanson, E.B.: Software Maintenance Management. Addison-Wesley Longman Publishing Co., Inc., Boston (1980)
9. Lopes, N.P., Menendez, D., Nagarakatte, S., Regehr, J.: Provably correct peephole optimizations with alive. SIGPLAN Not. 50(6), 22–32 (2015)
10. Lúcio, L., Amrani, M., Dingel, J., Lambers, L., Salay, R., Selim, G.M.K., Syriani, E., Wimmer, M.: Model transformation intents and their properties. Softw. Syst. Model. 15(3), 647–684 (2016)
11. Mens, T., Taentzer, G., Runge, O.: Detecting structural refactoring conflicts using critical pair analysis. Electron. Notes Theor. Comput. Sci. 127(3), 113–128 (2005). Proceedings of the Workshop on Software Evolution Through Transformations: Model-Based vs. Implementation-Level Solutions (SETra 2004)
12. Mosser, S., Blay-Fornarino, M., Duchien, L.: A commutative model composition operator to support software adaptation. In: Vallecillo, A., Tolvanen, J.-P., Kindler, E., Störrle, H., Kolovos, D. (eds.) ECMFA 2012. LNCS, vol. 7349, pp. 4–19. Springer, Heidelberg (2012). https://doi.org/10.1007/978-3-642-31491-9_3
13. Padioleau, Y., Hansen, R.R., Lawall, J.L., Muller, G.: Semantic patches for documenting and automating collateral evolutions in Linux device drivers. In: Proceedings of the 3rd Workshop on Programming Languages and Operating Systems: Linguistic Support for Modern Operating Systems, PLOS 2006. ACM, New York (2006)
14. Pawlak, R., Monperrus, M., Petitprez, N., Noguera, C., Seinturier, L.: Spoon: a library for implementing analyses and transformations of Java source code. Softw. Pract. Exp. 46, 1155–1179 (2015)
15. Redondo, J.M., Ortin, F.: A comprehensive evaluation of common Python implementations. IEEE Softw. 32(4), 76–84 (2015)
16. Rodriguez, L.R., Lawall, J.: Increasing automation in the backporting of Linux drivers using Coccinelle. In: 11th European Dependable Computing Conference - Dependability in Practice, Paris, France, November 2015
17. Schaefer, I., Bettini, L., Bono, V., Damiani, F., Tanzarella, N.: Delta-oriented programming of software product lines. In: Bosch, J., Lee, J. (eds.) SPLC 2010. LNCS, vol. 6287, pp. 77–91. Springer, Heidelberg (2010). https://doi.org/10.1007/978-3-642-15579-6_6
18. Syriani, E., Vangheluwe, H., Lashomb, B.: T-core: a framework for custom-built model transformation engines. Softw. Syst. Model. 14(3), 1215–1243 (2015)

19. Tun, T.T., Yu, Y., Jackson, M., Laney, R., Nuseibeh, B.: Aspect interactions: a requirements engineering perspective. In: Moreira, A., Chitchyan, R., Araújo, J., Rashid, A. (eds.) Aspect-Oriented Requirements Engineering, pp. 271–286. Springer, Heidelberg (2013). https://doi.org/10.1007/978-3-642-38640-4_14
20. Vlaanderen, K., Jansen, S., Brinkkemper, S., Jaspers, E.: The agile requirements refinery: applying SCRUM principles to software product management. Inf. Softw. Technol. **53**(1), 58–70 (2011)

Author Index

Printed in the United States
By Bookmasters